THE SCIENCE OF

SEXY

THE SCIENCE OF

SEXY

BY BRADLEY BAYOU

PRODUCED & DESIGNED BY
NUMBER SEVENTEEN

ILLUSTRATED BY
CHANELLE EMBREY

GOTHAM BOOKS

GOTHAM BOOKS Published by Penguin Group (USA) Inc. 375 Hudson Street, New York, New York 10014, U.S.A. Penguin Group (Canada), 90 Eglinton Avenue East, Suite 700, Toronto, Ontario M4P 2Y3, Canada (a division of Pearson Penguin Canada Inc.); Penguin Books Ltd, 80 Strand, London WC2R 0RL, England; Penguin Ireland, 25 St Stephen's Green, Dublin 2, Ireland (a division of Penguin Books Ltd); Penguin Group (Australia), 250 Camberwell Road, Camberwell, Victoria 3124, Australia (a division of Pearson Australia Group Pty Ltd); Penguin Books India Pvt Ltd, 11 Community Centre, Panchsheel Park, New Delhi – 110 017, India; Penguin Group (NZ), cnr Airborne and Rosedale Roads, Albany, Auckland 1310, New Zealand (a division of Pearson New Zealand Ltd); Penguin Books (South Africa) (Pty) Ltd, 24 Sturdee Avenue, Rosebank, Johannesburg 2196, South Africa Penguin Books Ltd, Registered Offices: 80 Strand, London WC2R 0RL, England

Published by Gotham Books, a member of Penguin Group (USA) Inc. First printing, January 2007
10 9 8 7 6 5 4 3 2 1 Copyright © 2006 by Bradley Bayou All rights reserved Gotham Books and the skyscraper logo are trademarks of Penguin Group (USA) Inc. Library of Congress Cataloging-in-Publication Data has been applied for. ISBN: 978-1-592-40260-1 Printed in the United States of America without limiting the rights under copyright reserved above, no part of this publication may be reproduced, stored in or introduced into a retrieval system, or transmitted, in any form, or by any means (electronic, mechanical, photocopying, recording, or otherwise), without the prior written permission of both the copyright owner and the above publisher of this book. The scanning, uploading, and distribution of this book via the Internet or via any other means without the permission of the publisher is illegal and punishable by law. Please purchase only authorized electronic editions, and do not participate in or encourage electronic piracy of copyrighted materials. Your support of the author's rights is appreciated. While the author has made every effort to provide accurate telephone numbers and Internet addresses at the time of publication, neither the publisher nor the author assumes any responsibility for errors or changes that occur after publication. Further, the publisher does not have any control over and does not assume any responsibility for author or third-party Web sites or their content. Photos: pages 8, 10, 12, 14, 16, 18, 20, 22, 26, 28 © WireImage.com

WELCOME

I'd like to start by telling you a little about myself and what this book can do for you.

THE SCIENCE OF SEXY
IS NOT LIKE
OTHER FASHION BOOKS

This book turns dressing into a science.

I want you to try an experiment. Pick up any women's magazine and look at all of the women inside. Flip through the pages while you are standing in line at the grocery store if you have to, and look at all the models, especially those in the ads. You will quickly notice something about these women: *Most of them are young, beautiful, tall, and very skinny.* The problem? **That shape is not normal.**

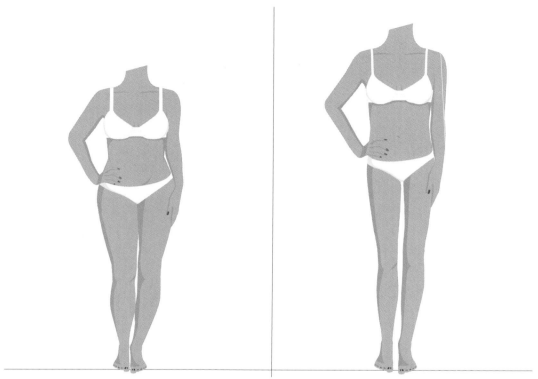

DIAGRAM 1.1 *Most women in this country look like the woman on the left, yet most clothes are created for the woman on the right. See the problem? I'll teach you how to use clothes to dress for YOUR body.*

Let's be real here for a second.

The average fashion model is about 5'10", 115 pounds, and a size 4 at most. Now, consider this: **The average American woman is 5'4", 164 pounds, and a size 14.** In fact, half the women in this country wear a size 14 or above. Yet most of the clothes you find in stores are designed for tall, skinny fashion models. The problem is, the majority of women might not even look good wearing those clothes!

**I've figured out a way to make
real women's bodies look beautiful.**

How? I've worked out a formula that will categorize your body into one of forty-eight distinct shapes. Then, I've created a unique Fitting Room for each shape that contains my secret strategies for dressing sexy. All you need to do is figure out which of the forty-eight profiles you fall into using my height, weight, and shape chart. Don't worry, I'll walk you through every step of finding your distinct shape—including how to measure yourself—so you know you're doing it right.

We've created twelve sections we call Fitting Rooms (with four different silhouettes in each), and they are all chock-full of information that will change the way you dress forever. I'll point out your body's blessings and curses to help you look at your figure in an objective way. So simply go to the appropriate Fitting Room for a personal dressing consultation.

*I'll tell you what to wear to balance your
figure, as well as what to reveal and what to
conceal to make you look your best.*

I'll provide you with three specific examples of outfits, from work to weekend, that bring your new dress-sexy rules to real life. And I'll tell you the one item that will instantly improve the look of your specific figure.

**Chances are, I've already dressed a celebrity who is
your height, your weight, and your shape.**

I've made her look her best on the red carpet, and I'm positive I can make you look your best, too.

FIGURE A

QUEEN LATIFAH

TRUST ME

I've been a couture fashion designer for eighteen years.

I have an atelier in Beverly Hills, California, where I fit and dress celebrities for high-profile events including the Academy Awards®, the Emmys®, the Grammys®, movie premieres, and many other red carpet events where looking gorgeous is mandatory.

Whatever your size, whatever your shape, I can make you look great.

Here's one example.

Before I dressed Queen Latifah for the Academy Awards, she was known mostly as a rapper and wasn't used to wearing glamorous gowns. In 2003, when she was nominated for Best Supporting Actress in *Chicago*, she wanted to make a grand entrance on the red carpet. She was nervous at the fitting because she's not thin like most actresses. Yet wearing my gown, she looked beautiful. I continued to dress her, and by 2004 she had appeared in *People* magazine's "Best Dressed" list and was called "among the year's most dazzling" in my dress at the Golden Globes®.

But Queen Latifah isn't my only sexy success story. I've also helped other stars look stunning on the red carpet. In recent years, some of the celebrities I've dressed include:

Oprah Winfrey, Kristin Davis, Barbra Streisand, Eva Mendes, Coretta Scott King, Mena Suvari, Donna Summer, Cynthia Nixon, Maggie Gyllenhaal, Mariah Carey, Mary J. Blige, Jenna Elfman, Regina King, Paula Abdul, Kerry Washington, Serena Williams, Felicity Huffman, Marcia Cross, Selma Blair, and Geena Davis.

On this and the following pages, I'll show you some of the red carpet dresses I've designed and how beautiful the stars looked in them. That's because I designed each dress specifically for the woman's individual body. And each of these women—and all women—are very different. One size does not fit all. Far from it.

FIGURE B

EVA LONGORIA

However, I do know something that all women have in common.

All my experience has confirmed how I approach dressing women. Deep down, you want to look and feel beautiful, gorgeous, and desired. In essence, sexy. You may never have thought about it, and you may not want to admit it, but I believe it's true.

All women want to look sexy.

Keep in mind, there are different kinds of sexy. There's a demure, coy sexy. A glamorous, mysterious sexy. And, of course, an overtly plunging sexy. The choice is entirely yours. Your version of sexy should fit your personality. Whatever sexy style you choose, I can help you dress to bring out your best.

Your individual body type affects how you should choose your clothes. After styling women of all shapes and sizes, I know a lot about body types. I've seen them all. Every woman has a unique combination of height, weight, and silhouette shape, and I've developed a style system custom-made to fit and flatter you, and you specifically.

My goal is to help you look your best.

That involves convincing you that not every style is going to look good on you. Just because something is in style doesn't mean you should wear it. Why spend your money on something that doesn't look great on you? Dressing well isn't about spending a lot on your clothes. The trick is learning what kinds of shapes will balance your body, and what parts of your body you should conceal and reveal. And that's what I'm here to teach you.

WHAT IS THE SCIENCE OF SEXY?

Consider it your unique fashion prescription.

Today, most fashion books and magazine articles fail to distinguish the differences in body types when it comes to giving fashion advice. And they use vague lists of descriptors for how to look taller or thinner.

I have turned dressing into a science, literally.

I began with a science called anthropometry. Anthropometry is the measure of the human form. It involves gathering statistical data on the variations in body dimensions across the population, all of which plays a huge role in clothing design. Cutting-edge scientific studies on anthropometry have proven the existence of many figure shapes. In fact, a national organization called SizeUSA conducted a study of 10,000 American men and women using a TC^2 machine. This machine scans the body in less

THE THREE FACTORS THAT DETERMINE YOUR BODY TYPE

1. SILHOUETTE

2. MEASUREMENTS

3. WEIGHT

DIAGRAM 1.2 *Keep all three factors into account if you want to look better.*

than six seconds, accurately measuring 200,000 data points on the body to produce a 3-D true-to-scale image of each human body. I have used this information to create a basic fashion formula that works for every type of figure.

The result? I can make women of all shapes and sizes look better. You're not the only woman who wants to improve her look. Believe me, even the most beautiful stars feel they need serious help. It's no wonder.

There's a lot of pressure on women to be thin, young, and beautiful.

In fact, one study on the perception of beauty published in the *Personality and Social Psychology Bulletin* found that being surrounded by beautiful people can make you feel considerably less satisfied with your own physical appearance. The study, conducted by psychologists Douglas Kenrick, Ph.D., Sara Gutierres, Ph.D., and Jenifer Patch at Arizona State University, concluded that, "If there are a large number of desirable members of one's own sex available, one may regard one's own market value as lower." And with the surfeit of tall, skinny, beautiful actresses all over the television, the movie screen, and magazines, it's easy for you to start feeling down on yourself.

But don't let it get to you.

Remember, all those famously perfect women you're used to seeing are being helped by a big bag of tricks: bright lights, professional makeup artists, costume designers, personal trainers, production magic, and photographic digital enhancements. They also have one more bonus in their back pocket: a professional stylist telling them what they should (and shouldn't) wear to look their best.

You may not have all those perks at your fingertips, but what you do have in your hands is a formula that can have a dramatic effect on how your figure appears. A simpler way to explain it may be the way I talk about it in real life with my clients. Basically, it's this:

The foundation of this "science of sexy" boils down to two simple things.

1
Dress to balance your body.

2
Learn to conceal your flaws and reveal your assets.

By doing both, you will create a figure that looks beautifully proportioned and that gets attention in all the right places. Like a couture gown for the Oscars®, I've developed a style system custom-made to flatter every inch of you.

DEBRA MESSING

The bulk of this book is devoted to giving you personal fashion advice based on your unique figure. I've taken into account all of the scientific research and paired it with mathematical ratios of both height and weight to create the shapes. Knowing which one of these forty-eight types you are will help you dress with confidence from this day forward.

My formula is your answer for dressing sexy.

Each of these forty-eight shapes is defined by both a numeric value (measurement of your height and weight) and a figure type (shoulder-bust-hip ratio). This isn't just any fashion advice, this is personal information based on your specific geometric body proportions. Consider it your unique fashion prescription.

48 SEXY SHAPES

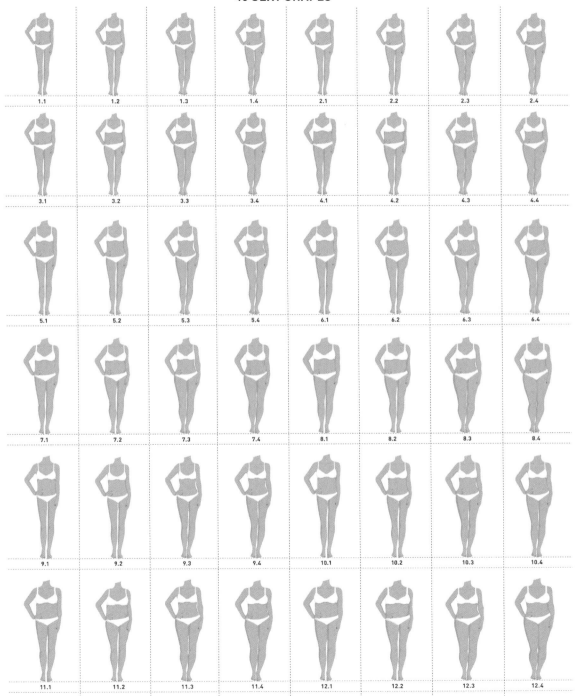

DIAGRAM 1.3 *Each of the forty-eight body types has its own unique combination of height, weight, and silhouette.*

BALANCE IS SEXY
As humans, we are attracted to balance.

Imagine looking at a landscape at one particular tree. The tree might be larger on one side, and it might bulge out a bit on the other. Branches and twigs twist around in imperfect ways, but overall, when you look at the tree, it

EXAMPLE 1

EXAMPLE 2

is balanced. In fact, when you look at all the trees on the horizon, even the overall landscape is balanced. How did this happen? The answer is because nature is symmetrical. It always has been. Each piece may not be perfectly symmetrical, but as a whole, it balances itself out. Yes, as it turns out, Mother Nature is the most amazing designer of all.

Artists have been trying to copy nature for centuries. My goal as a fashion designer is to

FIGURE F

CHANDRA WILSON

copy nature as much as I can, too. Because as humans, we want to balance human figures the way nature balances itself. As humans, we are attracted to balance.

Science, in fact, has proven there is one timeless evolutionary trait for sexy: symmetry.

Studies on the perception of beauty have proven that human beings demonstrate an innate preference for symmetrical features. Though the importance of symmetry continues to be studied, research has shown that people prefer mates with symmetrical traits, because this is equated with healthy genes and a strong immune system.

Clothing, like the human body, is created with symmetry in mind.

The good news? You can fake symmetry.

Imagine you've spread out a sweater flat on a table. Look at it. Notice the outline of the garment. If you were to pick up the sweater and fold it in half, it would fold perfectly, right? Would one side be larger than the other? Of course not. Both sides would be exactly the same. Clothing is symmetrical. And yet, when it comes to dressing from head to toe, it's so easy to offset the balance of your silhouette.

*The most basic balanced shape
is the hourglass.*

If you want to look better every day, you need to wear clothes that replicate the proportions of the hourglass silhouette. However, a woman with a perfectly balanced hourglass figure can look out of proportion by choosing the wrong clothes. Here's a formula that describes what I'm thinking mentally when I'm dressing a woman: Your body's silhouette, plus the right clothing proportions, equals sexy balance.

EXAMPLE 3

The translation? By learning your body's natural proportions, you can make the correct clothing choices, and create the illusion of being perfectly proportionate.

PERSONAL FASHION FORMULA

YOUR BODY **+** A BALANCED OUTFIT

DIAGRAM 1.4 *Once you learn the factors of both of these, you'll look better every single day.*

Perfect dressing is, simply, perfect balance.

Thanks to my experience helping women flatter their shapes, heights, and weights, I've developed a system that will make you look more balanced—and much, much sexier.

MY CONCEAL & REVEAL STRATEGY
Physical perfection is a myth.

You wouldn't believe some of the things I hear perfect-looking women say about their thighs, stomachs, butts, breasts, and cellulite. You name the body part; I've heard a woman complain about it.

In fact, let me ask you this: When's the last time you looked in a mirror and thought, "Wow, I look absolutely fabulous?"

Take your time…think about it.

Got your answer?

Well, that wasn't recent enough. You should be thinking that every day, in every mirror and in every department store window you pass. You should be the walking epitome of proud and sexy. And once you get the hang of using the conceal and reveal strategy, you'll find yourself feeling that way a lot more often.

A True Hollywood Story

EVERY WOMAN'S BODY IS DIFFERENT

One afternoon, I went to the home of a very famous movie actress—an Academy Award–winning actress— to begin designing a dress for an award ceremony. I took out my measuring tape and started fitting her, when she said to me, "Well, we have to hide my hips because they're too big."

I said, "Hips? What hips?" She was a perfect size four. Yet she was convinced she had a huge figure flaw that had to be covered up!

And she wasn't the only one. I've never once had a celebrity come into my studio and say to me, "Do what you want. I think my body's perfect and I think I look great." In fact, they're usually complaining about something within five minutes of starting the fitting.

The point is, every woman's body is completely different. And quite often, the differences that you consider flaws could actually be assets that set you apart as unique. Those flaws might not even be flaws at all.

FIGURE I

BEYONCÉ

Remember, this style system is about science, and it is vital that you look at your figure objectively so you can develop an honest understanding of your shape. To do so, we have to make a deal.

I will be honest with you about what to wear, if you agree to be honest with yourself.

Every woman has flaws on her body she might want to hide, and every woman has beautiful parts on her body she should want to flaunt. The number one complaint from stars? Their arms. They're the most beautiful women in the world, and nearly every one of them has issues with their arms. One girl said, "I'm getting grandmother arms." I said, "No, you're not. You're 23 years old!" It's ridiculous to feel this way. Don't get caught up in hating everything, including your good parts.

Yes, it's often harder to admit the good parts about yourself than the bad.

(God forbid you were caught admiring yourself in a mirror for a minute, right?) But if this book is going to work, you need to do both. I can start helping you right now with my **Conceal & Reveal Strategies.**

Here's how it works: After you complete steps 1 and 2 below, use your answers to refer to my "Conceal & Reveal Strategies" chart. There, you will find some quick dress-sexy solutions that will help you tone down your flaws and play up favorites. Keep these in mind as you continue reading the book, because these are tricks that work all the time.

A CONCEAL & REVEAL EXERCISE

STEP 1: Circle the three body parts you consider "flawed."

This is probably easy. If you're like every other woman, you've been overanalyzing yourself and pointing out your flaws your whole life. And no, you can't circle everything! You can only pick three.

YOUR NECK	YOUR SHOULDERS	YOUR BACK
YOUR BUST	YOUR WAISTLINE	YOUR STOMACH
YOUR ARMS	YOUR BUTT	YOUR HIPS
YOUR THIGHS	YOUR CALVES	YOUR FEET

STEP 2: Circle the three body parts you love the most.

This is probably harder, but it's just as important. Come on, really, what do you like?

YOUR NECK	YOUR SHOULDERS	YOUR BACK
YOUR BUST	YOUR WAISTLINE	YOUR STOMACH
YOUR ARMS	YOUR BUTT	YOUR HIPS
YOUR THIGHS	YOUR CALVES	YOUR FEET

CONCEAL & REVEAL STRATEGIES

	CONCEAL	REVEAL
YOUR NECK	High crew neck tops or turtlenecks will shorten a too-long neck.	V-necks and wide U-necks will elongate the appearance of your neck.
YOUR SHOULDERS	Dark colors on top and raglan sleeves on shirts make your shoulders seem slimmer.	Wide lapels or epaulets on your jackets will widen the look of your shoulders.
YOUR BACK	Dark, well-fitted jackets will de-emphasize your wider back regions.	Halters or plunging, backless dresses will show off this sexier side if you want to.
YOUR BUST	Semi-fitted styles, darted tops, V-necks, sweetheart cuts, and single-breasted jackets, will help a big bust look best.	Horizontal stripes, ruffles, ruching, and empire-waist cuts will make a small bust look best.
YOUR WAISTLINE	Tailored cuts, such as jackets with princess seams or peplum jackets, create the illusion of a waist.	Wrap dresses that tie at the waist or belts that cinch you will show off your slim middle.
YOUR STOMACH	Empire-waist shirts and dresses, or shirts with ruching, help disguise a bulging stomach.	Fitted tops and sweaters in a lightweight fabric fit snugly (not clingy) and show off a sexy stomach.

CONCEAL & REVEAL STRATEGIES

	CONCEAL	REVEAL
YOUR BUTT	Curve-skimming dresses in matte jersey will diminish the appearance of a full bottom.	Pants or jeans with interesting back pockets show off your natural curves.
YOUR ARMS	Three-quarter-length jackets will make your arms appear slimmer by hitting at the thinnest point on your forearm.	Sleeveless tops, halter tops, and strapless dresses will attract attention to pretty arms.
YOUR HIPS	Jackets that are tailored to hit at your waist and have wide shoulders balance large hips.	Pants with side pockets or pocket detailing add curves to straight hips.
YOUR THIGHS	Boot cut or flared-leg pants counter the width of your thighs and balance your legs. A-line skirts can disguise full thighs.	Stovepipe pants or skinny jeans reveal your shapely thighs.
YOUR CALVES	Avoid skirts that hit at mid-calf length, which will make your calves look wider.	A-line skirts that hit at knee-length make calves look slimmer, and high heels make your calves shapelier.
YOUR FEET	To conceal big feet, try a round-toe or square-toe cut.	A low-cut, high-heeled shoe will visually lengthen the look of your feet.

THE PSYCHOLOGY OF STYLE

Clothing has a language all its own.

Your clothes are sending complex messages.

Stop for a minute and look at what you're wearing. When you woke up this morning and put on that outfit, were you considering the fact that your style was displaying your economic status, social circle, sophistication level, morality, and mood? Probably not. And yet that's exactly what your clothes are saying about you.

A picture says a thousand words... and so does an outfit.

Clothing has a language all its own. It's like a shorthand to help read and contextualize people we encounter. Instantly. Clothing helps us make snap judgments about a person's tastes, habits, hobbies, social status, and more.

Another True Hollywood Story

CLOTHES CAN SPEAK FOR YOU

Recently, a young movie star walked into my atelier to be
fitted for a dress. She wanted something new to wear on the red carpet
at her movie premiere. This was a big deal. She knew she
would be photographed by paparazzi, and she knew her image would
be in all the magazines and in the minds of fans and potential
directors and producers for months to come. In essence, she needed
to make a very positive impression.

Do you want to know the first thing I asked her? I didn't ask her
what color dress she wanted or what length she wanted it to be.
Those questions came later. Instead, I asked her what split-second
first impression she wanted to make on the red carpet:
"What image are you trying to project?"

She told me she'd only been getting roles playing young
girls and she wanted to change her image. She now wanted to be
perceived as having grown up, as being mature, glamorous,
sophisticated, and drop-dead sexy.

After asking her a few more questions, I dressed her in something that
fit the bill, and the photos of her after the event were stunning.
She certainly didn't look like a young girl anymore, and directors saw
that. What was her next big film role? Playing an older, more sophisticated,
sexy woman. You probably saw the film. It was really good.

BAI LING

No, it's not always fair. And no, we don't always draw the right conclusions about one another based on clothing choices. But with so many people out there, it's one of the few tools we have to help edit our surroundings.

We judge others by their clothing, and they judge us. It's human nature.

Instead of being frustrated by it, why not embrace the idea? Consciously choose clothes that make you feel authentic, that say something about your personality before you say a word. Align your clothes with your personal and professional goals so your clothes can work harder for you. Clothing can change the professional attention you get, the kind of people who befriend you, and the kind of dates or partners you attract. You know how they say you should dress for the job you want not the job you have? That's because if your boss can picture you in a higher position—literally, through the clothes you're wearing—you're more likely to get the job.

Your clothes speak for you.

Make sure they know what to say.

Just because you decide you don't want to be judged by your clothes doesn't mean it isn't happening. It's happening all the time. It's happening right now.

Use your clothing as a form of social communication. Every single day, you have an opportunity to send whatever message you want about yourself. You get to pick the clothes from your closet that speak before you do. Choose what you put on your back carefully, because your clothes will keep right on talking about you behind your back!

THE RED CARPET
QUESTIONNAIRE

Celebrities use red carpets as advertising. They have to think carefully about what they're going to wear, because what they're selling is their image. The same goes for you. No, you may not be walking down an actual red carpet, but the minute you walk out your door, you are selling yourself and your image. Don't you want people to think you look fabulous and successful based on what you're wearing?

So let's pretend you're the woman in my atelier, looking to get fitted for a dress. You walk in, I greet you. Go ahead, put your jacket down. Now let's talk for a minute. Here is a sampling of what I would ask...

QUESTION ONE
WHAT IS THE IMAGE YOU ARE TRYING TO PROJECT?

A. sophisticated and glamorous
B. conservative and classic
C. trendy and cool
D. hippie chic
E. all-out sexy

*The answer you chose is the overall effect you want to project. You should keep this in mind the entire time you're getting dressed. For example, if you chose "**B**" (conservative and classic), you should be thinking Audrey Hepburn, which means you shouldn't be shopping for clothes or dresses at stores that focus on selling items that appeal to those who chose "**D**" (hippie chic). Don't contradict the image you want to project with items from another style.*

MY TIP: Shop your image! Each store out there focuses on one "style" of clothes. If you're shopping for a black jacket, you will find straight, classic cuts at Brooks Brothers and trendy, cool cuts at Dolce & Gabbana. Shop at the stores that project the image you want to send.

QUESTION TWO
HOW SEXY DO YOU WANT TO BE?

A. overtly, wildy sexy
B. playfully sexy
C. quietly, mysteriously sexy
D. very barely sexy

Think of your answer as relating to one of the characters from Sex and the City. *If you answered "**A**," think of yourself as going for an overtly sexy look like Samantha. If you answered "**B**," think Carrie. If you answered "**C**," think Charlotte. If you answered "**D**," think Miranda.*

MY TIP: To alter your vision of sexy, I work on two areas: how low I can go in the cleavage, and how high I can go on the skirt, or the slit in the skirt. (Again, you should never work both angles. The ultimate sexy means leaving something to the imagination.) To look the sexiest (Samantha), go low (pull the neckline down to a deep plunge and show more cleavage) or go high (pull the hemline of the skirt up, or raise the slit up toward your hip). To look less sexy (Miranda), do less.

And here's another added-value tip that increases the sexy: Consider the back of your dress! When you walk into a room, decked out and pretty, the men don't want to be obvious when looking at you, so they wait until you pass by. Then, as soon as you pass by or turn your back, they turn to look. If you give them something to remember you by on your back, you're doing even better than you were before.

QUESTION THREE
THERE'S PROBABLY SOMEONE YOU WANT TO MAKE AN IMPRESSION ON AT THE EVENT. IF SO, WHAT KIND OF RELATIONSHIP IS IT?

A. someone you love or want to drive wild
B. someone with whom you're comfortable showing off your sexy side
C. someone you want to tease with a small peek at your sexy side
D. someone you want to send a straightforward "not on the first date" look

Similar to Question 2, the answer you chose here can be traced to characters going out on dates in Sex and the City. *But here's the catch: This answer should match your answer to Question 2, so you're consistent about where you're aiming on the dress-sexy scale.*

MY TIP: Make sure your answers in Questions 2 and 3 match up perfectly! That means that if you picked "**A**" for Question 2, you should have picked "**A**" for Question 3; if you picked "**B**" for Question 2, you should have picked "**B**" for Question 3; etc. If your answers to both questions do not match, think a bit more about the look you're going for.

QUESTION FOUR
WHAT PARTS OF YOUR BODY DO YOU WANT TO DISGUISE?

A. arms and shoulders

B. waist

C. hips

D. legs

If you spend the whole day or night worrying about a flaw on your figure, it can really affect your confidence. This is why you'll need to figure out what to fix so you can move on to looking your best. Now that you've chosen what part of your body you want to cover up, don't go choosing styles that do the opposite. I've worked with many brides who will say they don't like their heavy arms…but say they want to wear a strapless dress. Or women who want to show off their slender figure…then consider billowing, puffy gowns. Keep your plans consistent.

MY TIP: Refer to the "Conceal & Reveal Strategies" part of this book. Dressing up should be about showing off the best you, and if you're worried about some part of your outfit, you can't relax and be your most confident, sexy self.

QUESTION FIVE
WHAT COLORS DO YOU THINK LOOK GOOD ON YOU?

A. intense rich colors such as black, navy, red, and hot pink
B. pale soft colors such as peach, camel, coral, and ivory
C. soft neutrals & pastels such as plum, mauve, lavender, and pale blue
D. rich, earthy colors such as olive, orange, gold, and brown

This is always an important question. Instead of thinking about what color you want to wear to your event, think about what looks good on you first—the color you've seen in photographs that makes your face brighter, or the color you've worn that got the most "you look great in that" compliments.

MY TIP: Find your guaranteed great color. If you know yellow looks stunning on you, you'll feel more stunning in that than, say, experimenting with brown for the evening. (If you really don't know what colors look good on you, ask your friends for help. Or, take snapshots of yourself dressed in different color tops and compare them to see which looks best on you.)

With the answers to these five basic questions, you can get a fairly strong idea of what to wear to your event. Sometimes you'll want to look subdued, and sometimes you'll want to look all-out smashing. But by reviewing this questionnaire and my suggestions, you'll definitely look and feel sexy each and every time.

My Ten
"Dress-Sexy"
Commandments

There are some rules that apply
to every woman, all the time, no matter what
your height, weight, or silhouette.

Heed them well.

Thou shalt choose the right undergarments

Before you put on anything, the very first things you need to get are a good bra and good underwear—especially if you're a full-sized or plus-size woman. There are stores full of bras and underwear with salespeople who can help you and experts who work in just bra fitting—take advantage of their knowledge. Get fitted for a bra. Make the effort to get this part right, and the rest of your outfit will benefit.

Now I could write a whole book on how to do this, but right now, I'll keep it simple.

The right bra

enhances your curves, holds in extra bounce,
and isn't so tight on any part of your torso that it creates lumps.

THE MOST COMMON PROBLEM?
Lumpy underarms and back fat.

TRY THIS TRICK
Try a lightweight, fitted cotton T-shirt on over your bra
to see if it lies smoothly over your bra area.

The right panties

covers up your bottom, and isn't so tight on any part of
your lower body that it creates lumps or bulges.

THE MOST COMMON PROBLEM?
Visible panty lines.

TRY THIS TRICK
Wear a pair of lightweight pants in a three-way mirror
so you can see what the people behind you do.

The right control garment

smoothes out your flabby spots without just shifting
your weight to another part of your body.

THE MOST COMMON PROBLEM?
Creating new bulges next to the ones you're covering up.

TRY THIS TRICK
If you're putting on a control garment (like Spanx®) to control the
lumps in your middle, make sure it's shifting the extra weight up.
If it has to go somewhere, it may as well be up toward your chest!

Thou shalt choose the highest quality fabrics thou can afford

It's tempting to spend $35 on a pair of pants on sale from a cheap store. Don't do it. Why? Because those pants will not give you a high ratio of cost to wear. Let me explain.

This week, you spend $35 on a pair of pants. You might wear them once a week for a month. But because they wear out quickly, pull at the seams, fade on the first wash, and probably drape in an unflattering way, you'll only wear them once more next month. Since you only wore them five times, your cost-per-wear ratio is $7. If you buy a pair of $35 pants every two months, over the course of one year, you will have spent $210 on

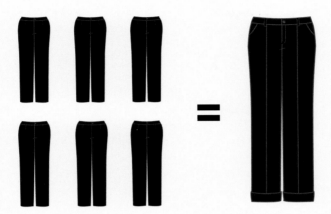

DIAGRAM 1.5 *For $210, you could buy six pairs of $35 pants or one pair of quality pants. And you'd wear those good pants for years to come. The more durable the quality of the item, the more wears for the buck!*

pants you can no longer wear that take up room in your closet. If, however, you spent that same $210 on a pair of quality, lightweight, black wool trouser pants that fit you ideally—meaning they don't crease, bunch, pull, or wrinkle—and that will wash and wear without conspicuous signs of use, I guarantee you'd wear that pair of pants twice a week. That's eight times per month. And, since these pants will last you all year, those 96 wears cost only $2.19 per wear. In essence, the cheap pants cost you more than three times as much as the expensive ones!

Buying cheap is like buying disposable clothing. Yes, it might hurt to hand over the money for quality items, but over time, it will ultimately save you money by eliminating the constant need for new things. You and your credit card will never have to "pay" for your mistakes again.

Turn the page to learn how to tell if something gets "The Bradley Bayou Seal of Quality."

The
Bradley Bayou
Seal
of
Quality

The 7-Step Garment Quality Check

STEP 1: **THE FABRIC**

Make sure the fabric feels good to the touch. Close your eyes and really concentrate on it. Fabrics can feel soft, smooth, rough, and hard. They can be heavy, medium, or light. They can be glossy, shiny, or matte. Beware of anything that feels cheap—especially knits and wools. Believe me, you want to at least make sure the fabric isn't itchy, because there's nothing worse than scratching like crazy in some cheap wool fitted sweater you've pulled on over your head.

Now, angle the fabric toward the light. When I pick out fabrics, I look carefully at the surface to make sure there isn't an undesired shine on it that makes it look cheap and, more important, creates a fattening effect on the body.

THE ULTIMATE TEST: Rub a section of fabric between your fingers to see if it pills (little fuzzy beads that collect and look awful over time). If it pills now, it will pill even more later.

STEP 2: **THE SEAMS**

Jackets, tailored shirts, and blazers all have visible seam lines that must be examined critically if you're buying a big-ticket item. Lightly tug at an area where different parts of the garment come together, like the shoulders. Make sure you can't pull apart the seam to reveal too much of the stitching. Then, check to see that the fabric matches up perfectly. Any pulling or bunching at the seam will mean it will look bad on you.

THE ULTIMATE TEST: Pay special attention if your garment is light-colored, because seams—good and bad—are more noticeable on light-colored fabrics.

STEP 3: **THE HEMLINE**

Look closely at the hemline on the bottom of each garment, whether it's a skirt, pants, or the bottom of a jacket or shirt, and check that the stitching is not conspicuous (unless of course it's meant to be). Generally, the threads should not be the first thing you see.

THE ULTIMATE TEST: Hold the hem up to eye level to be sure it's straight and even. Not all garments will pass this test.

STEP 4: **THE ZIPPER**

Check that the zipper is sewn in correctly. No part of the zipper should be coming undone or flapping around within the garment.

THE ULTIMATE TEST: Zip it! Start at the top, unzip it, then zip it back up. It should glide effortlessly. If it feels like a bumpy ride or if it snags any part of the fabric (like the lining) the item will not be worth the trouble over time.

STEP 5: **THE BUTTONS**

Bad buttons are a telltale sign of bad manufacturing. It's like going to an expensive restaurant with an unkempt bathroom—the quality behind the scenes is important, too. Check that the buttons are even, and sewn on securely. There should not be signs of loose or unraveling threads on the buttons or the buttonholes.

THE ULTIMATE TEST: Button it! It should feel secure, and be able to be unbuttoned and buttoned a good number of times.

STEP 6: **THE LINING**

Feel the material with which your garment has been lined. It should be soft, like silk or rayon—or it should at least feel soft. The softer the lining, the better it will drape over your body and the nicer it will make your natural silhouette curves. Stiff fabrics can give your body an unflattering, boxy shape.

THE ULTIMATE TEST: Try on the garment and make sure you can't feel the lining rubbing against your body.

STEP 7: **THE DETAILS**

If you want to dress up with a pretty garment covered with beading or sparkles, you don't want these pieces coming undone or falling off. Like loose buttons, it's a sign that behind the scenes, your garment was made cheaply. You can always add jewelry to a basic neutral to add desired pizzazz for the right price.

THE ULTIMATE TEST: Gently run your fingers across a few of the details. If a few sparkles fall off, or the beads hanging from a string appear ready to fall off, don't buy it!

COMMANDMENT
III

Thou shalt not force your figure into every style

𝕴 have some bad news for you. And I hate to be the one to break it to you, but I'm telling you this for your own good: All styles do not work for all women. In fact, certain styles will never look good on you. Period.

As you visit your personal Fitting Room, I'll be very clear about what you should wear and what you should avoid for your particular shape. But I wanted to be clear about this concept upfront. Just because a style is trendy—e.g., skinny jeans, slip dresses, tulip skirts—does not mean it will look good on you. Here are some examples of what I mean:

Shiny, charmeuse slip dresses should NOT be worn by women sizes 14 and up.

The glimmering fabric adds weight to your figure, and the revealing cut magnifies lumps and bumps.

❧

Low-rise jeans should NOT be worn by women with large hips or bulging stomachs.

Instead of smoothing your shape, you're adding bulges.

❧

Short women should NOT wear dark, knee-high boots.

These cut your look completely in half and make you look one-third shorter than you already are.

❧

If you don't have great legs, do NOT wear short skirts!

Just because your friends or the fashion models are wearing short skirts, it doesn't mean you should.

❧

Skimpy little tank tops? Busty women who need more support on top should NOT be wearing them.

This always makes me go "Aaaaaargh!"

I'm not telling you these things to inhibit your personal style or to hurt your feelings. I'm telling you because I want you to look sexier in everything you wear. Don't force your body into something that doesn't look fabulous on you.

Thou shalt use your skin to your advantage

When it comes to color, don't forget about the accessory you were born with: your skin. I'm not talking about wearing skirts up to here or shirts down to there, but about taking advantage of the natural, beautiful sight of bare skin. To a point.

A peek of flesh can instantly draw the eye straight to the spot you're showing off—and away from a flaw you're trying to conceal. So take advantage of this, and strategically reveal some skin to bring the eye toward your best assets. Just be sure that you're comfortable getting attention there—because, I assure you, you will.

If you were blessed with gorgeous legs, you can get away with a slightly shorter hemline. If you have a slender neck and a pretty collarbone, expose some skin there. If you have nice cleavage, wear a V-neck or U-neck that instantly attracts attention to one of your best features.

See how nice an open area can be? Your body can benefit, too. Really. Don't be afraid to show a little skin.

COMMANDMENT
V

Thou shalt not buy big-ticket trendy items

Before you spend your well-earned money on a trendy item, it's worth it for you to think twice, because navigating the "trendscape" can be a tricky thing. If you're not sure whether the item you want is worth spending your money on, run it through the quiz below. The rounds go from most to least important and will help you decide if it's worth buying.

The "To Trend or Not To Trend" Quiz

ROUND 1	
Does this style mirror my personality? Does it fit in the world of clothes I already own and wear? **YES OR NO**	Does this trend that everyone thinks is so fabulous actually suit my body? *(e.g., does it highlight my best parts and hide my worst?)* **YES OR NO**

RESULTS: If you answered NO to either of these questions, stop here. Do not buy the item. You will likely regret it. Instead, think about an accessory you can buy from the same style trend that can add flourish to a basic you already own—without spending a bundle (see COMMANDMENT VIII for more on this). If you answered YES to both questions, move on to the next round.

ROUND 2

Will this particular item be in style for the next six months? **YES OR NO**

Even if yes, will you be able to wear this item for the next two seasons *(e.g., a skirt may still be trendy in six months, but can you wear it in your cold climate?)*? **YES OR NO**

Do the buttons and seams, linings, zipper, and detailing look well made? **YES OR NO**

RESULTS: If you answered NO to one or two of these questions, you should either not buy the item or only buy it if you're spending very little money on it. It is never worth investing much money on something that will go out of style quickly or that is made poorly. If you answered YES to all three, move on to the final round.

ROUND 3

Can you wear this item a few times before someone notices a repeat or you get bored with it? **YES OR NO**

Is it something you can see yourself wearing in a few different ways *(e.g., a top that you can dress up with a blazer, or down with jeans?)*? **YES OR NO**

RESULTS: If you answered NO to both questions, you might not want to spend much money on the item. See if you can find a cheaper version of it at a discount store. If you answered YES to one or both of these questions, you may have found an item that, while trendy, will also withstand the test of time for you.

Hopefully, this quiz will get you thinking. More importantly, it will help you discern "fads" from "trends" from "fashion that's worth spending your money on." A $300 pair of beautiful leather boots will still look great in ten years. But if the trend is oversized dangling earrings or hoops, spend very little money on it (there are a lot of good, less-expensive imitations of a trend out there), because chances are it's a fad and will go out of style. Don't waste your money. If you look at something and have to ask yourself, "Do I really think this will look good in two years?" it probably won't.

Thou shalt select skinny fabrics and cuts

Not all fabrics are created to make your body look the same. And no matter what your body shape, some fabrics and cuts will make you look heavier, and some will help you look thinner. Your goal is to find the ones that drape over your body the way you need them to, to best accent your silhouette.

Generally speaking, fabrics with a stiff texture or a heavyweight or shiny surface will add either bulk or undue attention to the area. This stops the eye at a horizontal point on your body and makes you look wider or heavier than you are.

On the other hand, fabrics that gently flow and drape over your body create more of a vertical line on your figure, drawing the eye up and down. This makes you seem slimmer.

Sometimes, in order to create the perfect hourglass silhouette, you'll want to add volume to some areas, and help diminish others.

Here is your key to the fabrics and cuts that giveth and the ones that taketh away.

FABRICS THAT ADD WEIGHT (WHERE YOU NEED IT)

HEAVY STIFF FABRICS *wool, leather, denim, suede*

TEXTURED FABRICS *velvet, tweed, terry cloth*

SHINY FABRICS *taffeta, raw silk, charmeuse*

LIGHT-COLORED OR BRIGHTLY-COLORED FABRICS
white, hot pink, yellow

FABRICS THAT SUBTRACT WEIGHT (WHERE YOU DON'T WANT IT)

MID-WEIGHT FABRICS *matte jersey, fine-gauge knits, georgettes, crepes, soft cottons, polyester/spandex blends*

DARK FABRICS: *black, blue, and monochromatic outfits (that will create the tallest look).*

CUTS THAT ADD WEIGHT (WHERE YOU NEED IT)

GATHERING OF FABRIC *pleating, ruching, wrap-around skirts*

DETAILS *pockets, angles, appliqués*

CUTS THAT SUBTRACT WEIGHT (WHERE YOU DON'T WANT IT)

STRAIGHT, DRAPING FABRIC

VERTICAL DETAILS *princess seams, pressed seams*

Thou shalt ignore clothing tags— the fit is the thing

When I agree to make a dress for a woman going to a big event like the Academy Awards, the process goes something like this: I sketch out the item with my client. Then, a fit model who's the same height and weight as my client comes in. The fit model does three fittings before the client herself tries the dress on. Once my client does walk in? It takes three more fittings to get the dress just right.

The point is, there's a huge amount of personal fittings behind the scenes. Yet, how many times do you tailor the clothes you find on the rack to fit you? Probably not very often. And for most of you, never. But the fact is, choosing clothes is not about what size is on the tag in the back of those pants, it's about how well they fit you.

Keep in mind that all companies size clothing in different ways. Some companies even partake in something called vanity sizing. Have you ever heard of this? They actually add inches to their clothing so that when you try something on, you can fit into a size smaller than you are. That's why you can be a 32 waist in one brand and a 34 in another; a medium in one brand and a large in another. But all this does is add to the disparity between clothing sizes, and cause you grief.

But it proves my point: **The number on the little tag on the back of your pants or jacket is not important. Ignore it! Who even sees what size you're wearing anyway? Nobody. What people notice is how your clothes fit.**

Generally speaking, if there are wrinkles in the fabric when you try it on, the garment is either too small or too big. If it's too large, and your body seems to be swimming under the material, it will make you look even larger. And if it's too small or too tight, it will magnify flaws on your body, which will also make you look bigger.

DEFINITION OF THE IDEAL FIT: Clothing that traces your natural silhouette very closely without clinging, such that the fabric remains taut and unwrinkled. SYNONYM: Clothes that make people say, *"Wow, you look amazing, have you lost weight?"* ANTONYM: Big, baggy clothes that could be swapped for a burlap sack without noticing much difference; also, stretchy clothes that fit so tight, you body looks like sausage meat.

If clothes don't fit you off the racks, make it a habit to bring your clothes to a tailor to be fit to you. Yes, tailoring clothes costs a few extra dollars. But for the cost of a few dollars, you can feel like a million bucks every time you step out in public. If you're making an alteration, such as shortening a pair of pants, lengthening a sleeve, or taking in a skirt, a dry cleaner can usually do that for you at a very affordable price. If you need to adjust the fit on a jacket, a pair of pants, or a dress that's not fitting well, it's worth spending more to have it done right.

Thou shalt hail accessories

After the dresses at the Academy Awards, the next thing everyone wants to know about are the accessories. Because they, too, can make or break a single outfit. And chances are, you're not thinking as much about them as you should be. If you're not convinced of the power of accessories, let me explain **THE TOP 5 REASONS TO PAY MORE ATTENTION TO ACCESSORIES:**

REASON NO. 1

They can change an outfit from formal to casual (and vice versa) in just a few seconds

You can dress many outfits up or down depending on the garnishes you add. Take the little black dress, for example. Adding a pearl necklace will create a much different impression than adding a long strand of turquoise-colored plastic beads. Accessories also pack lighter in a suitcase, so you can create both classy and casual looks with one simple outfit.

REASON NO. 2

They're more affordable than clothes

Yes, some accessories are expensive, such as a nice leather handbag or expensive jewels. But many less-expensive accessories can still add colorful appeal or eye-catching touches to your basic wardrobe staples. For instance, you can add an embroidered belt to a pair of basic black pants or a beautifully patterned scarf to a plain white dress shirt, and you've changed your look for very little money.

REASON NO. 3

They can play up your sexiest assets

A beautiful, sparkling pendant necklace that hangs low on your chest can draw the eye to a very sexy area. If you have beautiful arms or wrists, a stunning bracelet can draw the eye there.

REASON NO. 4

They're a great diversion from your flaws

If you don't want people looking at your hips, bring their eye up to your face with pretty earrings, a brooch on your shirt, a scarf, or a pretty choker necklace. Or, if you're more proud of your legs than your arms, add subtle sex appeal to any outfit with one of the most beloved accessories of all: fabulous shoes.

REASON NO. 5

They can add a trendy touch to your neutral basics

Changing your accessories allows you to work many different "looks" without changing much at all. For example, you can take a classic white T-shirt and change its look simply by what you add. If you feel like looking feminine, choose flirty charms, lockets, or pendants. If you want to look bohemian, add accessories made of natural materials, like wooden beads, glass, or seashells. If you want to look elegant, add a pair of simple diamond or pearl stud earrings.

The prints and accessories must be in scale with the body

Just because you see a gorgeous, floral print on the mannequin in the window, doesn't mean it will look good on you. It might look better as a bedspread. Prints can have a drastic impact on making you look larger or smaller than you are.

This is news to many, many women, but it's true: The scale of your print pattern and the scale of your accessories must be in proportion to the scale of your body.

Let me explain with two more simple rules:

The scale of your print pattern must be in scale with your body

Here's what I mean by this. If you are a short, petite woman, and you wear a large floral print—such as oversized bright blooms on a spacious white background—your body will seem shrunken by the print. If you're a tall, plus-size woman, and you wear a dainty polka-dot print—like tiny royal blue dots on a white background—your body will seem disproportionately large in comparison to the small print.

If you want to make part of your body look larger or curvier, wear patterns with large spaces in between them, irregular print patterns, and strong color contrasts between the print and background.

If you want to make part of your body look smaller, wear patterns with regular spaces between them, regular patterns, and a low color contrast between the print and the background.

The scale of your accessories must be in scale with your body

Tiny girls who wear oversized bags, oversized necklaces, and oversized coats and sweaters look lost beside them, and seem even smaller in comparison. And large women who carry tiny bags (like delicate clutch purses) dwarf them, making themselves seem larger in comparison.

Put more simply, little things on big people look ridiculous. And big things on little people look ridiculous. Keep your accessories in proportion to your body. The more the items balance with the size of your figure, the better you will look.

Thou shalt wear the V-neck shape— it looks good on every woman

If all else fails and you find yourself in a "What to wear?" panic, choose a shirt with a V-neck cut. This includes V-neck sweaters and V-neck tops, dress shirts, wrap shirts, surplices, and wrap dresses.

Why? Because whether you're short, average or tall; whether you're slender, medium, full or plus size; whether you've got big shoulders, big hips, or big everything-in-between, a V-neck cut will help.

A V-NECK WILL

Draw attention to the center of your body and away from your trouble spots and create a slimming effect. By angling down toward your waist from both shoulders and meeting at a point in the middle of your chest, it mimics your torso. This will create the illusion of a slimmer, skinnier waist.

!

THE
FOUR STEPS
TO SEXY

*Now I'll show you how
to determine your
individual body type.*

MEASURE YOURSELF

To dress your body right, you have to
know your body. Don't just guess.
(Believe me, mirrors can be deceiving!)
So, grab a measuring tape and a
friend to help you, because it's very
difficult to measure some parts
of yourself and get it right.
The more accurate you are now,
the better you'll look later.

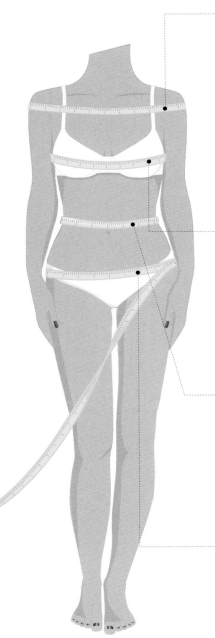

YOUR SHOULDERS
MEASUREMENT #1

This is the hardest measurement to do
by yourself, so you really should
ask someone to help. Place the measuring
tape at the tip of one shoulder and wrap
it all the way around you like a shawl
until it meets back at the same shoulder.
The tape should skim the top of
your shoulders so closely, it almost slips
off. This is the widest circumference
of your shoulders. Now, fill this in:

MY SHOULDERS ARE _____ INCHES/CM

YOUR BUST
MEASUREMENT #2

Stand up straight and wrap the measuring
tape around your back and across the fullest
part of your breasts, usually the middle of
them. Pull the measuring tape as taut as you
can without changing the shape of your
breasts. If things start to squish, you've gone
too far. Now, fill this in:

MY BUST IS _____ INCHES/CM

YOUR WAIST
MEASUREMENT #3

Wrap the measuring tape around your torso,
at the smallest part of your natural waist.
It should wrap flat around your back
without buckling and meet just above your
belly button. Now, fill this in:

MY WAIST IS _____ INCHES/CM

YOUR HIPS
MEASUREMENT #4

Hold the measuring tape at one hip,
below your hip bone, at the fullest part of your
hip. Then, keeping the tape flat, wrap
it around the largest part of your butt
(no cheating!), your other hip, and bring it back
to the meeting point. Now, fill this in:

MY HIPS ARE _____ INCHES/CM

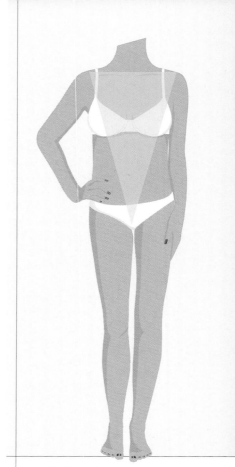

MATCH YOUR SHAPE

Now that you've measured yourself (shoulders, bust, waist, and hips), use those numbers to help determine your silhouette shape.

INVERTED TRIANGLE

Your shoulders or bust are larger than your hips.

JUST TO BE SURE,
CHECK THE NUMBERS:

Your shoulder or bust measurements are *more than 5% bigger* than your hip measurement.

FOR EXAMPLE:

*If your shoulders measure 36"
your hips will be 34 1/4"
or smaller.*

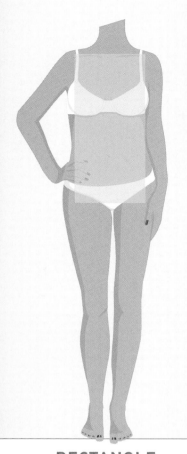
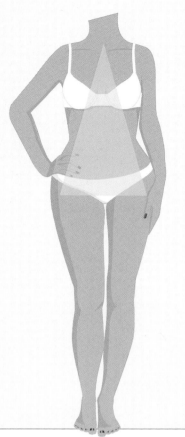
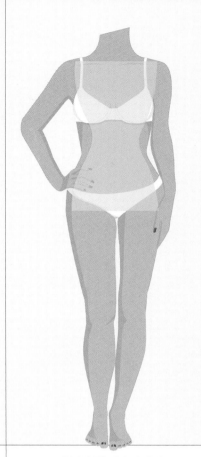

RECTANGLE

Your shoulders, bust, and hips
are around the same size,
with no defined waistline.

JUST TO BE SURE,
CHECK THE NUMBERS:

Your shoulder, bust,
and hip measurements are
within 5% of each other.

Your waist is
less than 25% smaller
than your shoulder
or bust measurements.

FOR EXAMPLE:

*If your shoulders measure 36″
your waist will be 27″
or more.*

TRIANGLE

Your hips are wider
than your shoulders.

JUST TO BE SURE,
CHECK THE NUMBERS:

Your hip measurement is
more than 5% bigger
than your shoulder
or bust measurements.

FOR EXAMPLE:

*If your shoulders measure 36″
your hips are 37 ³/₄″ or larger*

HOURGLASS

Your shoulders and hips are
around the same size,
with a very defined waistline.

JUST TO BE SURE,
CHECK THE NUMBERS:

Your shoulder and
hip measurements are
within 5% of each other.

Your waist is
at least 25% smaller
than your shoulder,
hip, and bust measurements.

FOR EXAMPLE:

*If your shoulders and hips
measure 36″ your waist
is 27″ or smaller.*

FIND YOUR COLOR

(AND ITS CORRESPONDING NUMBER)

WEIGHT (POUNDS)

HEIGHT (FEET & INCHES)	90	95	100	105	110	115	120	125	130	135	140	145	150	155	160	165
4'9"																
4'10"																
4'11"	1					2						3				
5'0"																
5'1"																
5'2"																
5'3"																
5'4"																
5'5"		5							6							
5'6"																
5'7"																
5'8"																
5'9"																
5'10"							9						10			
5'11"																
6'0"																
+																
	41	43	45	48	50	52	54	57	59	61	64	66	68	70	73	75

Stay with me, your science homework is almost done!
Now locate the section in the chart below that
lines up with your height and weight.
Once you have found your color, move on to STEP 4.

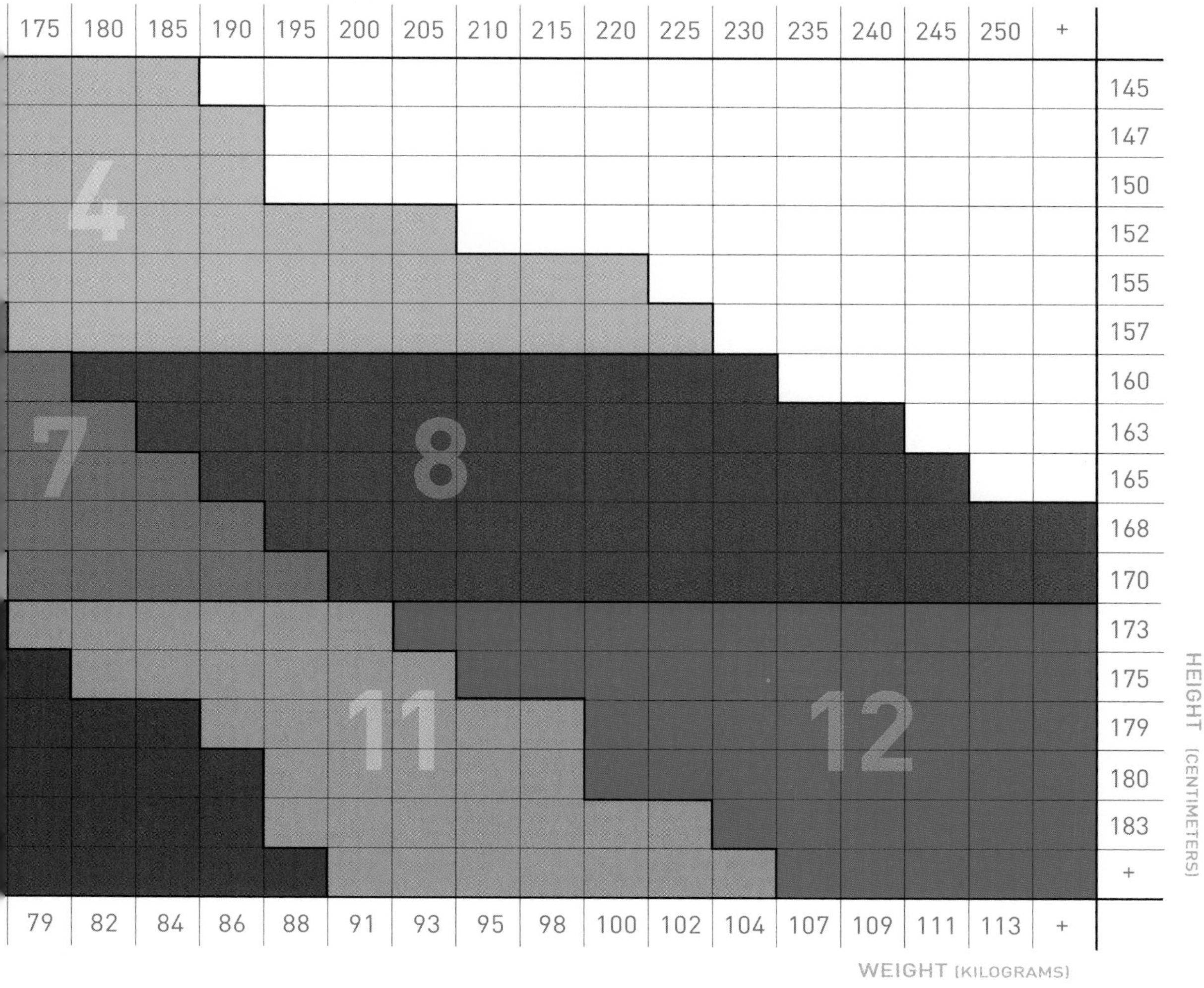

175	180	185	190	195	200	205	210	215	220	225	230	235	240	245	250	+	
																	145
																	147
																	150
																	152
																	155
																	157
																	160
																	163
																	165
																	168
																	170
																	173
																	175
																	179
																	180
																	183
																	+
79	82	84	86	88	91	93	95	98	100	102	104	107	109	111	113	+	

HEIGHT (CENTIMETERS)

WEIGHT (KILOGRAMS)

GO TO YOUR FITTING ROOM

FITTING ROOM 1

INVERTED TRIANGLE
PAGE
72

RECTANGLE
PAGE
76

TRIANGLE
PAGE
80

HOURGLASS
PAGE
84

FITTING ROOM 2

INVERTED TRIANGLE
PAGE
90

RECTANGLE
PAGE
94

TRIANGLE
PAGE
98

HOURGLASS
PAGE
102

FITTING ROOM 3

INVERTED TRIANGLE
PAGE
108

RECTANGLE
PAGE
112

TRIANGLE
PAGE
116

HOURGLASS
PAGE
120

FITTING ROOM 4

INVERTED TRIANGLE
PAGE
126

RECTANGLE
PAGE
130

TRIANGLE
PAGE
134

HOURGLASS
PAGE
138

FITTING ROOM 5

INVERTED TRIANGLE
PAGE
144

RECTANGLE
PAGE
148

TRIANGLE
PAGE
152

HOURGLASS
PAGE
156

FITTING ROOM 6

INVERTED TRIANGLE
PAGE
162

RECTANGLE
PAGE
166

TRIANGLE
PAGE
170

HOURGLASS
PAGE
174

Your Color + Your Shape = YOUR SECTION!

(And be sure to use the handy glossary in the back of the book for definitions and illustrations of some of the types of clothes I recommend for you.)

FITTING ROOM 7

INVERTED TRIANGLE
PAGE
180

RECTANGLE
PAGE
184

TRIANGLE
PAGE
188

HOURGLASS
PAGE
192

FITTING ROOM 8

INVERTED TRIANGLE
PAGE
198

RECTANGLE
PAGE
202

TRIANGLE
PAGE
206

HOURGLASS
PAGE
210

FITTING ROOM 9

INVERTED TRIANGLE
PAGE
216

RECTANGLE
PAGE
220

TRIANGLE
PAGE
224

HOURGLASS
PAGE
228

FITTING ROOM 10

INVERTED TRIANGLE
PAGE
234

RECTANGLE
PAGE
238

TRIANGLE
PAGE
242

HOURGLASS
PAGE
246

FITTING ROOM 11

INVERTED TRIANGLE
PAGE
252

RECTANGLE
PAGE
256

TRIANGLE
PAGE
260

HOURGLASS
PAGE
264

FITTING ROOM 12

INVERTED TRIANGLE
PAGE
270

RECTANGLE
PAGE
274

TRIANGLE
PAGE
278

HOURGLASS
PAGE
282

FITTING ROOM 1

If you're short and petite, you're in the right place. Just find your silhouette and prepare to get sexy.

SHORT PETITE INVERTED TRIANGLE

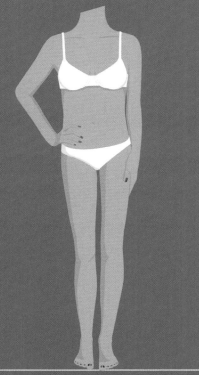

YOU

You are **SHORT**.
[BETWEEN 4'9" AND 5'2"]

You are **PETITE**.
[BETWEEN 90 AND 110 LBS.]

Your body forms an
INVERTED TRIANGLE
as your shoulders are
wider than your hips.

You have broad shoulders.
Your hips are small.
Your legs and butt are slim.

YOUR BLESSING

You have an adorable shape. Yes, you're shorter than average, but you're also very slender, which makes you appear slightly taller. You have beautiful, broad shoulders, and you have small hips and a tiny bottom. Also, because you're so petite, the difference between your shoulders and hips is minimal, which means it will require less effort to balance your body into a sexy silhouette. Your broad-shouldered figure is what most clothing manufacturers have in mind when they design their clothes. So I call inverted triangles like you "hanger girls," because clothes fall on you the same way they fall on a clothes hanger. That's great news, because it means most styles on the petite racks fall easily on your body. So when it comes to shopping, you can be confident that anything you aim for on the racks will fit you well—even in the children's section!

YOUR CURSE

As a SHORT, PETITE, INVERTED TRIANGLE, you have what's called a high balance, which means that the visual line of your silhouette reaches its broadest point at your shoulders. For this reason, you can appear top-heavy if you choose the wrong clothes. Also, you're fairly short and you lack curves on your hips and butt, so you sometimes look more "cute" than "sexy." Your other curse? You're the smallest on the height chart, which means you're often heading straight to the petite section of the store, which somewhat limits your choices. Additionally, when you do sneak into the children's section, it can be hard to find the sexy, mature styles you're looking for.

YOUR CELEBRITY BODY STAND-IN: Alyssa Milano

WHAT TO WEAR

*Your fashion challenge is to narrow your shoulders, to widen
your hips so they match your broad shoulders, and to reveal more
of your waist. You also want to add height overall.*

DRESSES

Wear **halter-neck, V-neck,** or **U-neck** dresses to draw the eye
in and away from your shoulders. Consider **wrap dresses,** which
do this while also adding slight volume to your hips. Choose small
and delicate prints in scale with your petite frame. Hem dresses
to hit just above or at your knee to lengthen your figure;
showing more leg will make you appear taller.

TOPS

Choose **halters, V-necks, U-necks,
sweetheart necks,** or **wrap tops**
that reveal a triangle of skin in your
chest area to draw the eye in from
your broad shoulders. Try a top with
straps that hit in the center of each
shoulder; this balances the skin
evenly on either side, making your
shoulders seem smaller. Wear
dark-colored tops with light-colored
pants to diminish your top half,
or try **monochromatic outfits** to
lengthen your figure overall.

SKIRTS

Wear **A-line skirts, circle
skirts, gored skirts,** and **wrap
skirts** that flare out to create
the illusion of fuller hips. Hem
skirts to hit just at your knee, or
shorter, to make you appear taller.
Choose skirts in light or bright
fabrics that draw the eye to
your bottom half. Also, choose
heavy fabrics to add more fullness
there. Pick skirts with front
pockets or side pockets,
to broaden your bottom half.

PANTS & JEANS

Try **low-rise pants**
with a wide waistband
to add volume there.
Choose pants with
**diagonal or chunky
pockets** at the hip
area that add curves
to your boy-shaped
hips. Hem your pants
to fit while wearing
mid-height heels
to elongate your look.

COATS & JACKETS

Wear **peplum
jackets** that cinch
at the waist and flare
out. Choose **A-line
jackets** and trench
coats with minimal-
to-no detailing in the
shoulder area that add
fullness to your hips.
**Three-quarter-length
coats** that show off
your legs will make
you appear taller.

JEWELRY &
ACCESSORIES

Wear delicate jewelry
that won't overpower
your petite frame.
Choose thin, **draping
necklaces** that draw
the eye in from your
shoulders. Add
hip-belts to add
curves there. Choose
handbags with long
straps that fall at
your hip to balance
your broad shoulders.

FIGURE 1.1.1
You, only sexier.

SHOES

Wear **peep-toe heels, open-toed slingbacks,** or **pointy-toed
stilettos** to draw the eye all the way to the bottom of your body,
which lengthens your look. Choose shoes with **thin heels** to
make your legs appear longer, and you taller.

WHAT NOT TO WEAR

Really. I mean it.

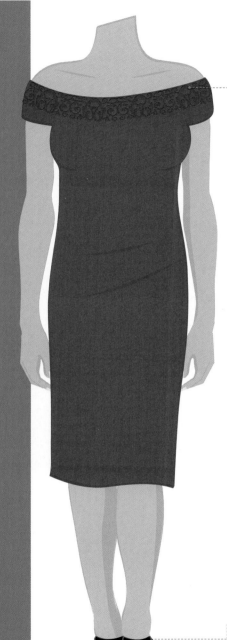

FIGURE 1.1.2
You, wearing the wrong things.

DRESSES

Avoid **off-the-shoulder dresses** that run straight down from your waist and make your hips seem shapeless. Don't wear dresses hemmed at ankle-length, which will make you appear shorter. Also, don't wear **corset dresses** that balloon out too much from the waist, which will make you appear young and girly.

TOPS

Avoid **boatneck tops** and **wide scoop necks,** which create a horizontal line from one shoulder to the other and make you appear wider on top. For the same reason, don't wear strapless tops unless you're going to balance out your shoulders with a full skirt on the bottom. Avoid **big, bulky sweaters** with large stitches that aren't in scale with your small frame and will make you appear top-heavy.

SKIRTS

Steer clear of **long skirts** that make your hips look flatter—and worse, cover up your great legs! Avoid pairing dark colors on the bottom with lighter colors on top, which will make you appear top-heavy. Don't wear **miniskirts** with **short jackets,** which will chop up your frame; varying the proportions of your clothing will lengthen you.

PANTS & JEANS

Avoid dark pants if you're wearing a bright, light, or bold top, as this can make you appear top-heavy. Don't wear tight, **tapered pants** that accentuate how small your hips are. Avoid **cuffs and pleats** on your pants, which shortens your legs.

COATS & JACKET

Steer clear of jackets with **shoulder pads** or extra detailing on the shoulder area, which include military epaulets, decorative buttons, or puff sleeves; they will make you appear top-heavy. Avoid coats with **oversize buttons,** which will dwarf your small frame.

JEWELRY & ACCESSORIES

Avoid jumbo-scaled jewelry, such as large, **long beads** that can make you look miniature in comparison. Don't wear **choker necklaces** that cut the vertical line at your neck in half and make you seem shorter. Avoid large, chunky handbags that aren't proportional to your small frame.

SHOES

Skip shoes with **ankle straps,** which cut off the vertical line of your body and make you appear shorter. Also, avoid too-tall stilettos; "the taller the better" does not hold true for you. Heels that are 3" or higher will seem too big for your frame. Don't wear **knee-high boots** with a skirt, as this covers up your slim legs and breaks the vertical line of your body.

THE NEW YOU

Three ways to put your dress-sexy rules into play.

CASUAL

The V-neck created by this wrap top draws the eye in from your shoulders. The contrasting-colored bow shows off your defined waist and falls toward your feet, adding a lengthening element. The pendant necklace draws the eye straight to your center. The jeans are hemmed to fit your high heels, which makes you seem even taller.

CAREER

The deep U-neck cut of the sweater creates a vertical line toward your center. The skinny belt is in scale with your small frame, and defines your waist. The light-colored skirt adds fullness to your bottom half. The flowing cut of the skirt creates the illusion of curvy hips. The pointy-toed heels help lengthen your look.

FORMAL

The straps of the sheath dress hits at mid shoulder, helping to balance the width on either side. The slight V-neck creates a vertical line pointing toward your waist. The jewel at the center of the dress draws instant attention to your center. The dress hugs your waist and flares slightly, completing the hourglass silhouette.

YOUR ONE FASHION MUST-HAVE: *pockets on your pants*

You can add the illusion of curves on your lower half without actually "adding" anything. Choose pants and jeans with angular front pockets, double pockets, and cargo pockets. The more detail at your hips, the better!

SHORT PETITE RECTANGLE

YOU

You are **SHORT**.
[BETWEEN 4'9" AND 5'2"]

You are **PETITE**.
[BETWEEN 90 AND 110 LBS.]

Your body forms a
RECTANGLE
as your shoulders are the
same width than your hips.

You have broad shoulders.
You have equally wide hips.
Your waist is undefined.

YOUR BLESSING

Great news: You already have the body parts that you need to create a sexy shape! You have slightly broad shoulders and slightly wide hips to match, which means you have a good figure to work with. You also have slim, pretty legs that are in perfect proportion to your frame. Keep that in mind when choosing skirt lengths, and consider being brave about what you reveal from now on. Your other blessing? Because your weight is on the low end of the scale, you don't have many obvious lumps, bumps, or flabby areas, so clothes fall beautifully on your figure. In fact, your body is actually the perfect shape for high fashion—I think of you as a shorter version of Twiggy! Even if you're not looking to become a runway model, you have the slender physique of women who are.

YOUR CURSE

As a SHORT, PETITE RECTANGLE, you lack a defined waist. For that reason, your silhouette almost has a boyish shape. You also have a flat, less-rounded butt than other women. This is great when it comes to fitting into all styles of clothes, but if you want your figure to seem balanced (remember, that is the essence of sexy), it lacks the feminine curves it needs. Your other curse? Because of your smaller frame, it can be hard to shop for clothes. You probably spend most of your time shopping in the petite sections of stores because the other sizes hang on you like bags! That makes it frustrating to find the styles you like in the sizes you need.

YOUR CELEBRITY BODY STAND-IN: *Kylie Minogue*

WHAT TO WEAR

Your fashion challenge is to accentuate your broad shoulders and your wide hips while cinching in your waist. You also want to add height to your look overall.

COATS & JACKETS

Wear **blazers with structured shoulders** to widen your shoulders. Choose blazers with **princess seams** that add shape to your waist to make you appear curvier. Pick **coats with belts** that tie at your middle. Wear **three-quarter-length coats** that hit above your knee and reveal more of your thin legs.

TOPS

Pick **boatnecks** and **wide scoop necks,** which will widen your shoulders, making your waist seem smaller. Or try narrow-set **halter tops;** exposing more skin on the outside of the straps will create the illusion of broad shoulders. Pick tops with **feminine details** to soften up your boyish shape. Or choose **monochromatic tops and bottoms** to lengthen your look overall.

DRESSES

Choose a **corset dress** that cinches in your middle. Or try an **off-the-shoulder dress** with a flared skirt to widen both your shoulders and your hips. Or try an **empire dress** that fits snugly around your chest, then flares out, creating the illusion of a high, defined waistline. Choose **small and delicate prints** for your dresses, which are in scale to your petite size.

SKIRTS

Wear a **circle skirt** or a **gored skirt** that subtly flares out from your waist, making it appear as if you have a cinched waist. Or wear a **trumpet skirt** that hugs your hips, topped with a **princess seam blazer** that adds hourglass curves to your torso. Hem skirts to hit at or above your knee, or choose skirts with side slits; showing more leg makes you appear taller.

PANTS & JEANS

Choose **pants with pockets** at the hip area, to add curves below your waist. Choose trousers with **pressed creases** down the front, which create a strong vertical line and make you appear taller. Dare to wear **short shorts** with pockets at the hips and butt that let you to show off your legs.

JEWELRY & ACCESSORIES

Wear minimal, chic jewelry that fits the scale of your tiny frame. Soften your straight shape with necklaces that fall in a soft curve, such as **delicate pendants or pearls.** Choose **small purses,** in scale with your small figure, that fall either at your bustline or hips to add volume there.

SHOES

Pick **peep-toe heels** or **pointy-toed heels,** which draw the eye to your toes, elongating your look. Heels make your calves appear shapely, implying your figure is, too. Choose heels in the same tone as your outfit, to lengthen your look.

FIGURE 1.2.1
You, only sexier.

WHAT NOT TO WEAR

Really. I mean it.

FIGURE 1.2.2
You, wearing the wrong things.

COATS & JACKETS

Avoid **boxy, cropped jackets** and **Chanel-style jackets** that hit at your waist; the shape exaggerates your rectangle frame and cuts your short figure in half. For the same reason, don't wear **boxy pea coats.** Steer clear of **long overcoats** that make you seem shorter.

TOPS

Avoid **too-short tops and cropped tanks;** showing off skin between your top and your pants breaks up the vertical flow of your figure and makes you appear wider in your stomach area (and there-fore shorter). Steer clear of **big, bulky knit sweaters,** which are too large in proportion to your small frame.

DRESSES

Don't wear **boxy shift dresses** that square off your shoulders then fall straight from your shoulders to your knees. Avoid **long, shapeless dresses** that fall past your knees without implying a waistline. Steer clear of **oversize florals or large, geometric prints** on your dresses, as they are not in scale with your petite frame.

SKIRTS

Don't cover up your great legs with **ankle-length skirts** or **prairie skirts,** which will add too much fabric to your bottom half and drag down your look. Avoid **skinny, pencil skirts** that emphasize how straight your figure already is. Don't wear skirts in fabrics that cling too snugly around your hips and butt, which will make your top seem larger in comparison.

SHOES

Don't wear shoes with **ankle straps or ties;** these will cut off the vertical line of your figure and make you appear shorter. Avoid **clunky, thick-soled shoes,** which will look out of proportion with your slim legs. Finally, avoid **too-tall stilettos.**

PANTS & JEANS

Don't wear **tapered stovepipe jeans, skinny jeans,** or **leggings;** these styles will all accentuate how thin your legs are, and you will appear top-heavy. Avoid **patterned pants** that draw too much attention to your bottom half, putting you off balance.

JEWELRY & ACCESSORIES

Don't wear **chunky choker necklaces** that drastically cut the slimming, vertical line from your neck to your chest. Avoid **oversized handbags** that are too large, proportionally, for your small frame. Don't carry handbags that hit at your waist, which adds unwanted bulk to your boxy middle.

THE NEW YOU

Three ways to put your dress-sexy rules into play.

CASUAL	CAREER	FORMAL
The U-neck cut of the top creates a soft line at your chest, adding curves to your straight frame. The angled short sleeves draw attention to your slim arms. The thin belt, in scale with your small frame, defines your waist. The boots add volume to your legs, bringing the eyes back out to complete the hourglass.	The puffy sleeves on this flouncy top widen your shoulders. The button front creates a subtle V-shape that points toward a small waist. The belt cinches in your middle. The semi-circle skirt tapers out from your waist, creating the illusion of curvier hips. The heels in the same tone as your top create a long, sexy look.	The off-the-shoulder style of this dress appears to broaden your shoulders, so your waist seems smaller in comparison. The contrasting band of fabric defines a waist where there isn't one. The dress flares slightly from your waist and hits above the knee; showing more leg helps you appear taller.

YOUR ONE FASHION MUST-HAVE: *belts to cinch in your waist*

Your waist may be undefined, but it's not big—in other words, it's perfectly cinchable. Wear thick belts, skinny belts, corsets that act as belts, and wrap dresses with belts that tie at your waist.

SHORT PETITE TRIANGLE

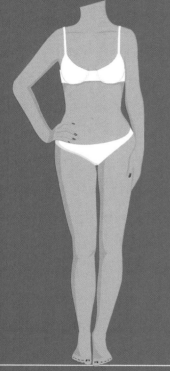

YOU

You are **SHORT**.
[BETWEEN 4'9" AND 5'2"]

You are **PETITE**.
[BETWEEN 90 AND 110 LBS.]

Your body forms a
TRIANGLE
as your shoulders are
wider than your hips.

You have a slim torso
and thin shoulders. Your hips
are wide-set. You have
a mildly shapely bottom.

YOUR BLESSING

You're one lucky woman. You have one feature that lots of women wish they had: You have curvy hips and a shapely behind. And, because of your petite weight, the difference between the size of your shoulders and the size of your hips is small. Instead of being oversized, you have just enough of a womanly shape to create the sexy silhouette you're aiming for. Your other blessing? You have a slender torso and small shoulders. You can wear tops that show off your slender top half, which helps create the slimming effect that makes you appear taller. And if you have a small bust, you get to show off your thin collarbone and a little skin—and that's always sexy.

YOUR CURSE

As a SHORT, PETITE TRIANGLE, you have what's called a low balance. This just means that the visual line of your silhouette reaches its broadest point at your hips. For this reason, you can appear bottom-heavy if you choose the wrong clothes. Also, because you have small shoulders, you look shorter at first glance than you may actually be. (As a short woman, you don't want to look shorter than you are.) Your other curse? Because of the combination of your short and petite frame, your shopping choices tend to be limited to what you can find in the petites section—and sometimes even the children's section—which makes it hard to find the styles you like in the sizes you need. Start befriending your local tailor, because your best bet is having your clothes personally fitted to your tiny figure.

YOUR CELEBRITY BODY STAND-IN: *Lucy Liu*

WHAT TO WEAR

*Your fashion challenge is to make your shoulders appear wider
to match your wide hips, while drawing attention away from your hips
and butt. You also want to add height to your look overall.*

DRESSES

Wear **wide scoop-neck dresses** or **strapless dresses** that show off your
collarbone and widen your shoulders. Choose **empire dresses** that add
volume to your bust area, then graze your hips to smooth out the transition from your waist. Choose **small prints** for your dresses, which are
in scale to your tiny size. When choosing a little black dress, try one
with **wide-set spaghetti straps** and an **A-line skirt** on the bottom.

TOPS

Try **boatnecks, square necks** and
wide scoop necks that rest far
on your shoulders, making your
shoulders look wider. For the
same reason, choose tops with **cap
sleeves,** which create a squared-off
structure to your shoulders. Wear
textured, **touchable sweaters,** such
as cable knit and mohair, or lightweight turtlenecks to draw the eye
up from your hips. Wear tops in the
same colors or tones as your pants
and skirts to create a long, lean look.

SKIRTS

Wear **circle skirts, gored skirts,**
or **A-line skirts** that cinch at your
waist then taper out to create an
illusion of an hourglass figure.
Or try **straight skirts** with buttons
down the front to draw the eye in and
away from your hips. Choose skirts
with prints that have dark backgrounds
and **tiny-scaled patterns,** proportional
to your petite frame. Hem skirts
either above the knee or just below
the calf at seven-eighths length—
a great length for elongating legs.

PANTS & JEANS

Wear **straight-leg** or
boot cut pants that
add fullness below the
knees and balance
your hips from below.
Try **cropped pants**
hemmed to hit just
above the widest point
on your calves so you
appear taller. Or wear
high-waisted trousers
that make your thighs
appear long and lean.

COATS & JACKETS

Choose **puff-sleeved
blazers** to add structure
to your shoulders and
make your waist look
slim in comparison.
Wear **cap-sleeved
jackets** on top of
a feminine camisole,
to add width to your
shoulders. Choose **tex-
tured jean, corduroy,
or velvet jackets** in tiny
shrunken cuts, scaled
to fit smaller frames.

JEWELRY & ACCESSORIES

Pick a **pendant,
charm necklace,** or
minimal, **delicate chain
necklace** that falls
to the top of your
cleavage and
attracts attention
to your slender neck.
Carry a small, **slim
clutch,** which is
proportional to
your petite frame.

SHOES

Wear **pointy-toed heels** in the same tone as your outfit
to elongate your look and make your hips appear
thinner. Or wear classic **ballet flats,** proportionate to your petite
leg length, paired with an **A-line skirt** or **slim-fitted pants.**

FIGURE 1.3.1
You, only sexier.

WHAT NOT TO WEAR

Really. I mean it.

TOPS

Avoid tops that contrast your bottom half and hit at the widest point on your hips, which draws unwanted attention there. Avoid **crew neck** or **raglan tops** that cover up the skin around your slender neck and appear to narrow your shoulders; this only makes your hips seem wider in comparison.

DRESSES

Don't wear **boxy, loose-fitting dresses** with no defined waist, as this will make you appear shapeless instead of sexy. Avoid **long, floor-length dresses** that hide your legs and make you look shorter. Steer clear of **full dresses** that bell out from the waist in stiff fabrics such as taffeta that make you look childish and wider than you are.

COATS & JACKETS

Steer clear of jackets in **soft fabrics,** such as linen, that lack strong shoulder construction and make your shoulders seem small and sloped. Avoid **long overcoats** that cover up your legs and make you seem shorter. Also avoid **double-breasted coats** in stiff fabrics that will make you look boxy instead of curvy.

SKIRTS

Skip skirts with **loud, bright, busy patterns** that emphasize your hips. For the same reason, avoid skirts in **stiff, heavy fabrics** such as leather or tweed that add volume to your full bottom half. Don't wear skirts with **horizontal details,** such as bright stitching or appliqués, or with ruching at the waist, which all work to widen your lower half and make you look shorter.

SHOES

Avoid shoes with **ankle straps,** which cut the vertical line of your legs and make you seem shorter. And steer clear of **too-tall stilettos;** heels that are 3" or higher will seem too large in scale for your petite frame.

PANTS & JEANS

Avoid **cuffed trousers,** which breaks the vertical line of your body and will make you look shorter. Don't wear **flared pants** that bring the eye a wide line at your feet, shrinking your stature. Don't choose pants with **side pockets** at the hip or thigh, which widens your hips.

JEWELRY & ACCESSORIES

Don't wear **chunky choker necklaces** that make your slender neck seem shorter. Steer clear of **long-handled handbags** that fall at the hip and draw attention to your widest area. Skip large, **bulky accessories** that aren't proportional to your slender frame.

FIGURE 1.3.2
You, wearing the wrong things.

THE NEW YOU

Three ways to put your dress-sexy rules into play.

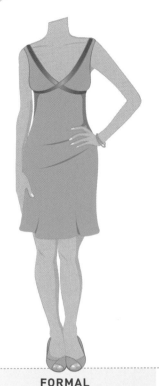

CASUAL

The cute cotton T-shirt with banded ribbing around the neck and sleeves shows off your slim torso. The poufy sleeves add feminine volume on your shoulders to balance your curvy hips. The straight-leg jean to your ankles creates an elongating effect, making you seem taller.

CAREER

The portrait collar on this suit blazer subtly helps widen your shoulders, but not too much for your petite frame. The horizontal band at your high waist creates curves where you want them. The monochromatic suit creates a long look that makes you appear taller.

FORMAL

The wide-set V-neck cut of this sheath widens your shoulders to balance out your hips. The ribbon detail at the chest draws the eye up toward your face. The skirt of the dress skims lightly over your hips to smooth out the fullness you already have there.

YOUR ONE FASHION MUST-HAVE: *boatneck & wide scoop-neck tops*

Tops that sit wide on your shoulders show off your slender collarbone and widen your neck. The wider the neck, the wider your shoulders will appear, perfectly balancing the width of your curvy hips.

SHORT PETITE HOURGLASS

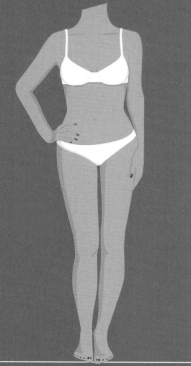

YOU

You are **SHORT**.
[BETWEEN 4'9" AND 5'2"]

You are **PETITE**.
[BETWEEN 90 AND 110 LBS.]

Your body forms an
HOURGLASS
as your shoulders are the
same width as your hips, with
a tiny waist in between.

You have a slim torso
and thin shoulders. Your hips
are wide-set. You have
a mildly shapely bottom.

84

YOUR BLESSING

Welcome to an easy road to sexy. Your figure is already very balanced, so you have an ideal start for a sexy body! You have thin shoulders which are also broad, and that makes you appear taller at first glance. You have slightly curvy hips and a shapely bottom. One of your strongest blessings is that you also have a very defined waist. Put those features together and what do you have? The hourglass silhouette that defines a sexy look. Your other blessing? Because you're so petite, the difference between your curvy hips and your tiny waist isn't large, which means you don't have to do much to keep yourself looking proportional.

YOUR CURSE

To be honest, as a SHORT, PETITE HOURGLASS, you don't have many downsides. Your main curse is that you're short, as part of looking sexy is about creating a taller, sexier figure. Being this petite can also be a curse when it comes to shopping, because most clothing is created for average-height women. Being as short and thin as you are, many styles in main department stores don't fit you off the rack—unless you're shopping in petite sections (or, like many petites, in the children's section). That alone can severely limit your style. Also, since looking sexy involves elongating your look, your short stature could use some help.

YOUR CELEBRITY BODY STAND-IN: *Salma Hayek*

WHAT TO WEAR

Your fashion challenge is to keep your broad shoulders and curvy hips balanced, while defining your waist. You also want to add height to your look overall.

DRESSES

Wear **fitted sheaths** with **V-neck** or **sweetheart necklines.** Try figure-fitting dress with a **high waist** that will make you appear taller. Or wear **wrap dresses** that reveal your hourglass figure. Choose dresses with **small prints** in scale to your tiny size. Hem dresses to just above your knee, as showing off your legs will make you appear inches taller.

TOPS

Choose **surplice tops** and **wrap tops,** which show off your collarbone and your small waistline. Wear **dress shirts** with the top two or three buttons open to create a V-neck that flatters your delicate top half. Wear **monochromatic tops and bottoms** that blend as an overall outfit and make you appear inches taller. Try fitted **sleeveless tops** or shells that show off your slender arms and square off your shoulders.

SKIRTS

Aim for **A-line skirts** with wide waistlines to accentuate your tiny waist. Or try **lightweight gored skirts** or **pleated skirts** sewn up to the hips; both reveal your small waist and curvy hips. Dare to wear **miniskirts** or skirts that hit just above or just below your knee. Or wear **handkerchief** or **asymmetrical** skirts; the uneven hemline elongates your legs, giving you the extra height you're looking for.

PANTS & JEANS

Wear high heels when you have your pants hemmed to lift your bottom while adding literal inches to your figure. Choose **straight-leg pants** that fit snug at your hips, then fall straight to your ankles, elongating your look. Or try **boot cut pants** that balance your hips from below.

COATS & JACKETS

Wear **corseted blazers** or **peplum jackets,** which cinch in at your waist then follow your natural curves out toward your hips. Try a **basic trench coat** that has subtly structured shoulders, a belt that pulls tight at the waist, and a bottom that tapers out toward your hips.

JEWELRY & ACCESSORIES

Wear **dainty necklaces** with a single focal point—such as a charm, a colored stone, a diamond, or a locket— to bring the eyes up to your slender neck. Use your hair as a sexy accessory: Styling it up creates a taller look while showing off your delicate neck and collarbone.

SHOES

Choose **peep-toed heels** or **pointy-toed heels** that draw the eye to the tip of your toes and lengthen your look overall. Pick shoes in the same color as your pants or skirt to create one, long vertical line on your body and make you look taller.

FIGURE 1.4.1
You, only sexier.

WHAT NOT TO WEAR

Really. I mean it.

DRESSES

Don't wear **empire dresses** that flow too loosely over your thin waist. For the same reason, steer clear of **drop-waist dresses** that square off your natural curves. Don't wear large bold prints that are proportionally too large compared to your small frame. Avoid hemming your skirts to hit at the widest point on your calf.

TOPS

Avoid **crew neck tops, raglan tops, turtlenecks,** or other high-necked styles that conceal your chest. When wearing button shirts, avoid buttoning them up to the top; for the same reason, avoid adding **scarves** or **brooches** to close the neck of your tops, which will only make you seem thicker around the neck and more top-heavy.

PANTS

Don't wear light-colored pants if you're wearing a dark shirt, as this can make you appear bottom-heavy. Avoid **baggy-fitting pants,** which will make you seem sloppy and short; you have incredible hips and should be showing them off! Don't wear pants with detailing at the hips without balancing out the volume you're creating on the bottom with a bright color or pattern on top.

SKIRTS

Steer clear of skirts with overly ornamental detailing in the hip area, which draws the eyes straight to your hips. Don't wear **circle** or **pleated skirts** in stiff fabrics that add too much volume to your bottom half, without balancing it on top.

COATS & JACKET

Stay away from **long, straight coats** that square off your shape and hide your curvy waistline. Don't choose jackets that hit at your hip or mid thigh, unless they have a waist-defining shape. Avoid **high-stance blazers** that button high on the neck; this makes you look heavier on top and shorter overall.

JEWELRY & ACCESSORIES

Avoid choosing **hip belts** that land at the largest part of your hips, making you seem more bottom-heavy. Don't cover the skin area around your neck with **scarves** or **chunky choker necklaces** that cover up your pretty collarbone and neck.

SHOES

Don't wear **too-tall stilettos;** heels that are 3" or higher will actually seem too large in scale for your petite frame. Avoid **bold, bright, shoes** that will distract from the tall, lean look you're aiming for. Don't wear **chunky heels,** which will make you appear shorter.

FIGURE 1.4.2
You, wearing the wrong things.

THE NEW YOU

Three ways to put your dress-sexy rules into play.

CASUAL

The deep V-neck of this fitted top emphasizes your pretty collarbone and broad shoulders. The bright yellow and small pattern draws attention to your top half, toward your chest. The dark, straight-leg jean hugs your hourglass curves and shows off the sexy shape you already have.

CAREER

The low-stance blazer creates a deep V-neck which lengthens your look and shows off your chest. The light-colored camisole draws attention to the center of your body. The fitted blazer reveals your small waist. The straight-leg pant in the same tone as your blazer creates a long, lean look overall.

FORMAL

The cap sleeves on this wrap dress accentuate your broad shoulders and slender arms. The bow around the waist accentuates your small, defined waist and falls toward your feet, adding a lengthening element. The subtle flare of the dress flows gently over your hips, completely balancing your look.

YOUR ONE FASHION MUST-HAVE: *a wrap dress*

This dress accentuates your broad shoulders and reveals as much cleavage as you're willing to show off. It also cinches in at your small waist and just grazes the gentle curves of your hips.

FITTING ROOM 2

If you're short and
of medium weight,
you're in the right place.
Just find your silhouette
and prepare to get sexy.

SHORT
MEDIUM
INVERTED TRIANGLE

YOU

You are **SHORT**.
[BETWEEN 4'9" AND 5'2"]

You are of **MEDIUM** weight.
[BETWEEN 100 AND 145 LBS.]

Your body forms an
INVERTED TRIANGLE
as your shoulders are
wider than your hips.

You have broad shoulders.
Your hips and butt are slim.
Your waist is not defined.

YOUR BLESSING

You've got a good thing going. The first element people will notice about your body are those beautiful, broad shoulders of yours. Yes, your top half is wider than your bottom half. But because you're of medium weight, you're not carrying very much on top. Proportionally, the difference between your shoulders and your small hips isn't drastic. What you have up top is worth showing off, and it's easy to balance your shape by adding volume around your bottom half. As far as those gorgeous shoulders go, here's another bonus: They make you seem taller than you are. And since creating height is part of building the sexy silhouette, you're off to a great start!

YOUR CURSE

As a SHORT, MEDIUM, INVERTED TRIANGLE, you have what's called a high balance, which means that you carry more of your weight in the top half of your body. For this reason, you can sometimes appear top-heavy—and in the wrong clothes, that means you can look heavier and shorter than you actually are. You can also run into problems finding clothes that fit. Why? Because your wide shoulders might not fit into petite clothes, but your tiny bottom half will. It's not difficult to balance out your shape, but it will take extra effort to mix and match sizes to suit your frame.

YOUR CELEBRITY BODY STAND-IN: *Julia Louis-Dreyfus*

WHAT TO WEAR

Your fashion challenge is to either play down your wide shoulders or add some curves to your hips to balance out your shape. You also want to add height overall.

DRESSES

Try dresses with **wide-set straps** that are proportional to your broad shoulders and will make your shoulders appear smaller. Choose dresses with detailing or **front pockets** at the hips to add fullness around your hips where you need it. Wear **corset dresses** that cinch in at the waist, then taper outward toward your knees.

TOPS

Wear dark colors on top and lighter colors on the bottom to draw the eye toward your bottom half. Or wear **monochromatic outfits** that elongate your entire silhouette and make you appear inches taller. Wear **V-neck** or **surplice tops** that draw the eye away from your wide shoulders. Try **tunic tops** or **untucked tailored tops** that hit at the hips. Wear shirts with **three-quarter-length sleeves** that hit the thinnest part of your arms, making your top half appear smaller.

SKIRTS

Choose **A-line skirts, circle skirts, pleated skirts,** or **full gored skirts** that create curves on your small hips. Or try **tulip skirts** that add fullness to your hips, taper in slightly, then flare out. Or pick skirts with horizontal details such as ruching or a **wide fabric belt** that will add the illusion of curves at your hips. Choose skirts in **thick fabrics** that hold their shape on your bottom half, where you want it.

PANTS & JEANS

Pick pants with **diagonal pockets** at the hip, which will create the illusion of wider hips. Or choose jeans with **distressing, bleaching, whiskering,** or **fading** on the hip area to draw attention there. Wear **straight-leg pants** that elongate your legs and make you appear taller.

COATS & JACKETS

Choose a **short, peplum jacket** that flares out from your waist toward your hip. If you have a large chest, wear **high-stance blazers** that button high at your chest to help contain your curves, creating the illusion of an hourglass figure.

JEWELRY & ACCESSORIES

Wear **bold cuffs** or **bangles** that add an element to your hips when your arms hang naturally. Wear **chandelier earrings,** which create vertical lines at your neck, counteracting the horizontal line of your shoulders. Carry a **tiny clutch** that lands at your thighs to draw the eye there.

SHOES

Wear **skinny high heels** to add inches to your height; even a **kitten heel** can help lengthen your look. Choose shoes with details at the toes, such as a **pointy toe** or a **peep toe,** which elongates your look and makes you appear even taller.

FIGURE 2.1.1
You, only sexier.

WHAT NOT TO WEAR

Really. I mean it.

TOPS

Don't wear **off-the-shoulder tops** that underscore just how wide your shoulders are in comparison to your bottom half. Avoid **baggy peasant tops** that make you seem top-heavy. Avoid **cowl neck sweaters** or **turtlenecks** that widen your shoulder area. Don't wear bright colors or textured fabrics on top without balancing it with a pattern on the bottom.

DRESSES

Avoid **boxy shift dresses** that fall on your straight hips and cover up your curves. Don't wear dresses hemmed from the mid calf down; this will cover up your legs and make you appear stumpier. Avoid **halter dresses** with straps that pull from the center of the dress, which will make your shoulders look wider than they are.

COATS & JACKETS

Avoid jackets or coats with **structured shoulders** or heavy detailing on the shoulders (such as **military epaulets** or **large buttons**); these will draw the eye outward and make you appear top-heavy. Don't wear **long coats** that cover your legs and make you seem short.

SKIRTS

Don't wear fitted **miniskirts** that diminish your bottom half and make your shoulders appear wider. Don't wear skirts in **clingy fabrics** or in **dark colors** that will make your top half stand out too much. Avoid fitted **pencil skirts** that emphasize how straight your hips are—unless you're adding a shapely peplum jacket to create imaginary curves from the waist down.

SHOES

Don't wear shoes with **ankle straps** that cut off the vertical line of your legs and make you appear shorter. Avoid **chunky heels** and **thick-soled shoes** that will make your thin legs and ankles actually appear pudgy.

PANTS & JEANS

Steer clear of **black skinny jeans, leggings,** or **pants** in stretch fabrics that emphasize how much slimmer your legs are in relation to your top. Don't wear jeans with **flat fronts** or no back pockets, which will make your bottom half too small to balance your wider top.

JEWELRY & ACCESSORIES

Don't wear **large hoops** or **oversized earrings** that will seem proportionally large compared to your short frame. For the same reason, don't carry **oversized handbags** that will lessen your stature; and don't choose bags that rest just under your arm, which adds weight to your upper half.

FIGURE 2.1.2
You, wearing the wrong things.

THE NEW YOU

Three ways to put your dress-sexy rules into play.

CASUAL	CAREER	FORMAL

The tailored top layered under your U-neck sweater hits at your hips, drawing the eye directly to your hips, adding fullness there. The boot cut jeans add fullness around your thighs and calves. Paired with pointy-toed high heels, the pants create a long, lean look, making you look inches taller.

This sleeveless sweater buttons down the length of the front, elongating your figure. The skinny belt at your natural waist emphasizes the hourglass shape. The circle skirt adds fullness to your hips and thighs to balance your shoulders. The pattern skirt on a light background does double duty to bring attention to your lower half.

The V-neck of this dress draws the eye to the center of your body, away from your wide shoulders. The wide cut of fabric on either side of your neck is in proportion to your wide shoulders, making them appear smaller. The semi-circle skirt adds a bit of fullness at the hips; hemmed above the knee, it also makes you appear taller.

YOUR ONE FASHION MUST-HAVE: *a full skirt hemmed above your knee*

The skirt cinches at your waist, then flows out, adding volume to your hips to balance your broad shoulders. Be sure to choose one in light to medium-weight fabrics rather than a heavy fabric that will balloon out and make you look childish.

SHORT MEDIUM RECTANGLE

YOU

You are **SHORT**.
[BETWEEN 4'9" AND 5'2"]

You are of **MEDIUM** weight.
[BETWEEN 100 AND 145 LBS.]

Your body forms a
RECTANGLE
as your shoulders are the
same width as your hips.

You have broad shoulders.
You have equally wide hips.
Your waist is undefined.

YOUR BLESSING

You have a lot to smile about. Without even doing a thing, you already have the hips and shoulders that are essential to building the hourglass structure that stands for sexy. Your shoulders are strong, your collarbone is pronounced, and you may even have a bit of cleavage to play with. And because you're of medium weight, you're not carrying too much extra meat around your belly area. That makes it easy to cinch in your waist with structured clothes and make you look like a sexy starlet in no time. Your other blessing? Your hips are already balanced by your shoulders, so as long as you keep your top and bottom halves proportional, you'll always look well-balanced.

YOUR CURSE

As a SHORT, MEDIUM RECTANGLE, you have an undefined waist. It can sometimes be difficult to create a waist where there isn't one, but it will be slightly easier for you since you have a medium frame. Also, because of your undefined waist, your body can look a bit boyish. And though it is easy to throw on comfortable clothes that fall loosely on your body, those wide shoulders and wide hips turn loose clothes into burlap bags! Your other curse? As a short woman, it can be hard to find clothes that fit you off the rack—and ones that don't fit can make you look shorter and dumpy. Prepare to befriend your local tailor, because you'll get a more flattering look when your clothes are taken in to fit your personal figure.

YOUR CELEBRITY BODY STAND-IN: *Reese Witherspoon*

WHAT TO WEAR

Your fashion challenge is to accentuate your broad shoulders and your wide hips while cinching in your waist. You also want to add to your height overall.

TOPS

Choose **wrap tops** or **surplices** that create a deep V-neck to draw attention to the center of your body. Or pick tops with **wide-set straps** to widen your shoulders, provided you balance it out on your bottom half with **shapely pants** or **full skirts.** Wear monochromatic tops and bottoms to elongate your look overall.

COATS & JACKETS

Pick jackets with **princess seams** that build in an hourglass silhouette to your torso; match the seams in your jacket to the seams on your pants to create a long, lean look. Wear a **trench coat** that has strong, structured shoulders; a band or a belt at the waist; and an **A-line cut** on the bottom to create the illusion of hips.

SKIRTS

Wear **A-line skirts** that taper outward and create the illusion of curves at your hips, or trumpet skirts that add feminine curves around your hip area. Choose skirts in **mid-to heavyweight fabrics** such as thick cotton to add volume on the bottom half; balance this out with light-colored or textured tops that tie at the waist. Wear **medium-size patterns** that are proportional to your medium frame.

PANTS & JEANS

Wear **straight-leg pants** or **boot cut jeans** with just a subtle flare to elongate your body and make you appear taller. Select pants with **contrasting stitching** to create a long, vertical line to your ankles. Or choose jeans with details around the hips, such as **side pockets, distressing, bleaching,** or **whiskering** around your hips and thighs to make them seem more shapely.

DRESSES

Wear **wrap dresses** with strong shoulders and a belt or tie that cinches in your waist. Or try **corset dresses** that cinch in your waist then flare out toward the knee. Or try a **sweetheart neck-line** that widens your shoulders and adds feminine curves to your boyish shape.

JEWELRY & ACCESSORIES

Draw the eye outward with a **hip belt** or a wide belt that sits at the broadest part of your hip. Carry a **medium-sized purse** in proportion to your medium frame that hits either just below your arm or at your hip, to add fullness to your top or bottom instead of your waist.

SHOES

Choose **pointy-toed heels** which change the angle of your bottom and make it appear perkier, while adding inches to your short figure. Wear shoes in the same color as your outfit to make you seem even taller overall.

FIGURE 2.2.1
You, only sexier.

WHAT NOT TO WEAR

Really. I mean it.

TOPS

Avoid tops with **dainty straps** that are out of scale with your large shoulders and make you seem more top-heavy. Skip tops that cling to the middle of your torso and accentuate your boyish shape. Avoid **sleeveless tops** that make your shoulders and arms seem thick. Don't wear **baggy peasant tops** that make your middle seem even wider.

DRESSES

Steer clear of dresses that fall straight from under your arms down to the hem. Avoid **narrow-set halters** and **square-necked dresses** that accentuate your broad shoulders without adding volume to your hips. Avoid **thin or stretchy fabrics** that cling around your middle and reveal the rectangle there; instead, aim for stiff or heavy crepe fabrics that hold you in.

COATS & JACKETS

Don't wear **double-breasted blazers** or thick **twill pea coats** that mimic your rectangular shape. Steer clear of **straight coats** that button from the neck to your knees without tapering at your waist, which will accentuate a lack of curves. Don't wear **long, ankle-length coats** that cover your slim legs, as this will drastically shorten your figure.

PANTS & JEANS

Don't wear **stovepipe pants, skinny jeans,** or **leggings** that hug your thighs, reveal your flat bottom, and taper toward your ankles. On the other hand, avoid baggy, wide-leg pants such as **palazzo pants** and **cropped pants** that accentuate your body's already boxy look.

SHOES

Don't wear **chunky heels** or thick-soled shoes that seem out of proportion to your medium-sized legs. Steer clear of **square-toed shoes** that underscore your boxy frame. Also, don't wear **slip-on mules with thick heels.**

SKIRTS

Avoid **pencil skirts** that run straight to your knee and emphasize your lack of curves. Avoid **straight, ankle-length skirts** that flatten your bottom and cover your pretty legs; this will make you appear shorter and dumpy, instead of sexy.

JEWELRY & ACCESSORIES

Don't carry **square handbags** that land at your waist and make you look wider there. And don't forget your belt! Wear one at the center of your waist, or wear a hip belt at the broadest point of your lower half to create the illusion of curves.

FIGURE 2.2.2
You, wearing the wrong things.

THE NEW YOU

Three ways to put your dress-sexy rules into play.

CASUAL

The bright yellow top draws attention to your top half, while the contrasting arch on the neckline brings a roundness to your boxy torso. The wide hip belt in a contrasting color adds volume to your hip area. The boot leg jean hemmed to the floor elongates your look and makes you appear taller.

CAREER

The flouncy, front-button top creates a V-neck shape that mimics the tapering you want to create toward your waist. The puffy gathers at the shoulders and elbows soften your boxy shape. The circle skirt hugs your hips and gently tapers out, creating the illusion that your hips have more volume than they do.

FORMAL

The wrap dress creates a flattering V-neck and ties at the waist, creating the illusion that you have one. The puffy short-sleeves add a bit of fullness at your shoulders, making your waist seem smaller in comparison. The peep-toe shoes create one long, monochromatic look which lengthens your look overall.

YOUR ONE FASHION MUST-HAVE: *a corset*

A corseted dress or a corset in your top helps you create a waist where there isn't one. And because of your medium frame, you're small enough for a corset to work its magic without pulling too tight and making it hard for you to breathe!

SHORT MEDIUM TRIANGLE

YOU

You are **SHORT**.
[BETWEEN 4'9" AND 5'2"]

You are of **MEDIUM** weight.
[BETWEEN 100 AND 145 LBS.]

Your body forms a
TRIANGLE
as your hips are wider
than your shoulders.

You have a defined narrow waist.
Your hips are full.
Your bottom is round.

YOUR BLESSING

The good news is that the place you carry most of your weight is in your hips. And that's one of two areas on the body that give off a strong, sexy silhouette (cleavage is the other one—but if you don't have it, you can fake it!). With gorgeous hips, a rounded bottom, and shapely thighs, you're already halfway there. Even if you have more booty than you wish you did, you can easily balance it with the right tops to make your body appear perfectly balanced. Your other blessing? You have a narrow waist and a small ribcage. This makes it easy for you to flatter your upper body and make your midriff look slim. At first glance, those small shoulders and your dainty collarbone sends the message that you're slim from head to toe. Overall, you have a beautiful, feminine shape. Be proud of what you have to work with!

YOUR CURSE

As a SHORT, MEDIUM TRIANGLE, you have what's called a low balance. This just means that the visual line of your silhouette reaches its broadest point at your hips. For this reason, you can appear bottom-heavy if you choose the wrong clothes. And because you're short, that weight sitting on your hips can make you appear squat if you're not careful. Your other curse? If you're like most short, medium triangles, you may have small breasts and narrow, sloped shoulders—they can make you look shorter than you are.

YOUR CELEBRITY BODY STAND-IN: *Jennifer Love Hewitt*

WHAT TO WEAR

Your fashion challenge is to make your shoulders appear wider, to match your wide hips; you also need to draw attention away from your hips and butt. You also want to add height overall.

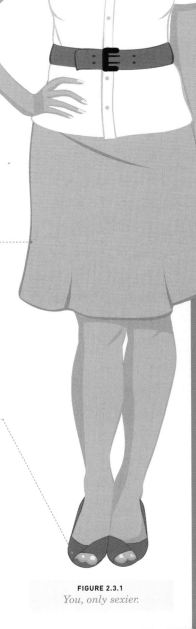

TOPS

Wear a **puffed-sleeve top** or **tailored dress shirt** with an eye-catching collar to widen your shoulders. Or choose wide **scoop-neck tops** that square off your shoulders in order to balance your hips. Wear **lighter colors** on top to bring out your top half. Or choose **monochromatic tops** and bottoms that will make you appear inches taller.

DRESSES

Pick **empire dresses,** which pull the eye up and make your legs seem a mile long. Wear **halter dresses** in fluid, mid-weight fabrics or wrap dresses in a matte jersey to downplay your bottom half. Wear **shorter hem lengths** to show off your legs, or wear **asymmetrical hemlines** that call attention to your legs—showing off more leg will make you look taller.

PANTS & JEANS

Pick **dark colored bottoms**— don't underestimate the slimming properties of black, charcoal, dark brown, navy, and dark green. Choose **high-waisted, straight-leg trousers** that make your torso appear shorter and your legs appear longer. On casual days, try **palazzo pants,** which fall with ease over your hips without adding volume to your bottom.

SKIRTS

Choose **gored skirts, godet skirts, trumpet skirts,** or **pencil skirts** hemmed at knee length that drape with ease over your hips and show off your legs. Or choose **A-line cuts** with a small or no waistband that flow easily over your hips and keep your silhouette looking defined. Try skirts with **side slits,** which make your legs seem longer and you, taller.

COATS & JACKETS

Wear **puff-sleeved blazers, military jackets,** or blazers with strong shoulders that form a distinct shoulder line. Choose jackets in **structured fabrics** such as denim, suede, tweed, or velvet, which add texture to your torso. Or wear **A-line trench coats** to disguise fuller hips.

JEWELRY & ACCESSORIES

Choose a **chunky necklace** to draw attention up from your hips. Or try **medium-sized chandelier earrings, drop earrings,** or **hoops** to flatter your neck. Carry a small and **simple clutch** under your arm, which is proportional to your short frame.

SHOES

Wear **pointy-toed heels** in the same tone as your outfit, to elongate your look. Or choose heels with **cutaway arches, peep-toes,** or pumps that are cut low at the toe to create a long line to your toes and make you appear taller.

FIGURE 2.3.1
You, only sexier.

WHAT NOT TO WEAR

Really. I mean it.

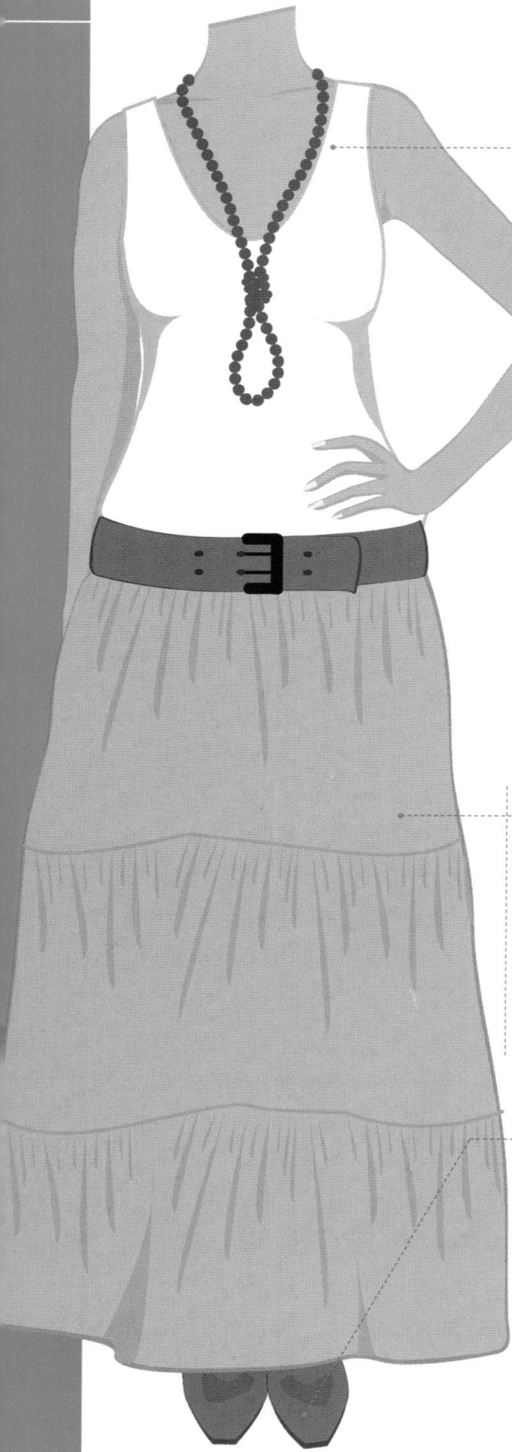

TOPS

Don't choose tops or sweaters that hit at your hips. Avoid **crew neck tops** or **raglan styles** that cover up your slender neck, narrow your shoulders, and can make you look heavier than you are. Skip **halter tops** if your shoulders are sloped, as they'll accentuate your bottom half. Don't wear **sleeveless tops** or tank tops that make your upper half seem even smaller.

DRESSES

Steer clear of dresses in **stiff, heavy fabrics** that bell out and add unwanted volume to your bottom half. Also, don't wear dresses that balloon out from the waist and can make your short figure look childish. Steer clear of **loud, busy patterns** that emphasize all the wrong regions as the print bends over wider sections on your body.

PANTS & JEANS

Don't wear **flared pants** that make your legs seem shorter and your thighs heavier. Avoid pants with details on your hips, which will draw the eye to the widest point on your figure. Don't wear **cuffs or pleats** on your pants, which take inches off your height. Skip **cargo pants** with big pockets at the hips and thighs.

SKIRTS

Don't wear **prairie skirts** or **long skirts** hemmed at your ankle, which pull the eye down to your bottom half and make you seem heavier and shorter. Avoid **horizontal details** on skirts, such as **tiers, ruffles,** and **front pockets** that break up your vertical line and make your hips seem wider. Don't wear **circle skirts** or **pleated skirts** that bell out, adding unwanted volume at your hips.

SHOES

Avoid **dark, knee-high boots** that will shorten your legs and make your hips seem wide. Don't wear **square-toed** shoes that cut off the vertical flow of your figure.

COATS & JACKETS

Don't choose **boxy jackets** hemmed to your hip, which will highlight your trouble zones. Avoid **front pockets** on your blazers that add unwanted volume to your hips. Avoid **soft fabrics** such as linen or flimsy jersey material, as this will make your shoulders seem too small and sloped.

JEWELRY & ACCESSORIES

Steer clear of **wide hip belts** that emphasize the largest part of your silhouette. Don't wear **jumbo-sized jewelry** such as long, chunky necklaces that aren't in scale with your short frame and draw the eye down toward your wide hips. Don't carry **large shoppers or totes** that draw attention to your hips and thighs.

FIGURE 2.3.2
You, wearing the wrong things.

THE NEW YOU

Three ways to put your dress-sexy rules into play.

CASUAL

The bright red top paired with dark bottoms adds fullness to your top half. The wide-set V-neck of this top appears to widen your shoulders to balance out your bottom half. The straight-leg jean elongates your look, making you appear taller and slimmer. The pendant necklace draws the eye up to your slender collarbone.

CAREER

The shoulders on this blazer add structure to your shoulders. The corset emphasizes your waist. The corseted blazer cinches your waist, emphasizing the curves there. The light-colored camisole and pretty necklace both bring the eye up to your chest, while the monochromatic suit makes you seem taller and slimmer overall.

FORMAL

The gathered scoop neck of this dress draws the eyes out toward your shoulders while adding fullness to your chest area to balance your curvy hips. The band at your high-waist makes you seem taller than you are. The skirt of the dress barely skims over your hips to smooth out your fullness on the bottom.

YOUR ONE FASHION MUST-HAVE: *wide scoop-neck tops*

The wider the neck, the wider your shoulders will appear, perfectly balancing the width of your curvy hips. Choose tops in the same tonal colors as your pants or skirts, and you'll lengthen your look and appear taller and sexier.

SHORT
MEDIUM
HOURGLASS

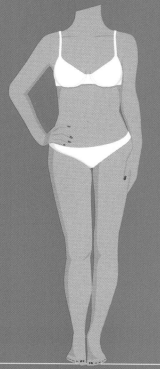

YOU

You are **SHORT**.
[BETWEEN 4'9" AND 5'2"]

You are of **MEDIUM** weight.
[BETWEEN 100 AND 145 LBS.]

Your body forms an
HOURGLASS
as your shoulders are
the same width as your hips,
with a tiny waist in between.

You have broad shoulders
and a shapely bust. Your hips
and butt are curvy. Your
waist is small and defined.

YOUR BLESSING

You have a lot to be thankful for. You were born with a great body with curves in all the right places. Though you're a petite woman, you have broad shoulders and might even have cleavage—though how much of it you show off is entirely up to you. You also have shapely hips and a round butt, which are vital to the sexy silhouette. To top it off, you have the hourglass waist of a belly dancer. In other words, you're all woman! Your other blessing? Even though you're on the shorter end of the height scale, your balanced body makes you seem taller. Those broad shoulders of yours are the first thing people notice, so instead of looking squatty, you look lean. Your only job is to keep your body balanced and show off the figure you already have. Lucky you!

YOUR CURSE

As a SHORT, MEDIUM HOURGLASS, you lack the height that helps define a tall, sexy silhouette. And because you're short, the curves you carry on your top and bottom halves can easily be thrown out of balance. Those of you on the very short end of the spectrum can easily add accidental weight to your hips and butt, making you look more bottom-heavy than you actually are. And, if you're not careful to accentuate your waistline, your whole silhouette will seem larger than it is. Your other curse? As a short woman, it can be hard to find the styles you want in the stores you want to shop in; you're often confined to shopping in petite areas, which lessens your options.

YOUR CELEBRITY BODY STAND-IN: *Jessica Simpson*

WHAT TO WEAR

Your fashion challenge is to keep your broad shoulders and wide hips balanced, while defining your waist. You also want to add height overall.

DRESSES

Wear **figure-fitting sheath dresses** that hug your hourglass curves. Hem your dresses at knee length or above to reveal more of your legs, which will make you look taller. Wear **wrap dresses** that cinch your small waist while flattering your shoulders and hips. Choose **asymmetrical** or **handkerchief dresses** that skim over your hourglass hips, then reveal different parts of your leg to lengthen you.

TOPS

Pick **wrap tops** and **surplices,** which draw the eye to your chest and wrap around your slim waist, accenting your hourglass shape. Choose fitted **V-neck, U-neck,** or **square-neck sweaters** that hug your torso. Wear **dress shirts** and unbutton two or three buttons for a neck-flattering V-neck. Wear **monochromatic tops and bottoms** to elongate your entire silhouette and make you appear inches taller.

SKIRTS

Wear **A-line skirts** that smooth over your hips steadily. Or try **gored skirts, godet skirts,** or **pleated skirts** that are stitched into place up to the hip line and then release into a flare; all of these allow you to show off your hourglass figure without adding pouf to your hips.

PANTS & JEANS

Choose **mid-rise jeans** instead of low-rise jeans, as they will create a smoother line from your waist through your hips. Try **stovepipe jeans** that hug your curves perfectly. Or wear **straight-leg pants** and **men's-cut trousers;** the fullness below the knee will balance your hips.

COATS & JACKETS

Wear **princess seam blazers,** which mimic your hourglass shape. Or wear **peplum jackets,** which cinch in at your thinnest point then flare out toward your hips. Try a **basic trench coat** hemmed to hit above the knee, so you reveal more leg and appear taller.

JEWELRY & ACCESSORIES

Choose **pendant necklaces** with a single focal point such as a small diamond that falls above your cleavage; the V-shape of the necklace mimics the angle you're trying to create toward your waist. Wear **small jewelry** that doesn't overpower your short frame.

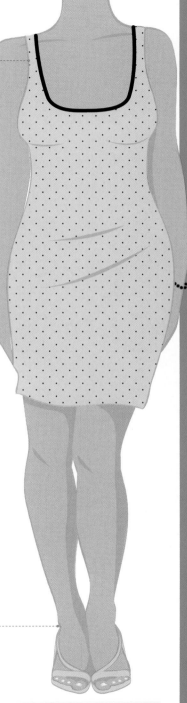

SHOES

Wear **strappy stiletto sandals** or **pointy-toed heels** in the same color as your outfit to elongate the vertical line of your body and make you seem taller. For extra detail, try **peep-toe shoes** or **low-cut pumps** that draw the eye straight to the tips of your feet. Or wear **classic ballet flats** with Capris to flatter your short figure.

WHAT NOT TO WEAR

Really. I mean it.

FIGURE 2.4.2
You, wearing the wrong things.

DRESSES

Don't wear **empire dresses, drop-waist dresses,** or **boxy shift dresses** that disguise your small waist and turn your hourglass figure into a rectangle. Avoid **ruching** or **busy prints** around the hip area of your dress. Don't wear dresses in **thick fabrics** such as heavy twill, wool, or tweed that flatten your sexy curves.

TOPS

Avoid **high crew necks, raglan tops,** and **turtlenecks.** As you are of medium weight and may have some bust on top, turtlenecks can create the dreaded "uniboob" that will make you appear top-heavy. Don't wear tops with pockets at the bustline or detailing at the shoulders without balancing the added volume on the bottom. Don't button tailored dress shirts up to your neck or cut off the open neckline with thick scarves.

PANTS & JEANS

Don't wear **low-rise jeans,** which hit at the widest point on your hips, unless you're balancing them with more volume on your top half. Don't wear **palazzo pants** or **cargo pants** with large pockets that land at the hip, offsetting the balance of your shape. Avoid **distressing** or **whiskering** on the thighs of your jeans which will make your thighs and hip area appear wider than they are.

SKIRTS

Don't wear **horizontal stripes** on your skirts, which will make your hips look dispropor-tionately bigger. Don't wear **large prints** on your skirts that aren't in scale with your short frame, making your bottom half seem big. As with dresses, don't wear skirts in **thick fabrics** that disguise your hourglass curves.

COATS & JACKET

Steer clear of **boxy cropped jackets** and **pea coats** with front pockets at your waist, both of which widen your torso. Avoid **long jackets** that land at your hip, which ignore your waistline and add weight to your broadest point on your bottom half. Don't wear **ankle-length coats,** which will shorten you.

JEWELRY & ACCESSORIES

Skip **hip belts** that land at the widest part of your hips, making you seem bottom-heavy. Don't cover the skin area around your neck with **scarves** or **chunky choker necklaces** that don't allow the eye to see some skin.

SHOES

Avoid shoes in contrasting colors from your pants or skirt that will distract from your curves. Don't wear **big chunky soles, wide heels,** or **square toed-shoes,** all of which will make you appear wider instead of taller.

THE NEW YOU

Three ways to put your dress-sexy rules into play.

CASUAL

The low-stance blazer over the light-colored camisole draws the eye up to your chest, while creating a deep V-neck that makes you seem slim and tall. The structured long sleeves keep your shoulders looking broad. The straight-leg jean hemmed to the floor elongates your look, making you seem taller.

CAREER

The tailored white shirt creates a V-neck that reveals your chest and cleavage. The sleeves rolled up to three quarter length hit at a thin part of your arm, making your upper half appear dainty. The pencil skirt is hemmed above your knees to show more leg, making you appear taller.

FORMAL

The V-neck of this bright sheath dress enhances your cleavage and hugs your waist, accentuating your hourglass curves. The dainty pendant necklace mimics the V-shape that tapers toward your waist. The hem of the skirt hits high to show more of your legs, which elongates your figure overall.

YOUR ONE FASHION MUST-HAVE: *a fitted sheath dress*

Choose one in an eye-catching color. Make sure the straps hit evenly on each shoulder to keep your top half balanced with your bottom. As it gently hugs your curves, it emphasizes all the best features of your hourglass shape.

FITTING ROOM 3

If you're short and full-figured, you're in the right place. Just find your silhouette and prepare to get sexy.

SHORT
FULL
INVERTED TRIANGLE

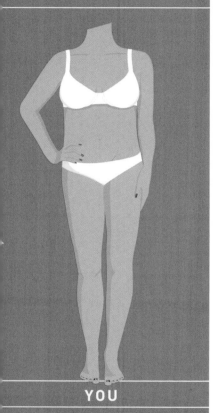

YOU

You are **SHORT**.
[BETWEEN 4'9" AND 5'2"]

You are **FULL**-figured.
[BETWEEN 135 AND 170 LBS.]

Your body forms an
INVERTED TRIANGLE
as your shoulders are wider
than your hips.

You have wide shoulders
and large arms. Your hips are not
as wide as your shoulders.

YOUR BLESSING

You have been naturally blessed with curves. In fact, as a full-sized woman, you may even have a big chest that you get to play up. (Do you know how many women would kill for body parts like yours?) You also have broad shoulders up top. And for a short woman, this is truly a great gift. That's because wider shoulders make you appear taller at first glance by pulling up the eyes to your top half and away from your hips. Your other blessing? Your butt and thighs are small, which means you can play up your bottom half instead of having to hide it. You're also lucky because beneath those narrow hips of yours are a pair of terrific legs. And though you have a full-size frame, don't be shy about showing off those legs. The more you show, the taller you'll appear.

YOUR CURSE

As a SHORT, FULL, INVERTED TRIANGLE, you have what's called a high balance, which means the visual line of your silhouette reaches its broadest point at your shoulders. You also lack curves in your butt and hips, which are essential in creating a sexy silhouette. Overall, that means you can appear top-heavy if you choose the wrong clothes. You need to pay extra attention in choosing undergarments that hold in and support your fuller figure up top. Also, if you dress the wrong way, any extra pounds you have can make you appear shorter and heavier than you are. Your other curse? While your bottom half fits more easily into clothes in the petite section, it can be difficult to find tops you want in your size.

YOUR CELEBRITY BODY STAND-IN: *America Ferrara*

WHAT TO WEAR

*Your fashion challenge is to narrow your shoulders, to widen your hips
so they match your broad shoulders, and to reveal more
of your waist. You also want to add height and look slimmer overall.*

TOPS

Wear **wrap tops** or **V-neck sweaters** layered over camisoles
and tailored dress shirts; allow the shirts to peek out underneath
at the hips to add extra fullness there. Try an **empire top** that
fits snugly around your bust, then gently tapers out toward
your hips. Choose **shallow U-necks** that draw the eye
to the center of your body, making you appear slimmer.

DRESSES

Choose dresses with **wide straps**
that are in proportion to your
wide shoulders (thin, dainty straps
will make your shoulders look
bulkier in comparison). Wear
A-line dresses, surplice dresses,
or **fitted sheath dresses**
that flare out, gently grazing
your hips to add subtle fullness
to your bottom half.

SKIRTS

Pick **gored skirts, godet skirts,**
or **circle skirts** that hug the waist
before flowing out to create the
illusion of hips. Choose skirts in **bright
or light colors** or **feminine patterns**
to bring up your bottom half. Pick
skirts with **front or side pockets,** both
of which instantly broaden your
bottom half. Hem your skirts at knee
length or above; the more leg
you show, the taller you will seem.

PANTS & JEANS

Stick with **dark-colored straight-leg jeans** or **pressed-crease
pants** that slim and elongate your figure; pair them with heels
to lengthen your whole look. Pick jeans with **full-size back pockets**
that are proportional to your full frame and make your bottom
look curvier to balance your top half. Try pants with **pockets at the
hips** or **angular pockets** at the hips to balance out your shoulders.

COATS & JACKETS

Choose **peplum
jackets** that flare
from the waist or
jackets with **princess
seams,** which nip in
toward the waist then
out toward the hips.
Wear jackets with
**three-quarter-length
sleeves** that cover
the widest part of your
arms and reveal
the thin lower half.

JEWELRY & ACCESSORIES

Wear pretty **pendant
necklaces** that
bring the focus toward
the center, away from
your wide shoulders.
Wear **handbags with
long straps** that fall
at your hip to balance
out your shoulders.
Pick **bold bracelets** or
bangles, in scale with
your full-sized frame,
that hit at the hip.

SHOES

Choose **pointy-toed
heels,** which make
you look taller and
slimmer—even a
small kitten heel
will help. Wear
shoes in the
same color as
your pants
to lengthen
your look.

FIGURE 3.1.1
You, only sexier.

WHAT NOT TO WEAR

Really. I mean it.

TOPS

Don't wear **too-tight tops** that cling to your squared-off torso. At the same time, don't cover up your top half with **baggy tops, crew necks, turtlenecks,** and **high-necked boatnecks,** which will only make you appear even more top-heavy. Don't **color-block** by creating tiers of different colors on your body, as this makes you seem wider and shorter.

DRESSES	SKIRTS
Don't wear **halters, dainty spaghetti straps, sleeveless dresses,** and **strapless dresses** that will only make you look thicker on top. Avoid **ankle-length dresses;** the more leg you show, the taller you will look. Don't wear **boxy dresses** that don't cinch in at the waist in some way, or your inverted triangle frame will become a rectangle.	Avoid **straight, tight,** or **fitted skirts,** which accentuate your small hips and make you seem more top-heavy. Don't wear **ankle-length skirts,** which cover up your calves and will make you look squat. Because you're short, don't wear skirts that balloon out at the hips in thick fabrics, which can make you look more girly than sexy.

PANTS & JEANS

Though you want to add volume at your hips, avoid **low-rise jeans,** which at your full-size weight will reveal too many curves. Don't wear **tight, tapered pants** that accentuate how small you are on the bottom; this will only accentuate how large your top is in comparison.

SHOES	COATS & JACKETS	JEWELRY & ACCESSORIES
Don't wear **chunky heels** or **flats** that make you seem short. Avoid **knee-high boots,** which break up the vertical line you're trying to build on your frame; they will make your legs seem thicker.	Avoid jackets with **shoulder pads,** which will only increase the width of your shoulders. Don't choose **boleros** that cut off your figure at your torso and make you seem thick in the middle. Avoid blazers with **tiny lapels** which will make your shoulders seem even larger in comparison.	Steer clear of **oversized earrings** that draw attention to your shoulders. Don't carry **oversized purses** or handbags that hit at your waist; though you have a full-size frame, you're still short, and big bags will weigh you down and make you seem shorter.

FIGURE 3.1.2
You, wearing the wrong things.

THE NEW YOU

Three ways to put your dress-sexy rules into play.

CASUAL

The U-neck cut of the shirt draws the eye away from your shoulders, exposing a more vertical area of your neck than horizontal, making you appear taller and slimmer. The dark straight-leg jeans lengthen your look to keep you from looking short and squat. The belt creates a waist where there isn't one.

CAREER

The dress shirt is unbuttoned to reveal a shallow V-neck that flatters your chest. The princess seams in the shirt create the illusion of hourglass curves. The shirt rolled up to three quarter length covers the thickest part of your arms. The circle skirt adds volume in your hip area, to balance out your shoulders.

FORMAL

The wide-set straps on the top of this dress is in proportion to your broad shoulders. The shallow V-neck holds in your full-figured bust. The belted waist creates the illusion of a curve there. The godet skirt bottom adds fullness at your knees to make your waist seem smaller in comparison.

YOUR ONE FASHION MUST-HAVE: *an A-line dress*

The shape adds steady volume over your hips to balance out your broad shoulders. A hem just above your knee allows you to show off your gorgeous legs— and the more leg you show on your short figure, the taller you will appear.

SHORT
FULL
RECTANGLE

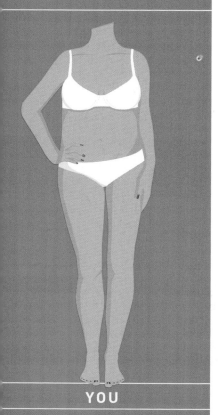

YOU

You are **SHORT**.
[BETWEEN 4'9" AND 5'2"]

You are **FULL**-figured.
[BETWEEN 135 AND 170 LBS.]

Your body forms a
RECTANGLE
as your shoulders are the same
width as your hips.

You have broad shoulders.
Your have equally wide hips.
Your waist is wide and undefined.

YOUR BLESSING

You, my dear, already have all you need to create a sexy silhouette. You have broad shoulders that you can accentuate with the right clothes. You also have wide hips. And if you have a full bust, you can choose to reveal a bit of attention-grabbing cleavage that always adds to looking sexy. Overall, your full figure offers plenty to work with. Your other blessing? You have nice legs in proportion to your body. Since you're short, it actually benefits you to show off your legs, because the more leg you show, the taller you'll appear. (Well, don't go overboard; a little leg goes a long way!) The only thing your figure is missing is a small waist, but lucky for you, that's not a difficult feature to fake.

YOUR CURSE

As a SHORT, FULL RECTANGLE, your undefined waist can become an issue. Basically, without a small waist between your wide shoulders and wide hips, your silhouette can look slightly male if you don't wear styles that show off your curves in the right way. Your other curse? You carry less weight in your hips and bottom than you do in your shoulders and middle. You may even have a somewhat flat bottom. For this reason, it may be hard to find clothes that fit, as most clothes are made for women with curvier hips and bottoms, and smaller waists. Also, as a full-sized rectangle, you have to be a bit more inventive in bringing your shoulders and hips out so that the waist looks smaller in comparison. Done the wrong way, you'll appear even shorter.

YOUR CELEBRITY BODY STAND-IN: *Missy Elliott*

WHAT TO WEAR

*Your fashion challenge is to widen both your shoulders and your hips
so that your waist looks smaller in comparison.
You also want to add height and look slimmer overall.*

DRESSES

Wear **off-the-shoulder dresses** or dresses with **shallow
V-necks** or **scoop necks** that make your shoulders seem
wider while holding in your full-sized torso. Choose
empire dresses that hug your bust, then taper out to
your hips, creating the illusion of a waist. Try **waterfall
dresses** that hang lower in the back or **fluted hems**
to make your legs seem longer and slimmer.

TOPS

Wear **wrap tops, surplices,** and
V-neck tops and sweaters to
create a vertical line at your chest,
making you seem taller and slimmer.
Wear **camisole tops under jackets**
to bring attention to your chest area
while still holding in your assets.
Or widen your shoulders with
boatneck tops, provided you wear
full, flowing or A-line skirts on the
bottom to balance yourself out.

SKIRTS

Wear **circle skirts, gored skirts,**
or **trumpet skirts** that hug your
waist, then flare out slightly to
create the illusion of a small waist
in comparison to your hips. Wear
an **A-line skirt** that tapers out from
your waist, making it appear as if
you have a cinched waist. Aim for
monochromatic skirts and tops, as
this will create a longer vertical line,
adding height to your short stature.

PANTS & JEANS

Wear **straight-leg
pants and jeans**
that elongate your body.
Pick pants with
detailing around the hip
area and **angled
or diagonal pockets**
that create the illusion
of curves at your hips.

COATS & JACKETS

If you have large arms,
wear **long-sleeve** or
**three-quarter-length
sleeve jackets** or
bolero jackets with
subtle structure in
the shoulders; this will
make your waist seem
smaller in comparison.
Wear **princess seam
blazers** or **peplum
jackets** that curve in
at the waist and flare
out toward your hips.

JEWELRY & ACCESSORIES

Carry a handbag
that hits at the hips to
add a slight bit of
volume there. Wear
pretty **pendant
necklaces** or **dangling
earrings** that draw
attention to your chest
and face. Put on
wide, pretty sash at
your waist to add a
feminine element to
your silhouette.

SHOES

Wear **pointy-toed heels, sexy peep-toed heels, cut-away arches,**
or **open-toed high-heel sandals** to draw the eye to the very tip
of your body—don't forget the great pedicure! If high heels are
uncomfortable under your full-size frame, try a **kitten heel;** even
the slightest lift will make you appear taller and slimmer.

FIGURE 3.2.1
You, only sexier.

WHAT NOT TO WEAR

Really. I mean it.

DRESSES

Don't wear **dainty halter dresses** that aren't in scale with your full shoulders. Don't wear **long dresses** that cover your legs, making you look shorter. Avoid **thin fabrics** that can be light and clingy around your middle; you're better off with heavier crepe fabrics that hold you in. Avoid dresses that cling to your shape, accentuating your undefined middle.

TOPS

Avoid **dainty halter tops** that aren't in proportion to your shoulders and arms. Don't wear **wildly patterned tops** that draw too much attention to your top half. Avoid **sleeveless tops** that cut the line of your arms at the shoulder, making them seem thicker. Don't wear **raglan tops** or **high-necked crewnecks** that can turn your chest into a "uniboob."

SKIRTS

Don't wear **trumpet skirts** that cling to your legs, making them look unproportionally thinner. Avoid **fitted pencil skirts** that minimize your lower half and emphasize your straight hips. Don't wear **large-pattern** or **brightly-colored skirts** which break up the color balance from top to bottom and will make you look shorter.

PANTS & JEANS

Don't wear pants in **clingy fabrics** that follow the line of your thin legs; these will make you appear top-heavy. And don't wear **bell bottoms** or **flared boot leg pants;** the extra flare draws the eye down and outward, making you appear short and squat.

COATS & JACKET

Avoid **double-breasted blazers and coats,** especially thick **pea coats** that will only make you look wider. Also, steer clear of **long, straight jackets** that hit at your thighs and **long coats** that button from the neck to your knees without tapering in toward your waist.

JEWELRY & ACCESSORIES

Avoid **square handbags** that land at your waist and make you look wider and boxier. And don't wear a **wide belt** around your waist unless it cinches your waist in considerably; otherwise, a belt only accentuates your undefined middle.

FIGURE 3.2.2
You, wearing the wrong things.

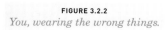

SHOES

Don't wear **square-toed shoes** that underscore your boxy frame. Steer clear of **chunky heels** and **thick soles** that make your ankles seem thick. Avoid **slip-ons** or **mules** that make your legs seem wide and unshapely.

THE NEW YOU

Three ways to put your dress-sexy rules into play.

CASUAL

The wide scoop neck on this blouse brings your shoulders out slightly so that your waist looks smaller in comparison. The full sleeves help cover the thickness in your arms. The sash at the base of the top makes it appear as if you have a smaller waist. The straight-leg jean elongates your look to make you appear taller.

CAREER

The wide-set neckline on this vintage-looking blazer helps widen your shoulders. The princess seams create the illusion of a waist where their isn't one. The trumpet skirt flares out below your hips, without adding too much volume to your full-size frame. The hem of the skirt reveals enough leg to add some height to your look.

FORMAL

The thick wide-set strap of this dress broadens your shoulders slightly to make it seem as if you have a smaller waist. The V-neck creates vertical movement that makes you look thinner and taller. The dress flows over your hips with a slight fullness to create the illusion of curvier hips.

YOUR ONE FASHION MUST-HAVE: *an empire dress*

This shape hugs and lifts your full-sized bust, then slowly tapers out toward your hips, making it appear as if you have a small waist in between. It also creates the illusion of a high waist, making you seem taller.

SHORT
FULL
TRIANGLE

YOU

You are **SHORT**.
[BETWEEN 4'9" AND 5'2"]

You are **FULL**-figured.
[BETWEEN 135 AND 170 LBS.]

Your body forms a
TRIANGLE
as your hips are wider
than your shoulders.

Your upper body is smaller
than your lower body. Your hips
are wide set and curvy.
You have a shapely bottom.

YOUR BLESSING

You've been blessed with one of the most desirable features of all: a nice, round booty! When it comes to having a sexy silhouette, this is a big help. You're the woman who walks down the street and can't help but send off a sexy vibe—provided you dress to flatter your figure. Basically, you have lots to offer on your lower half. But that's certainly not all. Your other blessing? You have a slender neck and lovely collarbone. Your small upper body makes you appear much slimmer than your weight suggests, and that really helps when it comes to finding clothing that fits you well. Because of this, you have no problems with clothes fitting your top half. You're just steps away from a sexy silhouette as you already have some great curves to work with.

YOUR CURSE

As a SHORT, FULL TRIANGLE, you have what's called a low balance. This just means that the visual line of your silhouette reaches its broadest point at your hips. For this reason, you can appear bottom-heavy if you choose the wrong clothes. And finding pants that fit your short height and full weight can be tough. Your other curse? Part of being a triangle means your shoulders are narrow, maybe even with a slight downward slope; your chest tends to be small in relation to your hips. This can make you look shorter. And since you're short, that's something you'll have to address when it comes to creating your sexy silhouette.

YOUR CELEBRITY BODY STAND-IN: *Kelly Clarkson*

WHAT TO WEAR

*Your fashion challenge is to downplay your oversized
lower half and to build up your cleavage.
You also want to add height and look slimmer overall.*

DRESSES

Wear **off-the-shoulder dresses** that create an unbroken
line at your shoulders, widening them. Choose dresses
with **princess seams** that define an hourglass shape
where there isn't one. Pick dresses in **mid-weight
fabrics** such as matte jersey, crepes, or soft cottons
that fall loosely from your waist and just skim the
curve of your hips and bottom.

TOPS

Wear **V-neck** and **U-neck
long-sleeve tops** that hit at the high
hip. Or wear **boatneck, wide scoop
necks,** and **sweetheart necklines,**
which broaden your shoulders
to balance your wide hips. Wear
tailored **dress shirts** with clean
vertical seams to help diminish
the fullness of your figure. If you're
small-busted, choose shirts
with shirring or ruching at the bust
to add volume there. Lightly layer
a sweater over a dress shirt to subtly
blend the curves on your body.

SKIRTS

Wear **dark-colored skirts**
in black, gray, navy, and brown.
I repeat: black, gray, navy,
and brown. Wear **A-line skirts** that
taper easily over your hips without
clinging. Or try fitted **gored skirts**
that hug your waist, then flow
gracefully over your trouble zones.
Wear skirts hemmed to the knee,
or just below the knee, to emphasize
your legs and make you look
taller. Choose **straight skirts with
princess seams** that minimize
the roundness of your lower half.

PANTS & JEANS

Wear **flat-front
trousers** and **straight-
leg jeans** with a
generous, fluid fit
through the hips and
thighs. Or wear **subtly
flared boot cut pants**
to balance out your
shapely thighs. Stick
with **dark-colored
pants** and **dark-wash
denims** to minimize
your lower half.

COATS & JACKETS

Choose **puff-sleeve
blazers** or jackets
with structured shoul-
ders to widen your top
half. Consider **bolero
jackets** or **cropped
jackets** worn at the
high hip and left open
to create a long unbro-
ken line. Try **A-line
coats** or **trench coats** in
bright colors to disguise
your fuller thighs.

JEWELRY & ACCESSORIES

Draw attention to
your slim neck and
collarbone with
long, necklaces that
slenderize your look.
Wear delicate
chandelier earrings
which will draw
the eye up to your
face, away from
your bottom half.

FIGURE 3.3.1
You, only sexier.

SHOES

Wear **peep-toe heels** or **pointy-toed stilettos** in the same color
as your outfit to create a slenderizing effect overall. Or for something
more comfortable, try a **wedge heel** with jeans, which still gives
you lift—but if the wedges have ankle straps or ties, don't wear them
with skirts, because the ankle strap will widen your legs.

WHAT NOT TO WEAR

Really. I mean it.

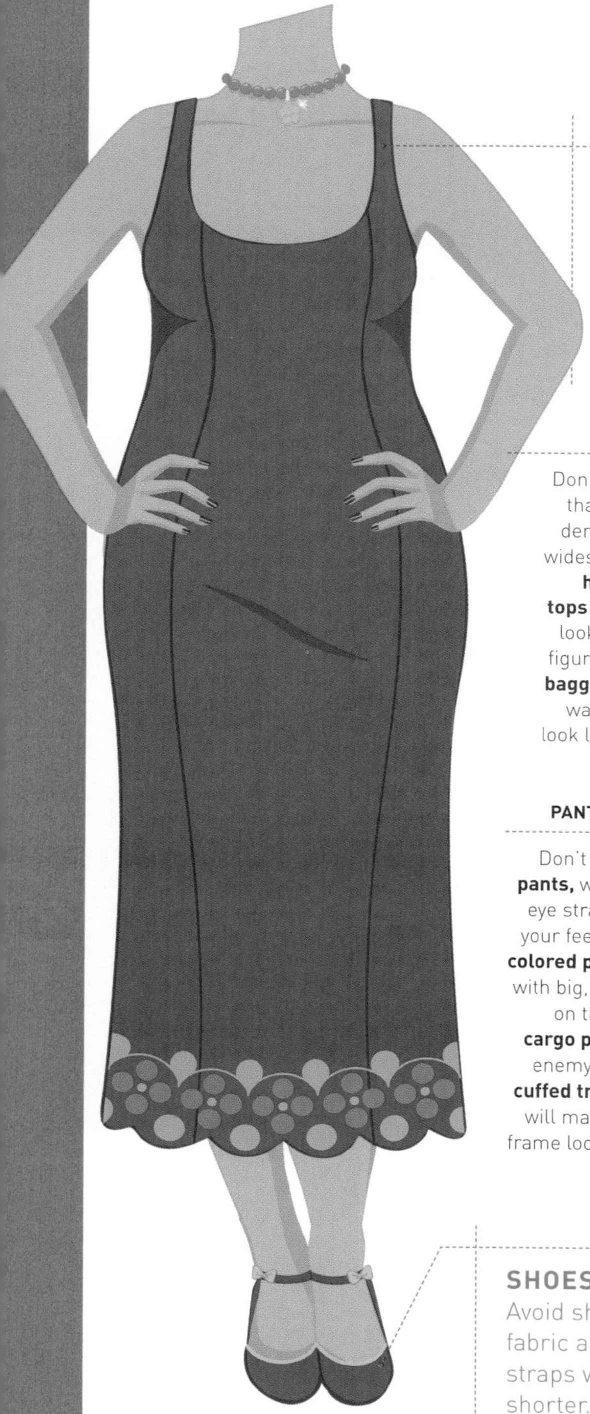

DRESSES

Avoid **ankle-length dresses** that drag down the bottom half of your body and make you seem heavier. Don't wear dresses with **thin shoulder straps** that aren't in scale with your frame. Avoid dresses that balloon out from the waist and make you look wide. Steer clear of **shiny, stiff fabrics** such as taffeta that add serious volume to your hips.

TOPS

Don't wear tops and sweaters that hit you across the mid derriere and accentuate the widest part of your figure. Avoid **halter tops** and **raglan tops** that make your shoulders look sloped and your overall figure look shorter. Don't wear **baggy tunic tops** that hide your waist and make your torso look like its lacking sexy curves.

SKIRTS

Avoid **pleated skirts** that will make your hips appear larger than they are. Steer clear of **busy patterns or stripes** on your bottom half at all costs—this will draw unwanted attention to your wide hips. Avoid **horizontal details,** such as fluted hems and tiers of fabric that break up your vertical line and reduce your height.

PANTS & JEANS

Don't wear **flared pants,** which bring the eye straight down to your feet. Avoid **light-colored pants** and those with big, baggy pockets on the sides—**cargo pants** are your enemy! Don't wear **cuffed trousers,** which will make your short frame look even shorter.

COATS & JACKET

Avoid jackets that hit at the mid derriere and make you seem wider than you are there. Don't wear **double-breasted coats** or **pea coats,** which widen your torso and cover up your waist. Avoid coats in **shiny leathers** that appear to add volume to your hips.

JEWELRY & ACCESSORIES

Don't wear **choker necklaces** that cut off your slender neck. Don't carry purses that are too small in relation to your figure; full-sized women should carry full-sized accessories. Avoid **shoulder bags** that hit at your hips, drawing attention to your broadest point.

SHOES

Avoid shoes with **ankle straps** or shoes that tie with leather or fabric around your ankles. The horizontal line created by the straps will make your ankles look wider and make you look shorter. Don't wear **chunky heels** or shoes with thick soles.

FIGURE 3.3.2
You, wearing the wrong things.

THE NEW YOU

Three ways to put your dress-sexy rules into play.

CASUAL

This top draws attention to your upper torso with its flattering open neckline. The contrasting ribbon hugs the base of your bust. The puff-sleeves cover only the thickest part of your arms. The dark, straight-leg pant makes you seem taller.

CAREER

The collared dress shirt creates a subtle V-neck shape which draws the eye upward. The puff-sleeves add feminine fullness to your shoulders. The princess seams in the top match the seams in the pencil skirt, creating a long, unbroken vertical line that makes you seem taller.

FORMAL

The off-the-shoulder style draws the eyes out toward your shoulders to balance your wide hips. The empire waist creates volume at your bust area and creates the illusion of a high waist, which makes you look taller. The bottom of the dress just grazes your hips, smoothing out the curves on your bottom half.

YOUR ONE FASHION MUST-HAVE: *a dark-colored dress*

A dark-colored dress in an off-the-shoulder or boatneck style with a fitted waist widens your shoulders to match your hips. The monochromatic look makes you appear both slimmer and taller.

SHORT FULL HOURGLASS

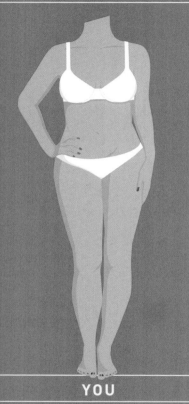

YOU

You are **SHORT**.
[BETWEEN 4'9" AND 5'2"]

You are **FULL**-figured.
[BETWEEN 135 AND 170 LBS.]

Your body forms an
HOURGLASS
as your shoulders are the
same width as your hips with
a small waist in between.

You have broad shoulders and a
shapely bust. Your hips and butt are
curvy. Your waist is defined.

YOUR BLESSING

You certainly are blessed alright! You were born with an hourglass silhouette, otherwise known as a perfectly balanced body in which your top and bottom halves match. You have a full bottom as well as beautiful, broad shoulders. Your other blessing? You have a defined waist. What that means is that no matter how big or small your chest is, and no matter how big your hips feel some days, with that small, defined waist of yours, you can look sexy! Plus, even though you're a full-sized woman, you actually look smaller than the sizes on your clothing indicate. A size 14 with a small waist can look like a size 10. Dressing sexy is all about looking proportional, and you were born that way. All you have to do now is learn how to keep balanced and accentuate what you already have.

YOUR CURSE

As a SHORT, FULL HOURGLASS, you have an extra issue to consider when you're getting dressed: making your figure look slimmer overall. You're already shorter than the average woman, and with your full-sized figure, you can look even shorter if you don't choose clothing that elongates your look. Your other curse? You might have a hard time shopping for clothes. You often have to shop in petite sections because of your height, yet your weight makes it harder to find sizes that fit. And once you do find them, you usually have to hem pants, skirts, and sleeves to fit your unique figure.

YOUR CELEBRITY BODY STAND-IN: *Lil' Kim*

WHAT TO WEAR

Your fashion challenge is to keep your broad shoulders and wide hips balanced, while defining your waist. You also want to add height and look slimmer overall.

TOPS

Wear **tailored dress shirts** with vertical seams to help diminish the fullness of your figure; the V-neck created by opening one or two buttons will point toward your defined waist. Choose tops with **three-quarter-length sleeves** to reveal only the thinnest part of your arms. Wear **wrap tops** and **surplices,** which bring the eye up to your chest and hug your waist.

DRESSES

Wear **single-color, dark dresses** that create one long vertical line from head to toe, making you look taller and leaner. Wear **A-line dresses** that hug your waistline then taper out. Choose dresses in **sturdy, stiff fabrics** that help contain and smooth out your full-sized curves.

PANTS

Wear **straight-leg pants and jeans,** which add a bit of volume on the lower part of your leg to balance your hips. Wear **mid-rise jeans,** which hit just above your hips and create a smooth line from your waist to your hips without adding bulk. Choose jeans with **full-sized back pockets** in scale with your full-sized body; if you choose small pockets, your butt will look big in comparison.

SKIRTS

Try **tulip skirts** or **godet skirts** that hug your thighs, then add curves at the hem to balance out your hips. Or wear **A-line skirts** that add steady volume over your hips. Wear **drapey skirts** that gently graze your curves. Hem your skirts just above or at your knee to show off your curvy calves; showing a bit more leg will also make you look taller.

COATS & JACKETS

Choose jackets with **princess seams** or wear **peplum jackets,** which show off your natural waist, then taper out toward your hips. For coats, pick a **basic trench coat** that defines your strong shoulders, pulls tight at the waist, then tapers out toward your hips in an A-line silhouette.

JEWELRY & ACCESSORIES

Wear necklaces that feature a single focal point—such as a **medium pendant necklace** that falls in a V-shape. Style your hair up when wearing skin-baring tops to show off your shoulders and collarbone; this guarantees you will instantly draws the eye up to your shoulders, which makes you seem taller.

SHOES

Wear a **pointy-toed heel** in the same color as your pants, to elongate your look. For something more comfortable, try a **wedge heel,** or at the very least try a **kitten heel** for a slight lift.

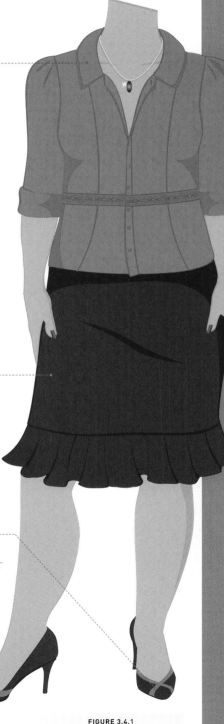

FIGURE 3.4.1
You, only sexier.

WHAT NOT TO WEAR

Really. I mean it.

TOPS

Skip the **oversized tunics, baggy tops,** or shirts that lack a defined shape; covering up your full torso like this will actually make you look larger on top. If you have large breasts, avoid **crew necks, raglan tops,** and **turtlenecks;** high-necked shirts can turn breasts into the dreaded "uniboob" that will make you appear top-heavy.

DRESSES

Don't wear **boxy, shift dresses** that turn your hourglass figure into in oval. Avoid **ankle-length dresses** that make your bottom half seem heavier and shorten you further. Avoid dresses with busy detailing or bunchy fabric around the hip area of your dress. Don't wear **flimsy material** like Lycra®-based cottons or thin jersey knits that will reveal your lumps and bumps.

PANTS & JEANS

Avoid **low-rise jeans** which won't contain your full-size frame, making you look even heavier. Don't wear **flared pants** or **gauchos** that drag the eye down to your calves and feet and make you appear a bit dumpy. Avoid **distressing or whiskering** on the thighs of your jeans, which will make you seem bottom-heavy.

SKIRTS

Don't wear **straight skirts** that flatten your sexy waist-to-hip area. And avoid hemming skirts to the thickest part of your calf, which will make you seem wider on your bottom half. Steer clear of **poufy circle skirts** that add unwanted volume to your hip area. Avoid **shiny fabrics and busy patterns or stripes** on your bottom half, which will draw unwanted attention to your hips.

SHOES

Avoid **square-toed shoes,** which will make you seem shorter. Skip shoes with **ankle straps;** the horizontal line created by the straps will make your full ankles look wider.

COATS & JACKETS

Skip the **Chanel-style jackets** and **mandarin blazers** that square off your torso and cover up your defined waist. Avoid blazers with **front pockets or bulky side pockets** that widen your hip area. Steer clear of coats that land at the hip; they widen your waistline and add weight to your broadest point.

JEWELRY & ACCESSORIES

Don't wear details such as **flowers, bows, and ruffles;** your full-size body is already so womanly, those feminine accents will make you look girly instead of sexy. Avoid **hip belts** that add unnecessary volume there. Don't cover the skin area around your neck with **scarves** or **chunky choker necklaces** that cover your skin and cleavage.

FIGURE 3.4.2
You, wearing the wrong things.

THE NEW YOU

Three ways to put your dress-sexy rules into play.

CASUAL

The open neck of this top draws attention to your chest and cleavage, accenting your collarbone. The long sleeves disguise your full-size arms. The beading at the chest draws the eye straight up toward your face. The straight-leg jean balances your curvy hips and elongates your figure, making you seem taller.

CAREER

The princess seams of this skirt suit mimic the hourglass curves of your figure. The matching seams from jacket to skirt create a long, vertical line, elongating your body and making you seem taller. The high stance notch blazer holds in your large chest while still hugging your sexy shape.

FORMAL

If you dare to bare your arms, the wide-set halter top creates a flattering V-neck and opens up your shoulders to balance your hips. The full skirt of the dress flows easily over your curves into a full shape that balances your shoulders. The black color is slimming to your figure overall.

YOUR ONE FASHION MUST-HAVE: *a tulip skirt*

This is a flattering skirt choice for your figure. It hugs your natural waist and hips, and then tapers in slightly to show off the curves you were born with. It then flares out at the hem to keep your silhouette perfectly balanced.

FITTING ROOM
ROOM
4

If you're short and
plus-sized, you're
in the right place. Just
find your silhouette and
prepare to get sexy.

SHORT
PLUS
INVERTED TRIANGLE

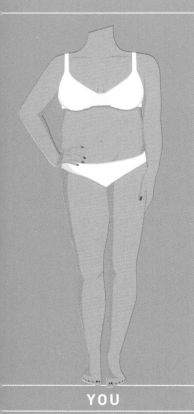

YOU

You are **SHORT**.
[BETWEEN 4'9" AND 5'2"]

You are **PLUS**-sized.
[BETWEEN 155 AND 225 LBS.]

Your body forms an
INVERTED TRIANGLE
as your shoulders are wider
than your hips.

You have wide shoulders. Your
hips are not as wide as your
shoulders. Your legs and butt are
not as wide as your shoulders.

YOUR BLESSING

When it comes to dressing sexy, it's important to show off your curves and you, my friend, have plenty of them! First off, because you're larger on top than on the bottom, you can probably create at least a little cleavage, which is one of the best tools for keeping all eyes centered on you. And because your shoulders are broad, you can look much taller than you are. And looking taller is your key to looking slimmer. (Slap some heels on, and you'll look even taller!) Your other blessing? You have slim hips and legs. In fact, though you're in the plus-size range, your small bottom half means you can get far more creative with pants and skirts and show off your legs a bit. Finally, you have somewhat of a waist to play up, which makes it easier for you to create the feminine, hourglass shape you're going for.

YOUR CURSE

As a SHORT, PLUS, INVERTED TRIANGLE, you have what's called a high balance. This means that the visual line of your silhouette reaches its broadest point at your shoulders. And as a plus-sized woman, you may carry extra weight in your arms, which means you can appear top-heavy if you choose the wrong clothes. If you don't dress to flatter the feminine side of you, you can appear to have a masculine build. Your other curse? You have to give your undergarments extra consideration when you're getting dressed. To be clear: You have a really important bra issue. For you to look sexy, you must first find bras that support you, lift you up, and don't create extra bulges around your upper half.

YOUR CELEBRITY BODY STAND-IN: *Roseanne Barr*

WHAT TO WEAR

Your fashion challenge is to narrow your shoulders, to widen your hips so they match your broad shoulders, and to reveal more of your waist. You also want to add height and look slimmer overall.

TOPS

Wear **U-necks, sweetheart, square,** and **shallow V-necks** to draw the eye in and away from your wide shoulders. Choose tops with **full-length** or **three-quarter-length sleeves** to conceal the thickest part of your arm. Choose tops in **structured fabrics,** such as thick cotton shirts that hold their shape off the hanger, to smooth out your lumps and bumps.

DRESSES

Wear **A-line dresses** in mid-weight fabrics such as matte jersey, georgettes, and polyester/spandex blends that aren't too thin, transparent, or clingy. Opt for dresses with **three-quarter-length** or **full-length sleeves** in heavy fabrics to help smooth out your torso. Hem your dresses at the knee to show some lower leg and elongate your body.

SKIRTS

Choose **A-line skirts** in thick fabrics such as heavy cotton or poplin. Or try **gored skirts** or **semi-circle skirts** that create volume at your hips and bottom. Choose skirts with **feminine details** at the waist, such as ribbons, ruffles, appliqués, or beading; this will help add volume where you need it and make your figure seem softer.

PANTS & JEANS

Pick **dark pants** for an overall slimming effect. Try pants with **front or side pockets** or with detailing around the hip area to add volume where you need it most. Choose **straight-leg pants** or jeans that skim your curves rather than cling to them, to elongate your look and make you seem taller and slimmer.

COATS & JACKETS

Wear **peplum jackets** that flare out from the waist toward the hips. Choose **low-stance blazers** in fitted, structured fabrics, as the V-shape created by one button is slimming. Pick jackets with **full-length** or **three-quarter-length** sleeves to reveal only the thinnest part of your wrists.

JEWELRY & ACCESSORIES

Wear a **pendant necklace** to draw the eye in from your shoulders and up toward your face. Add a **sash** or a **belt** at your high hip to add volume there and balance your wide shoulders. Wear **pretty details** such as flowery appliques, ruffles, and ribbons to add a feminine touch to your look.

SHOES

Wear a **substantial pump** in proportion to frame. Choose bold colors or interesting styles, such as **cut-away arches** or **peep-toe heels** that draw attention to your lovely legs and ankles.

FIGURE 4.1.1
You, only sexier.

WHAT NOT TO WEAR

Really. I mean it.

TOPS

Steer clear of **off-the-shoulder tops, boatnecks,** and **crew necks,** which will only make you appear even more top-heavy. Don't wear short sleeves that hit at the widest part of your upper arm—they will make them appear much heavier. Avoid **flutter sleeves** that flare out from your shoulders and create unnecessary volume there.

DRESSES

Avoid **Lycra®-based stretch fabrics;** as your body moves, stretchy fabric creates unflattering pockets and bulges that make you look larger than you are. Lumpy is not sexy. Avoid **spaghetti straps,** which are too delicate for your frame and will make you seem larger.

SKIRTS

Steer clear of **dark-colored skirts** on the bottom if you're wearing light colors on top; either keep your color tones consistent or stick with light, bright colors on the bottom to balance your wide shoulders. Don't wear fitted **pencil skirts** unless they flare out; you must balance your bottom half or you will look too heavy on top.

PANTS & JEANS

Don't wear **skinny jeans** or **leggings,** which hug your thighs and taper to your ankles; these will make you look top-heavy. On the other hand, don't wear **wide-leg men's-cut trousers** or **palazzo pants,** which will give your bottom half a masculine, boxy look. Avoid flared pants, which will make your frame appear short and stout, instead of long and lean.

SHOES

Avoid **strappy stiletto sandals** or other dainty shoes that will look out of proportion on your frame. Steer clear of **chunky soles** and **thick heels,** which make you look wider.

COATS & JACKETS

Avoid **cap sleeve jackets** and **short-sleeve jackets** that hit at mid arm and make your shoulders appear wider and your arms heavier. Don't wear jackets made of **thin, lightweight materials** such as thin cotton or linen, as it won't help hold in and structure your wide torso.

JEWELRY & ACCESSORIES

Don't cover up your chest area with **scarves** or **chunky chokers,** which will make your torso look thicker. Steer clear of **tiny clutches** and **dainty earrings,** which will look out of proportion on you. As a plus-sized woman, you need to wear and carry plus-sized accessories.

FIGURE 4.1.2
You, wearing the wrong things.

THE NEW YOU

Three ways to put your dress-sexy rules into play.

CASUAL	CAREER	FORMAL

The scoop-neck top draws the eye away from your shoulders and creates a soft line at your neck. The ribbon tie at the base of the shirt adds volume to your hips to balance your shoulders. The dark straight-leg jean adds fullness below the knee and elongates your look overall, making you seem taller and slimmer.

The low-stance blazer creates a long, vertical line at your center, drawing the eye away from your shoulders. The princess seams and fitted waist mimic the hourglass you're aiming for, while smoothing out any lumps and bulges on your torso. The semi-circle skirt adds volume to your lower half.

The square neck of this dress dips toward your sexy cleavage to bring attention there. The three-quarter-length sleeves reveal your slimmer forearms. The drop waist and the semi-circle skirt in the dress both add volume to your bottom half to balance your shoulders. The hip belt adds volume there.

YOUR ONE FASHION MUST-HAVE: *a structured jacket*

**Choose one with three-quarter-length or full-length sleeves.
Look for one with princess seams or peplum in a stiff fabric that can contain your curves and create the illusion of hips.**

SHORT PLUS RECTANGLE

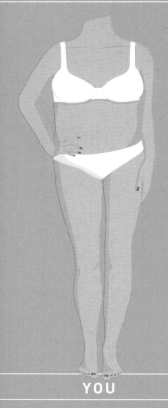

YOU

You are **SHORT**.
[BETWEEN 4'9" AND 5'2"]

You are **PLUS**-sized.
[BETWEEN 155 AND 225 LBS.]

Your body forms a
RECTANGLE
as your shoulders are the
same width as your hips.

You have broad shoulders.
You have equally wide hips.
Your waist is wide and undefined.

YOUR BLESSING

Luckily, you were born with some of the features known for having a sexy silhouette. You have hips, which you can dress up so they look even curvier than they are. And they are balanced by your shoulders, which you can also play up. Basically, you already have a balanced body. Because your hips and shoulders are the same width, all you need to do is create the illusion of a waist between the two, and you'll look like you have an hourglass silhouette. Your other blessing? Because of your full-size frame, if you have even a small amount of curves to work with at your bustline, you can turn what you have into sexy, eye-catching cleavage. Finally, your legs are slim in relation to the rest of your body, which means you can play them up and show them off—nothing says sexy like a little bit of leg on display.

YOUR CURSE

As a SHORT, PLUS, RECTANGLE, you lack a defined waist. That gives your silhouette almost a slightly male shape. Your other curse? As a plus-sized woman, the extra weight around your middle gives you more of an oval shape. This means it's important to find clothes that slim down your figure overall. Finally, with your silhouette, it can be hard to find clothes made to fit you. You land somewhere between large-sized clothes and the petite section. You also lack the height that can help make your plus-size figure seem lean and slim. (Thank goodness for high-heeled shoes!)

YOUR CELEBRITY BODY STAND-IN: *Angie Stone*

WHAT TO WEAR

*Basically, your fashion challenge is to widen your shoulders
as well as your hips, so that your waist looks smaller in comparison.
You also want to add height and look slimmer overall.*

TOPS

Wear **puffed-sleeve tops** to widen your shoulders slightly.
Try **wrap tops, surplices,** and **V-neck sweaters** layered over
feminine tops to create a flattering line at your chest area
while smoothing out your torso. Allow shirts to peek out
from sweaters and hit at the hips; this draws the eye
outward, making your waist seem small in comparison.

DRESSES

Choose dresses with wide open
necks, such as **boatnecks, scoop
necks,** and **sweetheart necks;** they
should also have full bottoms that
taper out from the waist in **stiff
fabrics** such as taffeta. Or wear
wrap dresses that tie around
your middle to create the illusion
that you have a shapely waist.

PANTS & JEANS

Wear **dark-colored straight-leg
pants** that elongate your body
overall and make you look taller.
Pick pants with detailing
or pockets around the hip
area, creating the illusion of
more curves there. Wear pants
in the same color as your
top half to elongate your look.

SKIRTS

Pick **semi-circle skirts, gored skirts,** or **godet skirts** that
add necessary fullness around your hips and bottom. Choose
skirts in **medium-sized patterns,** which are in scale with
your plus-size frame. Hem your skirts either above or at
your knee to reveal your great legs—showing some leg will
make your short frame seem taller and, therefore, slimmer.

COATS & JACKETS

Choose **high-stance
blazers** in a sturdy
fabric to widen the
appearance of your
shoulders and help
hold in your torso.
Choose **puffed-sleeve
blazers or jackets**
with small shoulder
pads to exaggerate
it more; the broader
you appear on top, the
taller you will seem.

JEWELRY & ACCESSORIES

Wear **long, pendant
necklaces** to create a
vertical line down your
center. Or wear **medi-
um-sized chandelier
earrings;** tiny studs
will look dwarfed by
your body. Keep your
purse in proportion to
your plus-size frame.
Try a shoulder bag
that hangs long
and hits at your hip
to add volume there.

SHOES

Wear **low-cut or
open-toed heels** to
add height to your
look, which will
instantly make you
appear slimmer. Or
consider a **hearty
pump with delicate
details.** Choose shoes
in the same color as
your pants to further
the slimming effect.

FIGURE 4.2.1
You, only sexier.

WHAT NOT TO WEAR

Really. I mean it.

TOPS

Avoid **big patterns** or **bright-colored tops** that draw attention to your torso. Don't wear fitted tops that cling to your torso and accentuate your thickness in the middle. Avoid **turtlenecks** that will create the dreaded "uniboob." Steer clear of **horizontal stripes** on top that will make your torso seem thick and boxy.

DRESSES

Don't wear **boxy shift dresses** that fall straight from under your arms without defining a waist. Don't hem your skirts at the widest part of your calf, which will make your legs seem short and a bit stumpy. Avoid **thin fabrics** that will cling and reveal lumps in your middle; also skip stretchy fabrics that will buckle and bunch around your middle as you move.

PANTS & JEANS

Don't wear **flared pants;** the extra widening at your ankles draws the eye down and outward, making you appear short and squat. Avoid fitted **skinny jeans, leggings,** and **stovepipe pants,** all of which accentuate your straight, flat bottom half and emphasize your lack of curves.

SKIRTS

Avoid **bright-colored** or **large-pattern skirts,** which add too much volume to your figure. Don't wear fitted **pencil skirts** or **long, ankle-length skirts** that emphasize your straight hips in comparison to your torso; this will make you look top-heavy. Don't wear skirts that are **overly poufy** on the bottom, which adds too much volume to your hips and makes you look heavier.

SHOES

Don't wear **square-toed shoes** that mimic your boxy frame and shorten your overall look. Don't wear shoes with **delicate straps** and details—they are out of proportion with your plus-size frame.

COATS & JACKETS

Avoid jackets with **weak shoulder lines** and those made from **thin fabrics** such as linen that don't square off your soft shoulders. Don't wear jackets that lack silhouette-defining seams. Avoid **double-breasted jackets,** especially pea coats, which will add weight to your already wide torso.

JEWELRY & ACCESSORIES

Don't carry **large handbags** that hit at your waist, making your middle seem rounder and wider than it is. At the same time, avoid **tiny clutches** that will look too small in proportion to your plus-sized frame. Don't force **tight belts** around your middle.

FIGURE 4.2.2
You, wearing the wrong things.

THE NEW YOU

Three ways to put your dress-sexy rules into play.

CASUAL

The high-stance blazer helps give shape to your torso while also drawing the eye to the flattering V-neck at your chest. The princess seams in the blazer add subtle shape to your round middle. The dark, boot cut pant adds volume beneath your knees to balance your hips and make you seem taller and slimmer.

CAREER

The wide-set boatneck helps widen your shoulders. The romantic bow at the base of the shirt adds a feminine touch. The semi-circle skirt adds volume at your thighs to balance your shoulders, while adding a feminine touch. The knee-length hem reveals your pretty legs and makes you seem taller.

FORMAL

The wide-set neckline of this dress dips into a shallow V-neck to draw the eye to your center. The puffed sleeves help broaden your shoulders. The empire style creates the illusion of a high waist, making your legs seem longer. The tiered skirt adds feminine volume around your hips to balance your shoulders.

YOUR ONE FASHION MUST-HAVE: *an empire dress*

An empire dress creates the illusion of not just a defined waist, but a high waist. This makes your legs seem longer and makes you taller.

SHORT PLUS TRIANGLE

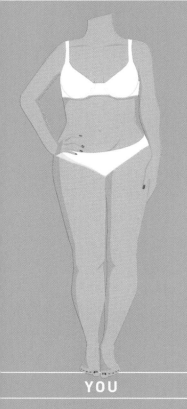

YOU

You are **SHORT**.
[BETWEEN 4'9" AND 5'2"]

You are **PLUS**-sized.
[BETWEEN 155 AND 225 LBS.]

Your body forms a
TRIANGLE
as your hips are wider
than your shoulders.

Your upper body is smaller than your
lower half. Your hips are wide-set.
You have a shapely bottom.

YOUR BLESSING

You have blessings galore. Basically, a sexy silhouette is all about having a full figure and lots of soft curves. Lucky for you, you have plenty of those! Also, your booty is where you carry your curves. The way I see it, if you're going to carry your weight somewhere on your body, that's a great place to carry it. Some women are even famous for their shapely behinds, so it's definitely something to be proud of. Your other blessing? Your torso is slimmer than your hips and thighs, which means you can show off your chest and collarbone. At first glance, your proportionally smaller top half can make you look as though you carry less on your frame than you actually do.

YOUR CURSE

As a SHORT, PLUS, TRIANGLE, you have what's called a low balance. This means that the visual line of your silhouette reaches out to its broadest point at your hips. Also, because you're short, your weight can make you look even shorter, so it's vital for you to add height wherever you can. You need to take your pants and skirts to the tailor to make sure everything is hemmed to best flatter your height-challenged figure. (Thank goodness for high heels!) Your other curse? Though your top half is smaller than your bottom, your shoulders are narrow and possibly sloped downward. Yet, because of your plus-size weight, your arms may seem heavy. This can be a difficult combination. It can also make you look shorter when people first see you.

YOUR CELEBRITY BODY STAND-IN: *Kim Fields*

WHAT TO WEAR

*Your fashion challenge is to downplay your oversized lower half,
to bring out your shoulders so it balances with your bottom, and to build up
your cleavage. You also want to add height and look slimmer overall.*

DRESSES

Wear dresses with **sweetheart necklines** that add curves to your chest to balance your curvy hips. Pick dresses with **flutter sleeves** or **fluted sleeves** to add volume on top. Wear **empire waistlines** to make your waist appear higher and your legs longer. Choose dresses with detailing at the bust or neck to draw the eye up. Pick a dress with a **fluted hem,** which balances out wide hips and full thighs.

TOPS

Choose **U-necks** and **V-necks** to expose your collarbone and draw the eye up. Wear **empire waist tops** with detailing beneath the bust to create the illusion of a high waistline. Try **semi-fitted cowl neck sweaters** in fine gauge knits to broaden your shoulders. Wear **tailored dress shirts** to create clean, elongating vertical lines; also, choose dress shirts with rounded shirttails to smooth out any imbalance between your top and bottom proportions.

SKIRTS

Wear **dark-colored, gored skirts** that drape over your hips and hit at or just above your knee. Or choose an **A-line skirt** that tapers over your trouble zone. Try **pencil skirts** with wide waist-bands that fall straight down from the hips. Wear similar colors on the top and bottom to streamline your look. Hem your skirts just above the knee to make you look inches taller.

PANTS & JEANS

Wear **straight-leg jeans** or **flat-front, wide-legged trousers** that graze to your hips. Or try a **palazzo pant** that drapes gently over your hips. Consider pants with vertical detailing or contrasting stitching to visually stretch your legs. Choose jeans with **large back pockets** in scale with your body.

COATS & JACKETS

Choose **military jackets** or **puffed-sleeve blazers** that widen the look of your shoulders. Or pick jackets with shoulder pads. Wear **single-breasted, low-stance blazers** to emphasize your neck. Wear **Chanel-style jackets** worn open to create the longest vertical line possible.

JEWELRY & ACCESSORIES

Carry a large **hobo bag** or **saddle bag** that you carry under your arm to balance your larger bottom half. Wear pearls or **pendant necklaces** that bring the eye up to your neck. Or wear **chandelier earrings** which draw the eye up to your face.

FIGURE 4.3.1
You, only sexier.

SHOES

Pick **open-toed shoes** or **pointy-toed stilettos** to lengthen the look of your leg; both shoes draw the eye to the furthest point on your leg, so they will appear longer and slimmer. If high heels are uncomfortable for you, even a **kitten heel** will give you a lift and will help elongate your look, making you appear slimmer overall.

WHAT NOT TO WEAR

Really. I mean it.

FIGURE 4.3.2
You, wearing the wrong things.

DRESSES

Don't choose dresses with ruffles, belts, or other flouncy, eye-catching details at the hipline that only widen your hips further. Steer clear of **dainty halters** or **spaghetti straps** that will look too delicate for your frame. Don't wear **shiny fabrics** that increase volume all over your body and add weight. Steer clear of **miniskirts** that show more leg than you need to.

TOPS

Avoid **raglan tops** and **crew neck sweaters** that narrow your shoulders. Don't wear **turtle-necks,** which hide your pretty neck and appear to double your chin. While light layering can help smooth out your plus-size curves, don't let the tail or bottom of your shirt peek out under your sweater, which will add extra bulk at the broadest point of your body. If you are small-busted, avoid shirts with darts that you don't fill in.

SKIRTS

Don't wear **white skirts or other light colors** on bottom that maximize weight and draw attention to your bottom-heavy proportions. Avoid **shiny, volumizing fabrics.** Steer clear of horizontal details that break up your vertical line and reduce your height. Don't wear **thick fabrics** such as suede or tweed, which will widen your hips. Don't hem your skirts to mid calf or ankle, which will widen your legs and make you look shorter.

PANTS & JEANS

Don't wear **flared pants,** which draw the eye to the ground. Yet also avoid **skinny jeans** and **stovepipe pants** that taper toward your ankles. Avoid **khaki** or **light-colored pants,** which add unwanted volume to your lower half. Don't wear **trousers with front pockets** that draw attention to the hips.

COATS & JACKET

Don't wear jackets made of **lightweight materials** such as linen and light cotton that will accentuate your narrow shoulders. Avoid coats that hit at the mid hip. Steer clear of **double-breasted coats,** which cover up your waist. Keep in mind that fur or faux fur coats have a volumizing effect on your figure overall.

JEWELRY & ACCESSORIES

Don't wear **choker necklaces** that cut off your slender neck. At the same time, don't wear **long, drapey necklaces** that draw the eye down. Avoid shoulder bags that hit at your hips. And don't carry **too-small purses** or clutches that seem tiny in relation to your plus-sized figure.

SHOES

Steer clear of **chunky-heeled shoes** or **square-toed styles** which make your whole look seem wider. Avoid high heels with **ankle straps,** as the horizontal line created by the straps makes you look shorter. And avoid **super-high stilettos.** Shoes 3" or higher will look disproportionate to your short frame.

THE NEW YOU

Three ways to put your dress-sexy rules into play.

CASUAL

The light-colored top draws the eye up to your torso. The V-neck with strong details broadens your shoulders to balance your hips. The fluted short sleeves adds more fullness at your chest. The straight-leg pant elongates your legs and makes you appear taller.

CAREER

The cropped blazer over the dress adds structure to your shoulders and torso, while creating a smooth line from your waist to your large hips. The belt at the base of the blazer defines your waist. The pencil skirt flows evenly over your hips, smoothing out your plus-size curves. The monochromatic look makes you seem taller and slimmer.

FORMAL

The wide-set scoop neck makes your shoulders look wider, and the puffed-sleeves add further volume there. The gathering at the bust of the empire dress adds fullness to your chest. The lightweight, flared skirt just grazes over your hips, rather than clinging to them, which smooths out your figure.

YOUR ONE FASHION MUST-HAVE: *a structured jacket*

**Choose one with strong shoulders and princess seams to
broaden your shoulders and accentuate your small waist. Pick one that
hits at your waist to balance out your hips.**

SHORT
PLUS
HOURGLASS

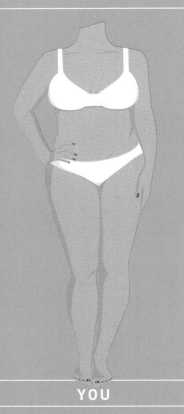

YOU

You are **SHORT**.
[BETWEEN 4'9" AND 5'2"]

You are **PLUS**-sized.
[BETWEEN 155 AND 225 LBS.]

Your body forms an
HOURGLASS
as your shoulders are the
same width as your hips.

You have broad shoulders.
Your hips and butt are very curvy.
Your waist is defined.

YOUR BLESSING

Lucky you! Your greatest blessing is your hourglass silhouette. Your top half and bottom half literally match. Your perfectly balanced body is the essence of the sexy silhouette. You have a gorgeous, full bottom. You have broad shoulders. And you may have a chest that you can make seem larger or smaller depending on what you choose to reveal. All in all, your body is the same as those voluptuous, womanly figures that artists have been painting for centuries. Your other blessing? You have a defined waist. It's the perfect optical illusion. Even though your body is plus-sized, showing off that waist of yours will always make you appear a size or two smaller. Your main goal is to keep yourself looking proportional by accenting what you already have. You're just steps away from sexy.

YOUR CURSE

As a SHORT, PLUS, HOURGLASS, you have wide shoulders. Though you're well-balanced and in proportion overall, your plus-size matches with your short height, so it can be difficult for you to find clothes that fit you properly. It's time to befriend your tailor, because hemming and tailoring to fit you perfectly is important. Also, because you're short, you can seem even heavier in some clothes, so you need to think about ways to dress to slim down your figure overall. Your other curse? You need to pay more attention than others when choosing bras and other undergarments—make sure they perfectly hold in and support your plus-size shape.

YOUR CELEBRITY BODY STAND-IN: *Carnie Wilson*

WHAT TO WEAR

Your fashion challenge is to downplay your oversized lower half and to bring out your shoulders so they balance with your bottom. You also want to add height and look slimmer overall.

COATS & JACKETS

Choose **high-stance blazers** that fit snugly at your waist, such as **princess seam blazers** that reflect your hourglass curves or **peplum jackets,** which cinch in at your thinnest point then flare out toward your hips. Wear **knee-length trench coats** that add structure to your shoulders and define your waist.

TOPS

Wear **wrap tops** and **surplice tops,** which bring the eye up to your chest. Wear **scoop-neck** or **boatneck-fitted sweaters** that sit wide on your shoulders and hug your waist. Wear bright-colored **camisoles** under your wrap shirts and blazers to bring attention to your gorgeous cleavage. Choose tops with **three-quarter-length sleeves** that reveal only the thinnest part of your arm.

DRESSES

Choose **A-line dresses** that cinch at the waist with a strong, wide waistline, then taper out. Or wear **wrap** or **surplice dresses** that accentuate your hourglass curves. Choose **fitted sheaths** in sturdy, stiff fabrics to control your plus-size curves. Wear **dark, single-colored dresses** that create a long vertical line, making you look taller and leaner.

SKIRTS

Wear **gored skirts, semi-circle skirts,** or other gently flared styles that graze your curves and flow out. Or try **A-line skirts** in a sturdier fabric to add steady volume over your hips. Hem your skirts at your knee or at the point just below the widest part of your calves; showing off a bit of your legs will make you look taller.

PANTS & JEANS

Wear **straight-leg** or **boot cut pants,** which add subtle volume on the lower part of your leg to balance your hips. Choose **mid rise jeans,** which hit just above your hips, creating a smooth line to your hips without adding bulk. Choose jeans with **large, round back pockets** in scale with your size.

JEWELRY & ACCESSORIES

Aim for necklaces that feature a single focal point such as a **pendant necklace** that falls in a soft V-shape. Wear **wide belts** to accentuate your waist. Carry **large accessories** proportional to your plus-size frame; tiny, clutches will make you seem larger in comparison.

SHOES

Wear a **pointy-toed heel** in the same color as your outfit to elongate your look and make you appear slimmer. For something more comfortable, try a **substantial pump** or at the very least a **kitten heel** with cutaway arches to add height.

FIGURE 4.4.1
You, only sexier.

139

WHAT NOT TO WEAR

Really. I mean it.

COATS & JACKETS

Don't wear **long, shapeless blazers** that land at the hip and add weight to the broadest point on your bottom half, while covering up your defined waist. Avoid **boxy jackets** with front or side pockets that widen your hip area. Don't wear **straight, ankle-length coats;** these hide your small waistline and cover your legs, making you seem shorter and heavier.

TOPS

Steer clear of **baggy tops** or those with fabric gathered in the middle, which cover up the skinniest part on your torso and makes you look boxy. Avoid **crew necks** and **turtlenecks** that cover up the skin on your chest and can morph into the dreaded "uniboob" that will make you appear top-heavy. Don't wear **horizontal-striped tops,** as the stripes will make your wide arms look heavier.

DRESSES

Don't wear **long, ankle-length dresses** that make you seem shorter, and therefore heavier. Avoid dresses with **large patterns,** especially huge florals; this will draw too much attention to your figure in general, making you seem larger than you are. Don't wear stretchy, **Lycra®-based fabrics** that will buckle and gather as you move; stick to sturdy, body-shaping fabrics.

SKIRTS

Don't wear too-poufy **bell-shaped skirts** that add unwanted volume to your hip area. Avoid **shiny fabrics** and **busy patterns** or stripes on your bottom half, which will draw unwanted attention to your hips. Don't wear very different colors on the bottom and top; the more monochromatic your look is from top to skirt, the more of a lean, vertical line you'll create.

SHOES

Skip delicate **strappy stilettos** that will be dwarfed by your frame. Avoid **ankle straps;** the horizontal line created by the straps will make your ankles look wider. Don't wear chunky heels or **square toes,** which will make you look shorter.

PANTS & JEANS

Avoid pants with big pockets that land at the hip, making you look bottom-heavy. Don't wear **low-rise jeans,** as your plus-size frame is bound to spill over. Avoid **flared pants,** which will make you appear short and dumpy. And skip **palazzo pants** and **gauchos,** which hide your sexy curves.

JEWELRY & ACCESSORIES

Don't cover the skin around your neck and cleavage with **scarves** or **chunky choker** necklaces. Don't wear accessories with too many **flowers, bows, ribbons, and ruffles,** which only adds fullness to your look overall. Avoid wearing **skinny belts,** which will be dwarfed by your size.

FIGURE 4.4.2
You, wearing the wrong things.

THE NEW YOU

Three ways to put your dress-sexy rules into play.

CASUAL

The off-the-shoulder top makes your shoulders appear wider and your collarbone look sexier. The pressed-crease Capri pants with heels creates a vertical line toward your feet. They hit at the knee, revealing some leg that makes you look taller and sexier.

CAREER

The blazer creates a wrap-top effect that controls your chest while defining your shoulders. The bright camisole peeking out at your chest draws attention to the center of your body. The full-length sleeves cover your arms. The pencil skirt shows just a little bit of leg, lengthening you.

FORMAL

The wide V-neck of this dress pulls out your shoulders, making you look taller. The three-quarter-length sleeves cover the largest part of your arms and reveal the thinnest part. The belt in a darker color acts like a visual corset to cinch your waist and show off your hourglass shape.

YOUR ONE FASHION MUST-HAVE: *a fitted blazer*

Choose one that hugs your natural waist as comfortably as possible. It will smooth out any bulges you have in your torso, while still allowing you to retain your sexy hourglass shape.

FITTING ROOM 5

If you're of average height and slender, you're in the right place. Just find your silhouette and prepare to get sexy.

AVERAGE SLENDER INVERTED TRIANGLE

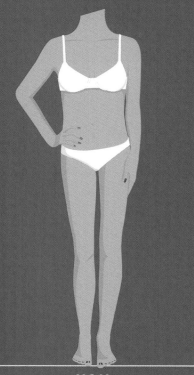

YOU

You are **AVERAGE** height.
[BETWEEN 5'3" AND 5'7"]

You are **SLENDER**.
[BETWEEN 90 AND 125 LBS.]

Your body forms an
INVERTED TRIANGLE
as your shoulders are wider
than your hips.

You have strong, wide
shoulders. Your hips are small.
Your legs and butt are slim.

YOUR BLESSING

Aren't you a lucky one? You have something so many women dream of having: a Hollywood body! By this, I mean that your slender figure, average height, and silhouette puts you in the company of women whose bodies grace the big screen. First of all, you have beautiful broad shoulders. That helps create the optical illusion that you are taller than you are. Also, because your hips are small, your figure resembles the one clothing manufacturers have in mind when they design clothes. That's why I sometimes call inverted triangles like you "hanger girls," because clothes fall on you the same way they fall on a clothes hanger. That makes shopping fairly easy for you. Also, because you're so slender, the difference between the width of your shoulders and your hips is still small, which means it will only require subtle tricks to balance your look into a sexy silhouette.

YOUR CURSE

Though your slenderness and shoulders make you appear taller than you are, you, like most Hollywood actresses, are not very tall. And because appearing tall is part of dressing sexy, high heels will really help out in that department. Also, you lack curves in your hips. While that makes it easy to fit into all kinds of clothes on your bottom half, it can be a curse when those clothes fall flat on you. When it comes to looking sexy, you could do with a little more shape on your hips to balance out your shoulders and turn you into an ideal hourglass.

YOUR CELEBRITY BODY STAND-IN: *Angelina Jolie*

WHAT TO WEAR

Your fashion challenge is to narrow your shoulders, widen your hips to balance out your strong shoulders, and reveal more of your waist.

DRESSES

Wear dresses with **narrow-set V-necks, U-necks,** and **sweetheart necklines** with straps that hit close to your neck to draw the eye vertically along your figure. Choose dresses with **horizontal detailing** at the base to balance your shoulders. Wear **corset dresses** or **A-line dresses** that hug your waist, then flare out toward the hem.

TOPS

Choose **surplice tops** and **wrap tops,** which create a flattering V-neck that pulls the eye in from your shoulders. For the same reason, wear **V-necks, U-necks, sweetheart necks,** and **square necks.** Pick tops with straps that hit at the center of each shoulder, which balance the skin on either side to help minimize the width of your shoulders. Wear darker colors on top than on the bottom to diminish your top half.

SKIRTS

Aim for **A-line skirts, wrap skirts, pleated skirts, gored skirts,** and **godet skirts,** all of which create a fuller look while holding a wide shape. Or wear **miniskirts** with an A-line shape to draw the eye to your slim legs, so you'll appear taller and sexier—provided you wear a shirt with fuller coverage to balance out your look. Choose skirts in **heavy cottons, bright fabrics,** or patterns to draw the eye to your hips.

PANTS & JEANS

Wear **low-rise pants** with a wide waistband to widen your hips. Pick **skinny jeans** that taper at the ankle, making your hips look larger in comparison. Try pants with **chunky pockets** at the hip such as fitted cargo pants. Aim for pants with embroidered or detailed pockets to add volume there.

COATS & JACKETS

Stick with **peplum jackets** that cinch at the waist and flare out to create the illusion of hips. Or wear a **corseted black blazer** to minimize your shoulders. Choose **A-line coats** and **trench coats** with minimal to no detailing in the shoulder area, that taper out from the belted waist.

JEWELRY & ACCESSORIES

Wear **hip belts** or **wide belts** worn low on your waist to widen your hips. Carry **handbags with long straps** that fall at your hip to add fullness to your shape there. Wear **drapey necklaces** that create a vertical line at your chest and bring the focus in from your shoulders.

SHOES

Wear **pointy-toed heels** in the same color as your outfit to lengthen your look—the taller, the better! Or wear bolder styles or boots to draw the eye to your bottom half.

FIGURE 5.1.1
You, only sexier.

WHAT NOT TO WEAR

Really. I mean it.

DRESSES

Avoid **wide-set V-necks** that sit far on your shoulders, making your shoulders seem wider. Steer clear of detailing around the neck of your dress. Avoid dresses that fall straight from your waist accentuating your flat hips. Don't wear **halter dresses** with straps that pull from the center of your chest, widening your top half.

TOPS

Avoid **boatneck tops,** which create a horizontal line from one shoulder to the other and make you appear even wider. Steer clear of **spaghetti straps** that sit far on your shoulders, which will contrast the width of your shoulders. Avoid **bulky, bright sweaters** in touchable knits like cashmere or mohair, which add too much volume on top.

SKIRTS

Steer clear of **long, ankle-length skirts** that accentuate how flat your hips and bottom are, which drags your look down—and worse, covers up your great legs! Skip **pencil skirts** that fall straight on your hips. Avoid skirts in **dark, slimming colors** that make your bottom half disappear.

PANTS & JEANS

Skip jeans that have few or no pockets, as you could use the extra detailing in the hip area where you need it most. Don't wear **leggings** that highlight how slim your bottom-half is compared to your top. Avoid **dark, straight-leg jeans** that make your hips seem too small to carry your shoulders.

COATS & JACKET

Steer clear of **military jackets, puffed-sleeve blazers,** and jackets with **shoulder pads, decorative buttons,** or **puff sleeves.** These styles will only make your shoulders appear even wider than they are. Avoid **light or white jackets** that draw the eye there.

JEWELRY & ACCESSORIES

Don't wear **choker necklaces** that leave too much skin on either side, widening your shoulders further. Avoid large or **chunky hobo handbags** that sit just under your arm, which only add to the heft on your top half.

SHOES

Skip shoes with **chunky heels** and **ankle straps,** such as Mary Janes, which add too much weight at your feet. Don't wear **slip-on mules** or **low wedges** that add chunk to your feet without adding much height.

FIGURE 5.1.2
You, wearing the wrong things.

THE NEW YOU

Three ways to put your dress-sexy rules into play.

CASUAL

The V-neck top creates a width-slimming vertical line between your shoulders. The bright skinny belt draws the eye down toward your hips and defines your waist. The skinny jeans taper toward the ankle, making your hips look wider in comparison. The bold, platform heels bring attention to your bottom half.

CAREER

The sweetheart neckline of this dark dress draws the eye to the center of your body, away from your shoulders. The A-line style gives shape to your hips. The horizontal detailing at the base of the dress draws the eye down. The boots adds weight to your bottom half, away from your wide shoulders.

FORMAL

The sweetheart-neck top brings the eye in to the skin between your shoulder blades. The vertically-shaped pendant necklace also helps bring the eye toward your chest. The flare in the skirt balances your shoulders, making it appear as if you have hourglass hips.

YOUR ONE FASHION MUST-HAVE: *pockets*

You can add the illusion of curves on your lower half without actually "adding" a thing! Choose pants and jeans with angular front pockets, double pockets, embroidered pockets, or cargo pockets...the more detail at your hips, the better!

AVERAGE SLENDER RECTANGLE

YOU

You are **AVERAGE** height.
[BETWEEN 5'3" AND 5'7"]

You are **SLENDER**.
[BETWEEN 90 AND 125 LBS.]

Your body forms a
RECTANGLE
as your shoulders are the
same width as your hips.

You have broad shoulders.
You have equally wide hips. Your
waist is wide and undefined.

YOUR BLESSING

Here's some great news: You already have the body parts you need to create a sexy silhouette. You have broad shoulders that square off along the top. And you have hips that are the same width as your shoulders, which means they balance each other. And balance, as I mentioned at the beginning of this book, is an important part of looking sexy. In fact, the more you accentuate your shoulders and hips, the more defined your waist will appear. Your other blessing? You have thin thighs and thin legs. That means you have a range of styles you can play up on your bottom half without worrying that you're overdoing it. Finally, because you have a slender physique, your waist isn't chunky. That means it will take well to styles that involve cinching it in, so you can create the hourglass figure you're aiming for.

YOUR CURSE

Yes, you have it all! But as an AVERAGE, SLENDER RECTANGLE, you do have a few issues to deal with. First, you have an undefined waist, which is vital to the hourglass silhouette that defines sexy. And if you gain weight, you tend to carry it around your middle. If you're like most women of this shape, your tendency is to try to cover up your trouble area with boxy or baggy clothing around your torso—but that only makes you appear even thicker in the center. Your other curse? Your wide torso gives you a slightly boyish shape, so one of your goals when dressing will be to soften your edges to give your figure a more feminine shape.

YOUR CELEBRITY BODY STAND-IN: *Demi Moore*

WHAT TO WEAR

Your fashion challenge is to accentuate your wide shoulders and your wide hips while cinching in your waist.

TOPS

Wear **wrap tops** and **surplices,** which add a feminine drape to your square torso. Choose tops with **puffed sleeves** or **flutter sleeves** to add some volume at your shoulders. Or wear **boatnecks,** tops with **wide-set spaghetti straps, camisole tops,** and **halter tops** that leave a large amount of skin on the outside of each strap, making your shoulders appear even wider.

DRESSES

Stick with **strapless dresses** or dresses with **sweetheart necklines,** all of which widen your shoulders so your waist looks smaller in comparison. Choose **wrap dresses** that cinch in at the waist with a belt or wrap. Or wear an **empire dress** that fits snugly on top, then tapers out gently over your stomach and hips.

PANTS & JEANS

Aim for **low-rise stovepipe pants** or **skinny jeans** that show off your slender figure while adding subtle volume at your hips. Pick pants with **small back pockets** and slight detailing around the hip area to fill you out there. Wear **Capris** that hit at a point just above the widest point on your calf, to keep you looking tall and slim.

SKIRTS

Choose a **full circle skirt,** a **full gored skirt,** or an **A-line skirt** that poufs or tapers out from your waist to fake the look of curvy hips. Or go the opposite direction and create a sexy silhouette with a **straight skirt** that cinches in at the waist, along with a fitted peplum jacket; choose a skirt with a sexy slit to add subtle attention below your hips.

COATS & JACKETS

Wear jackets that have **sharp, square shoulders** to exaggerate the width of your shoulders. Choose blazers with **puffed sleeves** to add fullness at your shoulders. Wear **low-stance blazers** that draw the eye into a long, sharp V-neck, making your waist seem smaller.

JEWELRY & ACCESSORIES

Choose jewelry that falls in a soft curve, such as pearls, or an angular V, such as a **pendant necklace,** both of which draw the eye toward your center. Soften your shape with **small purses** that fall either at your bustline or at your hips—not at your waist, which will widen your waist.

SHOES

Show off your sexy legs with **pointy-toed heels** or **high slingbacks,** which make your calves more shapely and imply that your figure matches. Elongate your look by choosing shoes the same color or tone as your outfit.

FIGURE 5.2.1
You, only sexier.

WHAT NOT TO WEAR

Really. I mean it.

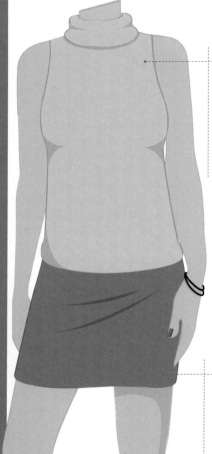

TOPS

Avoid **sleeveless tops** that cut off your arms too sharply, squaring off your look. Don't wear **crew necks, turtlenecks,** or **raglan tops** that cover up the skin at your chest. Avoid **short tops** and **cropped tanks;** by showing off skin between your top and your pants, you break up the vertical flow of your figure and draw attention to the horizontal line of skin at your stomach.

DRESSES

Don't wear **boxy shift dresses** that fall straight from your shoulders to your knees. Avoid **ankle-length dresses** that fall past your knees without implying a waistline. Don't wear **slip dresses** that hug your straight frame from top to bottom. Avoid **sheaths** that will fall flat on your figure.

PANTS & JEANS

Steer clear of **flat-front pants** without pockets; the lack of detailing at the hip and thigh area will flatten your hips and bottom. Don't wear **leggings** that will accentuate how thin your legs are.

SKIRTS

Don't wear **pencil skirts** that run straight down your flat hips, accentuating your lack of curves. Don't cover up your legs with **long, straight, ankle-length skirts.** Instead, take advantage of your strong suit and try short skirts that hit just above the knee, then leads the eye down toward your knees, giving the illusion of a shapely figure.

SHOES

Avoid **knee-high boots with skirts,** as they square off your shape instead of adding curves. Don't wear **chunky heels** or **square-toe heels** that look too bold on your bottom half.

COATS & JACKETS

Steer clear of boxy blazers, such as **Chanel-style jackets** buttoned from the collar to the waist that exaggerate your rectangle look. Don't choose jackets that run straight to your hips without defining your waist. Also avoid **long, straight coats.**

JEWELRY & ACCESSORIES

Don't carry **large handbags** that hit at your waist, which will only add more bulk to your middle. Instead, choose bags that land at your chest or your hips. Steer clear of **choker neck-laces** that cover up the curves in your neck and make you look boxy.

FIGURE 5.2.2
You, wearing the wrong things.

THE NEW YOU

Three ways to put your dress-sexy rules into play.

CASUAL	CAREER	FORMAL

The deep V-neck opens up your clavicle area to draw attention up and away from your waist. The bright pink top creates a focal point at the lowest dip in the V-neck, creating a slimming line toward the waist. The skinny jeans taper toward your ankles, making your hips seem wider, as if you have curves there.

The military-style epaulets and buttons at the top of this dress widen your shoulders. The belt over the gathered waist creates the illusion of curves at the center of your torso. The front pockets widen your hips, so your waist looks smaller. The flared skirt adds curves to the base of your silhouette.

The sweetheart neck of this dress draws the eye to the skin on your chest and face. The contrasting belt creates the instant illusion of a waist. The semi-circle skirt in this flowing fabric adds some fullness to your bottom half, making your waist appear smaller in comparison.

YOUR ONE FASHION MUST-HAVE: *cinchy belts*

Think wide belts, skinny belts, corsets that act as belts, and wrap dresses with belts that tie at your waist. Anything that pulls the eye inward from your shoulders and your hips will make it appear that you have a defined, sexy waist.

AVERAGE SLENDER TRIANGLE

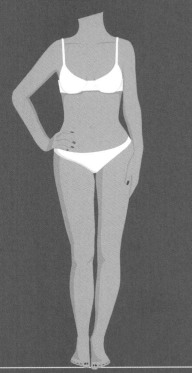

YOU

You are **AVERAGE** height.
[BETWEEN 5'3" AND 5'7"]

You are **SLENDER**.
[BETWEEN 90 AND 125 LBS.]

Your body forms an
TRIANGLE
as your hips are wider
than your shoulders.

You have a slim upper
body. Your hips are wide set.
You have a shapely bottom.

YOUR BLESSING

Well, you've certainly been dealt a pretty good hand! Though your hips are larger than your shoulders and bust area, your slender shape means that the proportion of the difference is small. This means you should make subtle steps in order to balance your body. Consider yourself blessed with your slender torso and small shoulders, which allow you to wear body-fitting tops that show off your slim shape. If you have a small bust, you can get away with wearing strapless tops that show off your sexy, thin collarbone, as well as deep V-neck and U-neck tops to show a little skin—and you can do some of this without the need for heavy-duty bras for support! Another bonus? The one place you'd do well to add curves happens to be the one place where fashion makes it the easiest: around your bustline. Thank goodness for push-up bras, padded bras, and low-cut tops.

YOUR CURSE

As an AVERAGE, SLENDER TRIANGLE, you carry your weight in your lower half. This means that you should avoid styles such as low-rise jeans that fall at the widest part of your hips or bright, bold skirts that might bring too much attention to the curves. Your fashion challenge? To bring the eye up to your top half, with tops and dresses that also make your shoulders appear wider, while at the same time taking the attention off of your bottom half. Adding weight to your top half and keeping it off the bottom will balance your look into an even more perfect, sexier you.

YOUR CELEBRITY BODY STAND-IN: *Halle Berry*

WHAT TO WEAR

*Your fashion formula is to make your
shoulders appear wider to match your hips; you also need
to draw attention away from your hips and butt.*

TOPS

Wear **off-the-shoulder tops, wide scoop necks,** and
boatnecks that rest far on your shoulders, all of which
create a horizontal line between your shoulders,
widening them. Wear **puffed-sleeve tops** or
sleeveless tops that let you show off your slender
arms. Add texture to your top half with cashmere,
mohair, or cable knit sweaters.

DRESSES

Choose **empire dresses** that gather
at the bust area to add volume
there, then flow outward, just
grazing your hips. Wear **strapless
dresses** that create a horizontal
line across your shoulders to widen
them, while letting you showcase
your gorgeous torso. Wear a
ruffled, feminine **halter dress** to
add weight to your bust area
and balance out your curvy hips.

SKIRTS

Wear **A-line skirts** that cinch in at
your waist, then taper forgivingly
over your hips and thighs. Choose
pencil skirts with princess seams
to create a long, lean look on
your bottom half. Wear **wrap skirts**
or **trumpet skirts** that flare out
slightly at the hem to balance
your hips. Choose **light, flowing
fabrics,** such as cotton jersey, that
drape easily over your lower half.

PANTS & JEANS

Aim for **straight-leg** and **boot cut pants** that flare just slightly
from the knee to balance your hips from below. Choose pockets
with little or no details. Wear **black pants** or **dark-colored
denims** with lighter or patterned tops to diminish the look of
your thighs. Wear **pressed-crease trousers** that elongate
your body with a steady, vertical line to your ankles.

COATS & JACKETS

Wear **puffed-sleeve
blazers** that make your
waist seem slim in
comparison. Try a
cap-sleeved jacket
to bring out your
shoulders. Choose
blazers with **wide
lapels** to draw the eye
outward. Or try a **short,
velvet, feminine blazer**
that nips in at the waist.

JEWELRY &
ACCESSORIES

Wear a **dainty pendant,
pearl, or charm
necklace** that falls
at your collarbone,
drawing the eye there
without overpowering
your slender
neck. Carry a **small
eye-catching clutch**
or a bright **hobo bag**
under your arm to
add fullness there.

SHOES

Wear **pointy-toed
mid-height to high
heels;** because you're
of average height,
you can go as high as
you want to increase
your stature,
making your hips
seem slimmer. Wear
pretty wedges
under your jeans.

FIGURE 5.3.1
You, only sexier.

WHAT NOT TO WEAR

Really. I mean it.

TOPS

Don't wear **narrow-set halters** that make your shoulders seem small and sloping compared to your wide hips. Avoid **drop-waist tops** or tops in contrasting colors that land at your hips and draw the eye down to your broadest area. Skip **crew neck** and **raglan sweaters** that cover up the skin on your top half and narrow your shoulders.

DRESSES

Avoid **sheath dresses** that run straight out from your shoulders down, bringing your silhouette out and exaggerating your triangle shape even more. Steer clear of full dresses that bell out from the waist in **stiff fabrics,** such as taffeta or crinoline, that make you look wider.

SKIRTS

Don't wear **circle skirts, gathered skirts, gored skirts,** or **pleated skirts** that add too much weight on your hips. Avoid skirts in **stiff, heavy fabrics** that add volume to your already fuller bottom half. Don't wear skirts in **shiny fabrics** such as silk or satin if you're not wearing the same on top; shiny fabrics will catch the light and make you look heavier there.

PANTS & JEANS

Skip **busy patterns** or bright and light colors on your pants; also avoid volumizing fabrics such as terry cloth—all of which emphasize the wrong region of your body. Avoid **pants with pockets** that draw the eye straight to your trouble spot. Steer clear of **skinny jeans** or **stovepipe pants** that taper at all toward your ankles, making your hips stand out in comparison.

SHOES

Avoid **chunky heels** and **round-toe flats** with pants, as this will make your legs seem heavier. Don't wear **knee-high boots** with skirts, as they break the vertical line and draw attention to your bottom half.

COATS & JACKETS

Steer clear of jackets in **soft fabrics,** such as linen, that lack strong shoulder construction and make your shoulders seem sloped. Avoid flap pockets on the hip of your jackets, adding extra weight where you don't want it. Steer clear of **large, oversized buttons** that don't match your slender frame.

JEWELRY & ACCESSORIES

Don't wear **hip belts.** I repeat: Don't wear hip belts. Avoid **chunky chokers** that make your slender neck seem shorter. Steer clear of **messenger bags, totes,** and **satchels** that fall at the hip and draw attention there. Skip large, **bulky accessories** that aren't proportional to your slender frame.

FIGURE 5.3.2
You, wearing the wrong things.

THE NEW YOU

Three ways to put your dress-sexy rules into play.

CASUAL

The short puffed-sleeve blazer turns your sloped, small shoulders into squared-off strong ones that balance your hips. The low-stance blazer over the U-neck top creates a sexy triangle at your chest that brings the eye up and away from your hips. The dark, straight-leg jeans lengthens your look, making your hips seem smaller.

CAREER

The princess seam pencil skirt in a dark charcoal color skims your hips—rather than clinging to them— to disguise your hips. The bright blue tailored top instantly draws the eye up toward your face. The puffed-sleeves on the top add fullness at the shoulders and arms to your shoulders.

FORMAL

The wide-set straps of this empire dress draws the eye outward toward your shoulders. The gathering at the bust area, combined with the sexy, low V-neck, adds fullness to your chest to balance out your hips. The light, flowing chiffon from the high waist doesn't add unnecessary weight to your hips.

YOUR ONE FASHION MUST-HAVE: *boatneck and wide scoop-neck tops*

Choose tops that sit wide on your shoulders to show off your slender collarbone. The wider the neck, the wider your shoulders will appear, perfectly balancing your hips.

AVERAGE SLENDER HOURGLASS

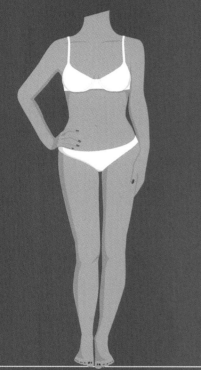

YOU

You are **AVERAGE** height.
[BETWEEN 5'3" AND 5'7"]

You are **SLENDER**.
[BETWEEN 90 AND 125 LBS.]

Your body forms an **HOURGLASS** as your shoulders are the same width as your hips, with a tiny waist in between.

You have broad shoulders and a slightly shapely bust. Your hips and butt are mildly curvy. Your waist is small and defined.

YOUR BLESSING

Wow, you should be pleased with what you were born with. You already have a very sexy body! Your shoulders and hips measure nearly the same width, which means your figure is already very balanced. And you have a very slim, defined waist, an element at the heart of a sexy silhouette. Rather than having to fake a small waist, your only job is to wear clothing that reveals what you have. Your other blessing? You're slender. Because you're so slender, the difference between your curvy hips and your tiny waist isn't very large, which means you only need to take subtle steps to keep yourself looking proportional. Finally, you have some height on your side. With even a slight dressing adjustment, you'll be looking taller and sexier in no time!

YOUR CURSE

As an AVERAGE, SLENDER HOURGLASS, your body is already well balanced, and your goal is to choose clothes that keep it that way. Unfortunately, this means you sometimes have trouble wearing new style trends that accentuate either your torso or your hips. To stay in balance, you need to avoid extremes. So if you want to wear low-rise jeans that land at your hips, you'll have to choose a top that widens your upper half equally. Even-steven, that's your aim. You just need to make sure that when you're getting dressed, you don't cover up any of the curves you were lucky enough to be born with. You already have the shape that means sexy, so now you just need to show it off.

YOUR CELEBRITY BODY STAND-IN: *Jessica Alba*

WHAT TO WEAR

*Your fashion challenge is to keep your broad shoulders and
curvy hips balanced, while defining your waist.*

COATS & JACKETS

Wear **peplum jackets,** which cut in at your thinnest point,
then flare out toward your hips. Or wear other shaped
blazers with **high waists** or **princess seams** that
follow your natural curves. Choose a **basic trench
coat** with subtle detailing at the shoulders, a belt
at the waist, and an A-line silhouette to your knees.

TOPS

Choose **low V-necks, wrap tops,
surplice tops, sweetheart necks,**
and deep scoop necks to show off
your gorgeous collarbone and slender
neck. For the same reason, wear
tailored dress shirts, leaving the top
two or three buttons open to create
a neck-flattering V-neck. Layer tops
under V-neck sweaters and blazers to
draw more attention to your chest.

DRESSES

Try a **halter dress** that reveals
your thin torso, thin collarbone.
and slender arms. Choose a fitted
sheath that traces your hourglass
curves. Wear a **wrap dress** in a
light- to mid-weight fabric, which
squares off your shoulders, creates
a flattering V-neck, cinches in
your small waist, and drapes gently
around your curvy hips.

SKIRTS

Wear **pencil skirts** with **princess seams** to reflect the
hourglass shape of your hips. Or wear **A-line skirts** with
strong, wide waistlines that taper out smoothly over your
curves. Pick skirts with **handkerchief hems** or **asymmetrical
hems** to accentuate both the curvy and thin parts of your
legs and make your average height seem even taller.

PANTS & JEANS

Wear **stovepipe
pants, skinny jeans,**
or **straight-leg pants**
that skim your hips
and reveal your slender
shape. Wear **low-rise
men's trousers** that
will fall beautifully
on your hips. Try
a **Capri** in a dark color,
paired with ballet
flats, to create a pretty
but still-sexy look.

JEWELRY & ACCESSORIES

Choose a **dainty
pendant, charm,**
or **locket necklace**
featuring a single
focal point to bring
attention to your
pronounced collar-
bone. Carry a **small
clutch** in proportion
to your slender frame.
Wear **small drop ear-
rings or studs** to draw
attention to your face.

SHOES

Wear **skinny
stilettos** with
interesting details,
such as **cut-away
arches** or **open-toes.**
Or try **slingbacks** and
wedges with high
heels. Elongate
your look by wearing a
shoe in the same
color as your outfit.

FIGURE 5.4.1
You, only sexier.

WHAT NOT TO WEAR

Really. I mean it.

COATS & JACKETS

Stay away from **boxy blazers** that square off your shape and cover up your natural gifts! Avoid **collarless jackets, mandarin collar jackets,** or **Chanel-style blazers** buttoned up that cover up your pretty chest area. Don't choose jackets such as **pea coats** that hit at your hip or your mid-thigh, unless they are built with a waist-defining shape.

TOPS

Don't wear **crew necks, raglan tops, buttoned-up cardigan sweaters, turtlenecks,** or other high-necked styles that hide your slim neck and chest. Avoid baggy **peasant tops** that completely cover the perfect curves at your small waist. Don't wear **empire tops** that flow out too much over your waist, once again covering your assets.

DRESSES

Steer clear of **drop-waist dresses** that disguise your beautiful waist. Avoid **thin or Lycra®-based fabrics** in styles that cling to your body; though you want to show off your curves, too much cling translates into too sexy. Steer clear of boxy **shift dresses** that run right over—and eliminate—your gorgeous waist.

SKIRTS

Avoid **circle skirts, full gored skirts, pleated skirts,** and **wrap skirts** that create too much fullness around your hips and thighs, covering up your slender curves. Don't choose skirts with ornamental detailing or pockets in the hip area, which will bring too much focus to your hips. Avoid bright colors on the bottom if you're not balancing it out with a bright or light color on top.

SHOES

Don't wear **big chunky soles** or wide heels, which will make you look dumpy. Avoid bold or bright shoes that will distract from your figure.

PANTS & JEANS

Don't wear **light-colored pants** if you're wearing a dark shirt up top—they will make you appear bottom-heavy. Instead, stick with monochromatic shades (such as a dark denim pant with an eggplant top), so you're not overemphasizing your top or bottom half.

JEWELRY & ACCESSORIES

Avoid **hip belts,** which accent your hip area too much, making you seem bottom-heavy. Don't cover the skin area around your neck with **scarves** or **super chunky choker** necklaces that don't allow the eye to see some skin. Don't carry **oversized handbags** that hit at your waist and disguise your figure.

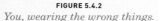

FIGURE 5.4.2
You, wearing the wrong things.

THE NEW YOU

Three ways to put your dress-sexy rules into play.

CASUAL	CAREER	FORMAL
The V-neck created by this surplice top draws the eye up to your chest. The surplice hugs your waist, revealing your hour-glass curves. The dark, stovepipe jean fits slim around your hips to show off your slender figure.	The shaped blazer follows the curve of your waist. The low-stance creates a flattering V-neck over the bright, tailored dress shirt. The pencil skirt starts in at your waist and skims your hips and thighs. The hem hits above the knee to show more of your slender legs, making you appear taller.	The sweetheart neckline on this halter dress widens your shoulders and hugs your thin torso as it thins toward your waist. The mid-weight fabric of the dress just skims along your hips and plays up your shapely figure without adding extra weight to it.

YOUR ONE FASHION MUST-HAVE: *wrap dresses*

Average, Slender Hourglass, we'd like you to meet Diane von Furstenberg,
because wrap dresses are your figure's best friend!
They create a flattering V-neck, cinch in at the waist, and graze your curvy hips.

FITTING ROOM
6

If you're average height
and medium weight,
you're in the right place.
Just find your silhouette
and prepare to get sexy.

AVERAGE
MEDIUM
INVERTED TRIANGLE

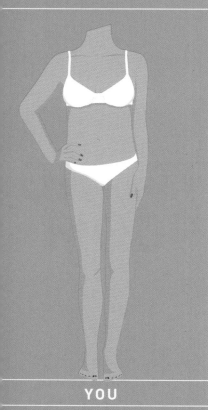

YOU

You are **AVERAGE** height.
[BETWEEN 5'3" AND 5'7"]

You are **MEDIUM** weight.
[BETWEEN 115 AND 170 LBS.]

Your body forms an
INVERTED TRIANGLE
as your shoulders are wider
than your hips.

You have broad shoulders and
arms. Your hips and bottom are slim.
Your waist is undefined because
it is the same width as your hips.

YOUR BLESSING

Well, you certainly have something to be proud of! Your most prominent feature is your wide, broad shoulders, which can be very sexy—especially on someone with a medium build like you. You look gorgeous in clothes that show off your shoulders. And those shoulders make you look taller at first glance. Your other blessing? Your body is the template for most of the clothes sold in large production, because thanks to your small hips, your shape is flattering to most styles. For instance, because you have a small bottom, thin thighs, and small hips, you can wear nearly any style of pants or skirts without worrying about them clinging to your hips, thighs, or bottom. You can even wear modern jean styles, which tend to have more detailing than ever on the front and back pockets.

YOUR CURSE

As an AVERAGE, MEDIUM, INVERTED TRIANGLE, you have what's called a high balance, which means that you carry more of your weight in your top half than you do in your hips and thighs. For this reason, you can sometimes appear top-heavy. Certain styles that cover up your chest area can make you appear larger on top than you really are. Your other curse? You may not have many curves in your bottom half, and it can be frustrating if "baby has no back." Finally, if you're on the short end of average, you need to add more height to your look to keep you looking tall and sexy!

YOUR CELEBRITY BODY STAND-IN: *Denise Richards*

WHAT TO WEAR

Your fashion challenge is to play down your wide shoulders and widen your bottom half to balance your figure overall.

TOPS

Aim for **V-necks, U-necks,** and **low scoop necks** to reveal a vertical line of skin at your chest, drawing the eye away from your shoulders. Wear **tailored dress shirts** with two buttons open to reveal a flattering V-neck. Allow your shirts to peek out from beneath sweaters and blazers, or wear contrasting tops that hit at the hip to widen your bottom half.

DRESSES

Wear a **halter dress** with thick straps that are proportional to your big shoulders, which makes them appear smaller. Try a **corset dress** that cinches your waist, then tapers outward toward your hips. Or wear a **drop-waist dress** that skims your curves and hits at the hip, adding shape there. Choose **flutter sleeve dresses** that make your arms appear slender as they peek out beneath.

PANTS & JEANS

Choose **straight-leg pants** that lengthen your look overall. Pick jeans that have **distressing, bleaching, whiskering, or fading** on the hip area, which all draw attention to your bottom-half. Wear **cropped pants, gauchos,** or **Capris** that hit at the knee to draw the eye to your hips and revealing some leg. Choose pants with pockets at the hip to create curves there.

SKIRTS

Wear **circle skirts, gored skirts, pleated skirts,** and **A-line skirts** that create fullness around your hips where you want it. Choose skirts in **medium-size patterns, lighter colors,** or **thick, textured fabrics** to draw the eye to your bottom half. Hem your skirts just above, just at, or just below the knee to show off your slim legs and make you seem taller.

COATS & JACKETS

Pick **peplum jackets** that flare out from the waist to make it appear as if you have hips. Or wear jackets that hit at the hip to add weight there. Choose **low-stance blazers** to create a deep V-neck, making you look curvier than you are.

JEWELRY & ACCESSORIES

Wear **sizeable pendant necklaces** that hit low to draw the eye down toward your hips. Try long **chandelier earrings,** which break up the horizontal line of your wide shoulders. Wear **cuffs** or **bangle bracelets** that draw attention to your hips.

SHOES

Choose **pointy-toed heels, peep-toe heels,** or shoes with flattering **cut-away arches** that lengthen your look. Because you're average height, you can wear heels as high as you want. The taller the better!

FIGURE 6.1.1
You, only sexier.

WHAT NOT TO WEAR

Really. I mean it.

FIGURE 6.1.2
You, wearing the wrong things.

COATS & JACKETS

Avoid **puffed-sleeve blazers,** coats with shoulder pads, **denim jackets with pockets at your chest,** and **military jackets** with detailing on the shoulders, such as epaulets or large buttons; all of these will broaden your shoulders too much and make you appear top-heavy. Don't wear light, bright colors or patterns on top paired with dark colors on the bottom.

TOPS

Avoid **narrow-set halter tops** and **off-the-shoulder tops** that underscore your wide shoulders. For the same reason, avoid **large cowl neck sweaters.** Don't wear short-sleeved tops that cut across the widest part of your arm, which can make a medium build woman like yourself seem larger than you are.

DRESSES

Skip **shift dresses** that fall on your straight hips like a burlap bag and take away any curves you might have. Also, avoid dresses with **dainty spaghetti straps** or **halter straps** that pull from the center of the dress and up around your neck, which will make your shoulders look much wider than they are.

SKIRTS

Don't wear dark-colored skirts paired with bright tops, which minimize your lower half further. Don't wear **fitted pencil skirts** that emphasize how straight your hips are, unless you're adding a **shapely peplum jacket** to create imaginary curves from the waist down. Avoid **straight, ankle-length skirts** that emphasize your flat hips and bottom, and drag down your look.

SHOES

Avoid **chunky, thick-soled shoes** that draw the eye down and make your thin legs and ankles appear pudgy. Don't wear **square-toed** heels that make you look shorter.

PANTS & JEANS

Steer clear of **dark-colored skinny jeans, leggings,** or **stovepipe pants** in stretch fabrics that emphasize how much slimmer your legs are in relation to your top. Avoid jeans with **flat fronts or no pockets,** which will make your bottom too skinny to balance on top.

JEWELRY & ACCESSORIES

Don't wear **tiny stud jewel earrings** that will seem small in proportion to your large shoulders. Also, avoid **tiny clutch purses** held at your hips, because the combination of small bag with your small hips will make your bottom half practically disappear.

THE NEW YOU

Three ways to put your dress-sexy rules into play.

CASUAL	**CAREER**	**FORMAL**
The V-neck top sits wide on your shoulders, making them seem smaller than they are. The drop-waist top hits at the hip to add weight there. The boot cut jean creates a long line to your ankles, while providing a very subtle flare below the knee to add more curves to your bottom half.	This tailored dress shirt is darker than the skirt to diminish your top half. The contrasting top hits that widest point on your hips to bring the eye there. The wide belt emphasizes your waist. And the circle skirt brings plenty of fullness to your hips and bottom to balance your shoulders.	The crisscross style of this top offers a V-shape at your cleavage, bringing the eye in from your shoulders toward the center of your chest. The wide strap makes your broad shoulders look smaller in proportion. The corset creates the illusion of a waist and turns your figure into an hourglass.

YOUR ONE FASHION MUST-HAVE: *pants with detailed pockets*

Side pockets, front pockets, or embroidered pockets all
help to widen your hips. Even the bulky hip pockets on fitted cargo pants
will make your silhouette sexier on a Saturday afternoon!

YOU

You are **AVERAGE** height.
[BETWEEN 5'3" AND 5'7"]

You are **MEDIUM** weight.
[BETWEEN 115 AND 170 LBS.]

Your body forms a
RECTANGLE
as your shoulders are the
same width as your hips.

You have broad shoulders.
You have equally wide hips. Your
waist is wide and undefined.

YOUR BLESSING

Lucky you, you've got a pretty great body to work with on the road to sexy. Without even doing a thing, you already have the wide hips and wide shoulders that are essential to building the hourglass structure that stands for sexy. This means that you can wear wild combinations of styles as long as you keep yourself balanced from top to bottom. With those broad shoulders, you look taller at first glace. And you can look stunning in shapes that show off some skin at your chest. Do you want some even better news? Because your wide hips are balanced by your wide shoulders, you get to enhance your shape instead of diminishing it! As long as you keep your top and bottom proportional, you'll always look great. Finally, you're average height, which means that it won't take much lifting to turn your silhouette into a taller, sexier one.

YOUR CURSE

Your biggest curse as an AVERAGE, MEDIUM RECTANGLE is that your waist is undefined, meaning it tends to be the same width as your hips and shoulders. It is difficult to create a waist where there isn't one, but luckily there are plenty of options to trick the eye (and more important the mirror!) into seeing a much slimmer waist than is already there. Since you are of medium build, it can be hard sometimes to find clothing that isn't clinging or adding boxy baggage to your body. You're really only one trouble-spot away from turning your silhouette into the perfect hourglass.

YOUR CELEBRITY BODY STAND-IN: *Laila Ali*

WHAT TO WEAR

*Your fashion challenge is to bring your shoulders
further out and add curves to your hips and
bottom so that your waist looks smaller in comparison.*

DRESSES

Wear **A-line dresses** with puffed-sleeves to make your
shoulders and hips look wider and your waist smaller in
comparison. Choose **wrap dresses** that tie in the center
to create the illusion of your waist. Wear **empire dresses**
that hug your bust and create an imaginary high waist.
Or wear **corset dresses** that fully cinch your figure.

TOPS

Choose **V-necks** or **U-necks**
that draw the eye up to your chest
and create the illusion of a curvy
silhouette. Try a **tunic top** that runs
beautifully past your stomach area
and lands at a spot on your hips. Pick
a **peasant top** or a **drop waist** top
with detailing such as fabric bands,
bows, or ribbon at the hip to make
you seem wider where you want it.

SKIRTS

Go with **A-line skirts** that have a
wide waistband and taper outward,
making it appear as if you have
a curved waist. Wear **gored skirts**
or pleated skirts sewn up to the hip
to make it look like you have hips.
Choose skirts in **mid- to heavy-
weight fabrics,** such as thick cotton,
or in **medium-size patterns** that add
fullness to your hips and bottom.

PANTS & JEANS

Wear **low-rise jeans**
that hit at the broadest
point on your body to
fake the look of curvy
hips. Or choose **boot
cut pants** to add a
bit of fullness below
the knee. Color-block
your look by wearing
the same color on top
and bottom, divided
by a dark color in
the middle to create
the illusion of a waist.

COATS & JACKETS

Wear a **trench coat**
with structured shoul-
ders and detailing such
as decorative flaps,
epaulets, or buttons; it
then cinches your waist
and tapers outward,
faking an hourglass
silhouette. Or wear
peplum jackets to add
curves to your torso.
Choose jackets
that hit at the hip
to add volume there.

JEWELRY & ACCESSORIES

Go for a **hip belt** that
sits at the broadest
part of your hip and
brings the eye there.
Choose **bangles**
or **cuffs** to add weight
to your top and
bottom half without
adding fullness to your
waist. Similarly, pick
a medium **clutch**
that either sits under
your arm or at your hip.

SHOES

Wear **pointy-toed heels, peep-toe heels,** or heels that dip low toward
your toes to create a long line to your ankles. As a woman of average
height, you should wear 2" heels to 3" or more, all of which will add
curves to the shape of your bottom, making it perkier.

FIGURE 6.2.1
You, only sexier.

WHAT NOT TO WEAR

Really. I mean it.

DRESSES

Don't wear a high-neck **sheath dress** that highlights your boxy shape. Avoid detailing at your middle that merely draws attention to your torso without cinching it in. Avoid **square-neck dresses** that accentuate the straight lines of your figure. Don't hem your dresses at the widest part of your calf, which makes your legs look thicker than they are.

TOPS

Avoid **sleeveless tops** that cut straight off at the edge of the shoulder and make your shoulders and arms seem thicker. Steer clear of **crew necks** and **raglan necks** that make your shoulders seem sloped and small. Don't wear **boxy cropped sweaters** that add more volume to your waist. Avoid tops in fabrics that cling to your torso and accentuate your squared-off shape.

SKIRTS

Don't wear **pencil skirts** that run straight from your torso to your knee. Avoid **straight, ankle-length skirts** that weigh down your hips and completely flatten your bottom. Skip **miniskirts** if you're wearing a waist-length, cropped shirt or jacket; choosing items of the same length proportionally will make you look boxy, instead of long and lean.

PANTS & JEANS

Don't wear thigh-hugging or Lycra®-based pants such as **leggings** or **skinny jeans** that reveal your flat bottom and small hips. At the same time, avoid wide-leg pants such as **palazzo pants** and **men's trousers** that accentuate your body's boxy shape.

COATS & JACKET

Avoid **double-breasted blazers** or thick twill pea coats that square off your shape. Steer clear of **long, straight coats** that button from the neck to your knees without tapering in toward your waist, as this will accentuate your lack of curves.

JEWELRY & ACCESSORIES

Don't carry **square handbags** that land at your waist and make you look wider there. Avoid **choker** necklaces that chop your neck in two and make your shoulders look masculine. And don't forget your **waist** or **hip belt!**

SHOES

Steer clear of **square-toed shoes** that underscore your boxy frame. Also avoid **round-toe flats** or **flat slip-on mules** that don't give your legs any lift, leaving them looking stick-straight and unshapely.

FIGURE 6.2.2
You, wearing the wrong things.

THE NEW YOU

Three ways to put your dress-sexy rules into play.

CASUAL

The off-the-shoulder peasant top widens your shoulders, so your waist looks smaller in comparison. The belt at the hips adds volume there. And the subtle boot cut jean adds a small flare below the knee, compounding the illusion that you have an hourglass figure.

CAREER

The bright-colored top under this blazer brings the eye straight up to your face. The V-neck created by the blazer fools the eye into thinking you're angling toward a waist. The pockets at the base of the blazer add a touch of necessary fullness to your hip area. And the very subtle boot cut pant completes your long, lean look.

FORMAL

The wide straps of this dress sit just on the edges of your shoulders to widen them. The empire style hugs your bust with a contrasting ribbon, making it appear that you have a small, high waist. The ruching under the bust adds volume to your cleavage that you might not already have.

YOUR ONE FASHION MUST-HAVE: *a peplum jacket*

This jacket slightly broadens your shoulders and flares at the hip, making your waist appear smaller in between. Wear one with pants, skirts, and dresses to make it appear as if you have a perfect hourglass figure!

AVERAGE
MEDIUM
TRIANGLE

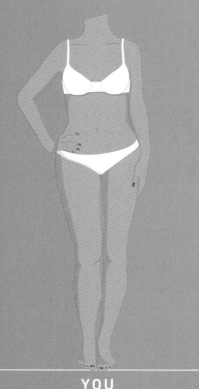

YOU

You are **AVERAGE** height.
[BETWEEN 5'3" AND 5'7"]

You are **MEDIUM** weight.
[BETWEEN 115 AND 170 LBS.]

Your body forms a
TRIANGLE
as your shoulders are
narrower than your hips.

You have a defined,
narrow waist. Your hips are full.
Your bottom is round.

YOUR BLESSING

Lucky you, you were born with amazing curves! And because your hips are the primary visual element on your body, giving you a strong silhouette, you're already halfway to sexy. You have gorgeous hips. You also have a full, rounded bottom and beautiful, shapely thighs. Your other blessing? You have a narrow waist and a small ribcage, which make it easy for you to flatter your upper body and make your midriff look slim. Your slender neck and small bust are perfect for tops that show off your neck, including dramatic, plunging V-necks—but maybe not as dramatic as the infamous Versace dress that your "celebrity body stand-in" once wore to the Grammys®. By drawing attention to your small torso, you look even slimmer than you are.

YOUR CURSE

As an AVERAGE, MEDIUM TRIANGLE, you have what's called a low balance. This just means that the visual line of your silhouette reaches its broadest point at your hips. For this reason, you can appear bottom-heavy if you choose clothes that highlight the area. Your hips appear especially wide in tight, straight skirts; in jackets or coats that fall to the low hip; and in tapered pants or jeans that blatantly show off your wide hips. Your other curse? While you may have full breasts, many Average, Medium Triangles have small breasts and narrow, sloped shoulders.

YOUR CELEBRITY BODY STAND-IN: *Jennifer Lopez*

WHAT TO WEAR

Your biggest fashion challenge is to restore balance in your silhouette by creating a strong shoulder line, playing up the charms of your short torso and de-emphasizing your lower body.

TOPS

Wear **V-necks** that sit far on your shoulders, **boatnecks, wide-set scoop necks,** and off-the-shoulder tops that widen your shoulders to match your hips. Wear **wrap tops** and **surplice tops** that show off your slender neck and reveal your narrow torso. Choose tops with **fluted sleeves, flutter sleeves,** or **puffed sleeves** to add volume to your shoulders. And whether you have a little cleavage or a lot, show it off!

DRESSES

Choose **empire dresses,** which add ruching and volume to your bust, then flow gently over your hips. Choose **halter dresses** in fluid, mid-weight fabrics, **wrap dresses** in a matte jersey, and **sheath dresses** in delicate patterns with a dark background. Hem your dresses to knee length or above to make your legs seem longer and your hips look smaller.

SKIRTS

Aim for **dark, neutral-colored skirts** paired with lighter tops to bring your top out and diminish your bottom half. Wear **knee-length pencil skirts** with no waistband in structured, firm fabrics to hold your curves in. Or choose **A-line skirts** in light fabrics that flow over the lower half of your figure flirtatiously.

PANTS & JEANS

Pick **straight-leg jeans** or **boot cut jeans** that add a very slight flare below the knees to balance your hips. Choose pants in black, dark colors and jeans in dark denim to play down the thighs help your lower half recede into the background. If you're on the slimmer side, try **stovepipe pants** that will slim you even more. Pick pants with medium-sized back pockets in scale with your frame.

COATS & JACKETS

Wear **puffed-sleeve blazers** or jackets with strong shoulders, such as a **Chanel jacket,** if you wear it open. This adds structure to your torso which will balance out your hips. Aim for **A-line coats** that skim over your thighs and bottom to disguise the broad curves.

JEWELRY & ACCESSORIES

Try **colorful, feminine scarves** around your neck to add volume to your top half. Or wear **drop earrings, short necklaces,** and **brooches** to draw the eye up. Carry a bright **medium-sized handbag** that tucks under your arm to add volume there.

SHOES

Wear **pointy-toed high heels** or **peep-toe stilettos** as tall as you want to make your legs appear longer, your thighs appear slimmer, and your backside appear raised and perky. Or **low-cut shoes** to visually lengthen your legs.

FIGURE 6.3.1
You, only sexier.

171

WHAT NOT TO WEAR

Really. I mean it.

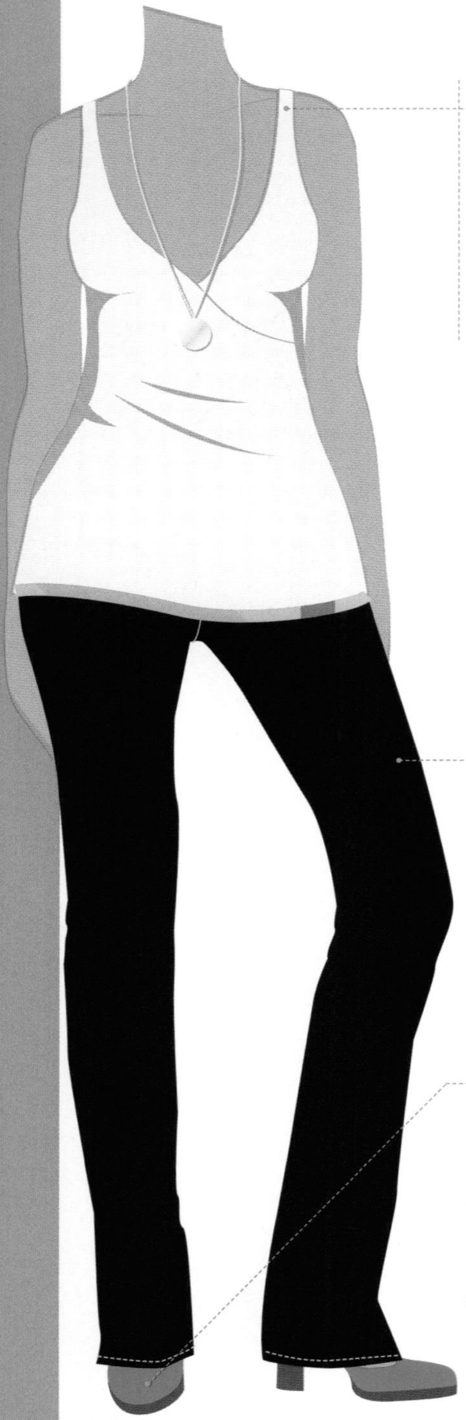

TOPS

Don't choose tops or sweaters that hit at the widest point on your hips—especially tops with horizontal accents at the hem—as this accentuates your wide hips. Steer clear of **crew neck** or **raglan tops** that cover up your slender neck and make your shoulders seem narrow. If your shoulders are sloped, skip **halter tops** that will make you look bottom-heavy.

DRESSES

Steer clear of **drop waist dresses** that add bulk to your hips without revealing a small waist. Don't wear a fitted **halter dress**—especially in shiny fabrics such as silk or satin—which will make you look bottom-heavy. Avoid **shiny dresses** that pick up light and visually add weight to your hips and bottom. Avoid fabrics that are too tight or clingy such as Lycra®.

SKIRTS

Avoid **prairie skirts** that add unnecessary bulk to your hips and thighs. Don't wear long skirts hemmed at your ankle, which only pulls your body down and makes you seem heavier. Avoid **full skirts** that bell out and **stiff fabrics.** Steer clear of horizontal details on skirts that break up the vertical line and make your lower half seem wider.

PANTS & JEANS

Avoid **cargo pants** and trousers with bulky side pockets or details on your hips, which will draw the eye straight to your wide hips. Don't wear **low-rise jeans** with a bulky waistline at your widest point. Steer clear of **textured fabrics,** such as terry cloth, that add unwanted volume to your hips, thighs, and bottom. Skip bright colors on the bottom if you're wearing dark tops.

SHOES

Don't wear **chunky heeled shoes.** Avoid dark, **knee-high boots** that will shorten your legs and counteract the slenderizing effects of your clothes, making your hips seem wide.

COATS & JACKETS

Steer clear of jackets hemmed to your hip, which highlight your trouble zones. Avoid **soft fabrics** such as linen or flimsy jersey material that don't hold up structure on the shoulders, as this will make you look bottom-heavy. Don't choose jackets with front pockets at the hip.

JEWELRY & ACCESSORIES

Stay away from super-long **pendant necklaces** that draw the eye down toward your hips. Avoid wearing **opaque tights** in the same color as your skirt, which will make you look shorter. Don't carry **large bags** that hang to the hip and draw attention to the broadest portion of your body.

FIGURE 6.3.2
You, wearing the wrong things.

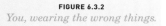

THE NEW YOU

Three ways to put your dress-sexy rules into play.

CASUAL

The wrap top sits far on your shoulders, making them appear wider. The puffed-sleeves add more volume on your top half to balance your hips. The bow at your waist accentuates your small torso. The dark denim jeans have a very subtle boot cut, to balance your hips from below.

CAREER

The monochromatic skirt suit slenderizes your figure, creating a vertical line along your figure. The shoulders on the jacket create a structured, strong horizontal line that balances your hips. The bright yellow top beneath the blazer draws the eye in toward your center. The open wedge heels give you sexy lift.

FORMAL

The wide open V-neck of this dress draws attention to your neck area and slender collarbone. The fluted sleeve adds more width to your shoulders to balance out your hips. The lightweight, drapey skirt just skims the hips, smoothing out the transition around your curves.

YOUR ONE FASHION MUST-HAVE: *a dark, boot cut jean*

This jean grazes your hips with a straight cut, then flares slightly from your knees to your ankles, which provides a perfect counterbalance to your hips. You will look taller and slimmer instantly!

AVERAGE
MEDIUM
HOURGLASS

YOU

You are **AVERAGE** height.
[BETWEEN 5'3" AND 5'7"]

You are **MEDIUM** weight.
[BETWEEN 115 AND 170 LBS.]

Your body forms an
HOURGLASS
as your shoulders are the
same width as your hips, with
a tiny waist in between.

You have broad shoulders
and a shapely bust. Your hips
and butt are curvy. Your
waist is small and defined.

YOUR BLESSING

Wow, you are one lucky woman! You know what your body reminds me of? A Playboy bunny—but in a good way. You have curves in all the right places. Honestly, you have one of the sexiest shapes of all the forty-eight shapes! You have broad shoulders and some flesh on your arms you can be proud to show off. You might even have a little bit of a bust, which you can turn into cleavage if you want. Your hourglass curves mean you can wear body-contouring items that show off your figure, as well as clothes that reveal some skin (and that's always sexy). You can wear plunging V-necks that bare your cleavage, boatneck or halter tops that show off your stunning collarbone, or short skirts that bare your shapely thighs and calves. Your other blessing? You have gorgeous hips, a full, rounded bottom, and shapely thighs.

YOUR CURSE

Though it's not much of a curse, as an AVERAGE, MEDIUM HOURGLASS your problem is that you have a perfect amount of weight in your arms, as well as in your hips, thighs, and bottom, but you're so well-balanced that if you're not thoughtful about what you choose to wear, you can easily add accidental weight to the wrong places. For example, if you choose the wrong pants or skirt, you'll instantly look more bottom-heavy than you actually are. It's a small margin of error. Also, if you're not careful to accentuate your waistline, by inadvertently making your torso appear thicker, your whole silhouette will seem larger than it is.

YOUR CELEBRITY BODY STAND-IN: *Drew Barrymore*

WHAT TO WEAR

*Your fashion challenge is to keep your broad shoulders and
wide hips balanced, while defining your waist.*

TOPS

Wear fitted **off-the-shoulder tops, boatnecks,** or **wide scoop
necks** to reveal your broad shoulders, provided you balance the
width on your bottom half. (If you're big on top, don't forget the
strapless bra!) Add texture to your top half with **fitted sweaters**
or ruching at the bustline. Try **wrap tops** and **surplice tops,** which
bring the eye up to your cleavage and wrap to your slim waist.

DRESSES

Wear **wrap dresses** that tie around
your small waist, then flow gently
over your hips. Similarly, choose
A-line dresses that cinch at the
waist with a strong, wide waistline or
belt. Or wear **fitted slip dresses** and
sheath dresses that hug the shape of
your body from top to bottom. Ideally,
wear **single-color dresses** that
let your silhouette speak for itself.

PANTS & JEANS

Pick **mid-rise jeans,** rather than
low-rise jeans, to create a smoother
line from your waist through your
hips. Choose **pressed-crease
trousers, stovepipe jeans,** or pants
with vertical stripes to keep your
figure long and lean. Or wear
figure-hugging **Capris** hemmed
above the widest point on your calf,
so your legs seem slim and long.

SKIRTS

If you have great legs, choose a **miniskirt** that hugs your hips and
reveals a lot of sexy leg, paired with a top that covers more of
you. Choose **pencil skirts** or **high-waisted skirts** that hug your
waist and run smoothly to your legs. Or try a **pleated skirt** in which
the pleats are stitched into place and release below the hips,
so you don't add unnecessary pouf to your hips.

COATS & JACKETS

Choose a blazer that
is shaped around
your torso and hits at
the hips, so as not to
break up the beautiful
line of your figure.
Wear **princess seam**
styles that mimic
the hourglass curves
you already have.

JEWELRY & ACCESSORIES

Try a **bright beaded
necklace** or
pearls to draw the
eye toward your face.
Similarly, wear a
medium-size pendant
or **charm necklace**
that falls in a soft
V-shape to reflect
the flattering angle
toward your waist.

SHOES

Pick a **pointy-toed
shoe** in the same
color as your pants
to strengthen the
vertical line of your
hourglass shape
and keep you
from looking too
horizontally
curvy.
The taller the better!

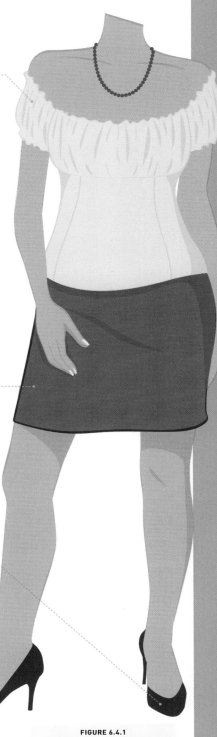

FIGURE 6.4.1
You, only sexier.

WHAT NOT TO WEAR

Really. I mean it.

TOPS

Avoid baggy **peasant tops** that cover your defined waist. Don't wear tops that hit at your low hip or **drop-waist tops** that fail to hug your hips. Steer clear of **crew necks, raglan tops,** and **turtlenecks,** especially if you have a full bust, as the tops can turn your breasts into a dreaded "uniboob" that will make you appear top-heavy. Don't cover your arms with **fluted sleeves.**

DRESSES

Don't wear **boxy, shift dresses** that make a square out of your hourglass figure. Avoid busy detailing or bunchy fabric focused around the hip area of your dress, as with a drop-waist dress. Don't wear **empire dresses** that flow loosely over your torso and cover up the waist you were born with. Avoid **prairie skirts** and **ankle-length skirts,** which weigh you down.

COATS & JACKETS

Don't wear boxy jackets such as **Chanel-style jackets** or **mandarin blazers** that square off your torso. Avoid blazers with pockets that fall at your waist or hips, widening the area. Don't wear **double-breasted coats** and **pea coats** that widen your torso. Steer clear of long coats hemmed at the widest point of your calf, making you appear heavy.

SKIRTS

Don't hem your skirt at **knee length,** which makes your legs look wider than they are and makes you look much shorter. Avoid **horizontal stripes** or details on your skirts, which will make your hips look disproportionately bigger. Also, avoid skirts with detailing at the hem, which draws the eye too far down.

SHOES

Skip **knee-high boots** with skirts, because they cover up your sexy legs. Don't wear **big chunky soles** or **wide heels,** which will make you appear wider, breaking up your vertical line.

PANTS & JEANS

Don't wear **low-rise jeans,** which hit at the widest point on your hips and will set your lower half slightly off balance. Avoid pants with side pockets on the hip. Avoid **drastic distressing or whiskering** on the thighs of your jeans, which will make your thighs and hip area appear wider than they are.

JEWELRY & ACCESSORIES

Steer clear of **hip belts** that land at the largest part of your hips, making you seem bottom-heavy. Avoid **long, chunky necklaces** that land at your middle and distract from your sexy silhouette. Don't cover your neck with **scarves** or **chunky choker necklaces** that don't allow the eye to see some skin.

FIGURE 6.4.2
You, wearing the wrong things.

THE NEW YOU

Three ways to put your dress-sexy rules into play.

CASUAL	CAREER	FORMAL

The shaped blazer hugs your torso all the way toward your hips, showing off your slim waist. The V-neck created by the blazer paired with the bright top peeking out draws the eye up to your chest. The dark denim stove-pipe jean over the strappy stiletto sandal keeps your figure long and lean.

The scoop neck top dips to your cleavage and hugs your torso, following the natural contour of your hourglass shape. The three-quarter-length sleeves reveal the thinnest part of your arms. The pencil skirt follows your curves. The above-the-knee hem on the skirt paired with the pointy-toe pumps makes you look taller.

The off-the-shoulder dress shows off your bare, broad shoulders, balancing your curvy hips. The slimming black sheath dress hugs your natural curves to just above the knee. The black peep-toe heels completes the long, vertical line on your figure, making you look tall, slim, and very sexy.

YOUR ONE FASHION MUST-HAVE: *a wrap dress*

Like your Average, Slender Hourglass sister, a wrap dress emphasizes your shoulders, waist, and hips—all the best features of an hourglass shape. What's not to love?

FITTING ROOM 7

If you're average height
and full-sized, you're
in the right place.
Just find your silhouette
and prepare to get sexy.

AVERAGE
FULL
INVERTED TRIANGLE

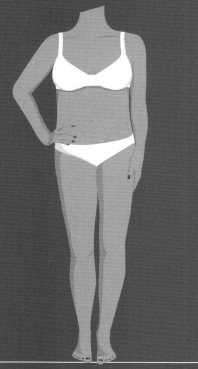

YOU

You are **AVERAGE** height.
[BETWEEN 5'3" AND 5'7"]

You are **FULL**-sized.
[BETWEEN 155 AND 195 LBS.]

Your body forms an
INVERTED TRIANGLE
as your shoulders are wider
than your hips.

You have wide shoulders. Your hips
are not as wide as your shoulders.
Your legs and butt, though full, are
not as wide as your shoulders.

YOUR BLESSING

Wow, you were been born with full, sexy curves! First, you have broad shoulders. And, if you have a full chest, you're blessed to have curves that can be turned into great cleavage, instead of having to buy push-up bras to invent cleavage. And since you have it, you should play it up! The fun for you when you get dressed is that you can use your sexy cleavage as a tool to draw the eyes in and away from your trouble spots. Your other blessing? Your hips and thighs are smaller than the top half of your body, which means you can fit into most styles of pants without a problem. And beneath those narrow hips of yours are a pair of knockout legs. Once again, if you've got 'em, you should flaunt 'em. If your legs look great in short skirts, don't be shy about showing them off. The more leg you show, the taller you'll look; the taller you look, the slimmer you'll look. It's another way to say that you're just steps away from sexy!

YOUR CURSE

As an AVERAGE, FULL, INVERTED TRIANGLE, you carry some extra weight—and you carry most of it on your top half. That's because you have what's called high balance, which means the visual line of your silhouette reaches its broadest point at your shoulders. For this reason, you can appear top-heavy if you choose the wrong clothes. In addition, just like the camera adds ten pounds to every actress, any pounds on your figure can make you look shorter. Your other curse? You lack curves in your butt and hips, which are essential in creating a sexy silhouette.

YOUR CELEBRITY BODY STAND-IN: *Whoopi Goldberg*

WHAT TO WEAR

*Your fashion challenge is to narrow your shoulders, to widen
your hips so they match your broad shoulders, and to reveal more
of your waist. You also want to appear slimmer overall.*

TOPS

Choose **tailored dress shirts, V-necks,** or **wrap tops** that
show a triangle of skin in your chest area; by revealing a
hint of cleavage, you draw attention to the center of your
body and appear slimmer. Or try an **empire top** that
fits snugly around your bust, then gently tapers out
toward your hips. Wear dark-colored tops with lighter
colored pants to make your top half seem slimmer
in comparison to your bottom.

DRESSES

Wear **A-line dresses** or fitted styles
with **pleated skirts, gored skirts,**
or **semi-circle skirts** that taper or
flow over your hips, adding subtle
volume there. Choose dresses with
thick straps in proportion to your
wide shoulders, which will make
your shoulders seem smaller. Wear
shallow V-necks to contain
your curves while revealing skin.

PANTS & JEANS

Wear **boot cut** or **slightly flared
pants** to add volume below
the knees to balance your shoulders.
Choose **palazzo pants, wide-
leg pants,** or **trousers with pockets**
at the hips to add volume to
your hip area. Pick jeans with **large,
round back pockets** in proportion
to your full-size frame to
make your bottom look curvier.

SKIRTS

Wear **flared** or **semi-circle skirts** in thick fabrics such as
heavy cotton or poplin to add subtle volume at the hips. Or
try **gored skirts** that hug the waist before flowing out in a slight
bell shape to create the illusion of hips. Choose skirts in **feminine
patterns** or **lighter tones** to bring up your bottom half or go with
monochromatic tones from top to bottom to look slimmer overall.

COATS & JACKETS

Choose **peplum
jackets** that flare at
the hips. Or try a
princess seam jacket,
which mimics the
shape of an hourglass.
Pick **high-stance blaz-
ers** that button close
to the neck such as a
mandarin collar or a
Chanel-style jacket that
you wear open. Jackets
should hit at your hips
to add volume there.

JEWELRY & ACCESSORIES

Wear **large, dangling
earrings** proportional
to the size of your
shoulders. Put on a
hip belt that hits at the
widest point of your
hips to add volume
where you need it.
Carry a **full-sized
satchel, shopper,** or
tote that hangs at
your hip and adds
imaginary weight
to your lower body.

SHOES

Choose **peep-toe heels,
pointy-toed heels, tall
slingbacks,** or heels with
detailing like **cut-away
arches,** all of which will
make you look taller
and slimmer. Because
you're of average
height, you can wear
2" heels or higher—
the taller the better!

FIGURE 7.1.1
You, only sexier.

WHAT NOT TO WEAR

Really. I mean it.

TOPS

Avoid **puffed-sleeve tops** that accentuate your shoulders. Avoid **crew necks, turtle necks,** and **boatnecks,** which will make you appear top-heavy. Don't wear **baggy peasant tops** that make your middle look even thicker. On the other hand, don't wear **too-tight tops,** which will cling to your torso and don't wear **dainty, spaghetti straps,** which will make your shoulders seem unproportionally large.

DRESSES

Don't wear **off-the-shoulder dresses** which create a horizontal line across the broadest point of your body and make your shoulders look big. Avoid **dainty halters, sleeveless sheaths,** and **strapless dresses,** which will also make your arms and torso look heavy. Steer clear of **short sleeves** or **cap sleeves** on dresses that hit at your bust-line and make you look top-heavy.

PANTS & JEANS

Avoid **low-rise jeans,** which at your full-size weight, reveal too many curves. Don't wear **skinny jeans** or **dark, tight, tapered pants** that accentuate how small you are on the bottom. Avoid **Capris.** which hug your smaller thighs as they taper to your knees, making you appear top-heavy.

SKIRTS

Don't wear **long pencil skirts** or **tight miniskirts,** which will make your hips look so thin you'll appear top-heavy. Don't wear **long, straight ankle-length skirts,** which flatten your hips and bottom. Avoid long **prairie skirts,** which don't allow you to show off some leg and look taller. Steer clear of **circle skirts** that add too much fullness at your hips.

SHOES

Avoid **chunky heels and thick soles,** which make you look heavier. Don't cover up your slim, sexy legs with **knee-high boots;** not only will they make your legs seem thicker, but they'll break up the slimming, vertical line of your look and make you appear wider overall.

COATS & JACKETS

Don't wear **puffed-sleeve blazers** or **jackets with shoulder pads,** which widen your shoulders. Don't choose jackets with **huge portrait collars;** at the same time, avoid those with tiny lapels, as all of these options will make your shoulders seem large in comparison.

JEWELRY & ACCESSORIES

Steer clear of accessories that run horizontally across your shoulders, such as **scarves** or **sashes.** Avoid **tiny clutches** and **dainty earrings,** which will look out of proportion on you. Steer clear of **hobo bags,** which add weight to your top half.

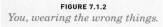

FIGURE 7.1.2
You, wearing the wrong things.

THE NEW YOU

Three ways to put your dress-sexy rules into play.

CASUAL

The V-neck top pulls
the eye in toward the center
of your body and away
from your broad shoulders.
The light layering smooths
out any bulk on your
torso. The boot cut jean adds
necessary volume below
your knee, which balances
out your wide shoulders.

CAREER

The monochromatic
skirt suit creates a slimming
effect. The princess seam
blazer adds curves to your
figure, while the front pockets
add subtle volume to your
hips. The blue top draws the
eye straight to your center,
making you look slimmer. The
gored skirt adds flare at the
base of the skirt to
balance your shoulders.

FORMAL

The rounded V-neck
on this dress reveals some
sexy cleavage. The thick
straps are in scale with your
wide shoulders, making
them seem smaller. The flare
at the hem balances
your shoulders. The dress
is hemmed just above
the widest part of your calf,
which allows you to
reveal your slim calves.

YOUR ONE FASHION MUST-HAVE: *a gored skirt*

**Resist the urge to wear pencil skirts to show off your slim legs, as they will make
you appear top-heavy. Instead, a gored skirt with a subtle flare built into the pattern will
balance your shoulders perfectly while showing off your knockout legs!**

AVERAGE **FULL** RECTANGLE

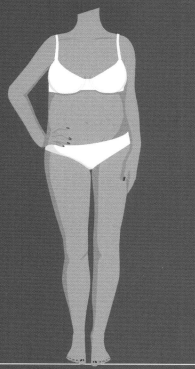

YOU

You are **AVERAGE** height.
[BETWEEN 5'3" AND 5'7"]

You are **FULL**-sized.
[BETWEEN 155 AND 195 LBS.]

Your body forms a
RECTANGLE
as your shoulders are the
same width as your hips.

You have broad shoulders.
You have equally wide hips. Your
waist is wide and undefined.

YOUR BLESSING

First and foremost, your blessing is that as a full-sized woman, you have some gorgeous, sexy curves. Your full figure offers plenty to work with when it comes to looking sexy. If you have large breasts, then you have one of the best tools to help you build a sexy silhouette; if you don't, you can wear even lower cut tops and dresses to up your sexy factor. Your other blessing? You have nice, long, slim legs in proportion to your body. It's worth it for you to show them off now and then. In fact, you're one of the few shapes that look great wearing boots! Start thinking about zipping some up and making fall your new favorite season. Finally, you have small hips and a small bottom. This means you fit easily into jeans without worrying about pulling them over your hips.

YOUR CURSE

As an AVERAGE, FULL RECTANGLE, you lack a defined waist. And because of your full size, your middle tends to take on a slightly oval shape. That means that your silhouette almost has a slightly male shape. Also, you have a flat, less-rounded butt. That's why it can be hard to find clothes that fit you well—most clothes are made for women with curvy hips and bottoms and smaller waists. Because cinching in your waist to fake the hourglass silhouette is difficult, you have to be a bit more inventive in creating the optical illusion of sexy, hourglass curves.

YOUR CELEBRITY BODY STAND-IN: *Jennifer Coolidge*

WHAT TO WEAR

Your fashion challenge is to define a waist where there isn't one by widening your shoulders and hips, so that your waist looks smaller in comparison. You also want to look slimmer overall.

DRESSES

Wear **V-neck dresses, wrap dresses,** or **surplice dresses** that tie or pull in at the waist. Or wear **empire dresses** that hug your bust, then flow out in a steady line toward your hips, making it look as if you have a thin, high waistline. Choose **full dresses** that flare from the waist in **stiff fabrics,** such as taffeta, to define your waist.

TOPS

Wear **wrap tops, surplices,** and **V-neck tops and sweaters** to open up your chest area and draw the eyes in from your wide shoulders. Wear **camisole** tops under jackets to bring attention to your chest area—if you have cleavage, show it off! Or widen your shoulders with **boatneck tops,** provided you wear poufy skirts on the bottom to balance yourself out.

SKIRTS

Pick **semi-circle skirts** or **gored skirts** that hug your waist, then flare out to add volume to your hips and bottom. Wear **monochromatic skirts** and tops to slim your body. Or color-block your look by wearing the same color skirt and top with a wide, dark belt in a contrasting color at your waist—this creates the instant illusion that your waist is smaller than it is.

PANTS & JEANS

Wear **straight-leg pants and jeans** that elongate your body. Pick pants with **pockets or horizontal detailing** at the hip area to create the illusion of curvy hips. Select jeans with **distressing, bleaching, whiskering,** or **fading** around your hips and thighs to make them seem more shapely.

COATS & JACKETS

Wear blazers with **princess seams** that curve in at the waist or jackets with **peplum seams** that flare out toward your hips. Or wear boxy **Chanel-style jackets** with shoulder pads to widen your shoulders, paired with flared skirts. Choose **trench coats** that cinch in your waist.

JEWELRY & ACCESSORIES

As a full-sized woman, choose **full-sized accessories:** Carry a handbag that hits at the hips to add weight there. Wear **large, bright necklaces,** colored beads that dip toward your cleavage, or **large, dangling earrings** that draw attention to your chest and face.

SHOES

Wear **peep-toe heels, pointy-toed heels, tall slingbacks,** or heels with **cut-away arches** to add height to your look, which will instantly make you appear slimmer—don't forget the fabulous pedicure! A little attention to your legs and feet goes a long way.

FIGURE 7.2.1
You, only sexier.

WHAT NOT TO WEAR

Really. I mean it.

DRESSES

Don't wear **fitted, full-length dresses** that accentuate your round middle. Steer clear of dress bottoms that taper in, making your torso look wider in comparison. Avoid **thin fabrics** that can be light and clingy around your middle. Don't wear **boxy shift dresses** that fall straight from your bust to your hips without revealing some shape on your figure.

TOPS

Avoid **sleeveless tops** that cut straight off at the edge of the shoulder and make your shoulders and arms seem thicker. Don't wear **baggy peasant tops** to cover up your torso, because this only makes you look bigger. Avoid shirts with Lycra® or stretch in it, as the puckers and bulges created by the pulling of the fabric will make your middle look heavier.

SKIRTS

Avoid fitted **pencil skirts** that minimize your lower half and emphasize your straight hips. Steer clear of **long, ankle-length skirts** that flatten your bottom and thighs, making you appear top-heavy. Don't wear **prairie skirts** that add unflattering ruffles to your figure while also covering up your gorgeous legs.

PANTS & JEANS

Don't wear **leggings, skinny jeans,** or **stovepipe pants** in clingy fabrics that taper down your thin legs. Many women with a shape like yours are tempted to wear flowing tops and tight leggings to show off your thinner legs. Don't do this! Tight pants will make you appear top-heavy.

COATS & JACKET

Avoid **double-breasted blazers** and coats, especially thick cotton, twill, or **wool pea coats; square jackets** will make you look wider. Also, steer clear of **long, straight coats** that button from the neck to your knees without tapering in toward your waist, as this will accentuate a lack of curves.

JEWELRY & ACCESSORIES

Avoid **square handbags** that land at your waist and make you look wider and boxier. Don't wear **long, chunky necklaces** or **pendant necklaces** that hit at your middle, drawing the eye there. Steer clear of **small stud earrings,** which will look out of scale with your full-size frame.

SHOES

Steer clear of **square-toed shoes** that underscore your boxy frame. Also avoid **wedge heels** with ankle ties or straps; the wedge adds too much weight to your slim legs, and the ankle straps cut the long line of your leg, making you look shorter.

FIGURE 7.2.2
You, wearing the wrong things.

THE NEW YOU

Three ways to put your dress-sexy rules into play.

CASUAL	CAREER	FORMAL

The surplice top creates a flattering V-neck that mimics the angle you want to see tapering toward your waist. The wrap of the surplice defines your waist. The lightweight fabric drapes over your middle—it doesn't cling!—to gently cover up lumps and bumps. The straight-leg pants elongate and slim your figure.

The princess seam blazer adds structure to your shoulders and creates the illusion of an hourglass shape. The monochromatic match of the top and skirt creates a lengthening, slimming effect. The godet skirt has a slight flare at the hem to balance your shoulders.

The V-neck of the empire dress opens up your chest area, while the beaded necklace draws the eye up and away from your middle. The empire style makes your waist look small and high, then flows out toward your hips. The slight flare of the godet skirt balances your shoulders. The black color is slimming overall.

YOUR ONE FASHION MUST-HAVE: *a surplice top*

The wrap effect of the surplice will automatically create a defined waist on your full-sized torso. It also lets you reveal a bit of cleavage, which is always sexy.

AVERAGE
FULL
TRIANGLE

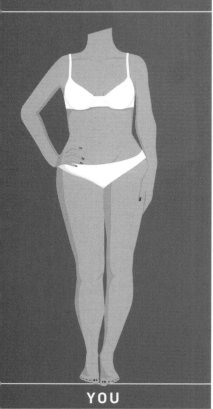

YOU

You are **AVERAGE** height.
[BETWEEN 5'3" AND 5'7"]

You are **FULL**-size.
[BETWEEN 155 AND 195 LBS.]

Your body forms a
TRIANGLE
as your hips are wider
than your shoulders.

You have a smaller upper
body than lower body. Your hips
are wide set and curvy.
You have a shapely bottom.

YOUR BLESSING

You have something a lot of women envy: booty! Some women are famous just for having big curves on their bottom like you, so revel in it! Your other blessing? You have a gorgeous, slender neck and a beautiful collarbone that you can show off. Because your top half is slimmer than your bottom half, you have beautiful arms that you should show off, rather than cover up. At first glance, your thin torso makes you look like you have a much slimmer figure than the numbers on your bathroom scale suggest. Finally, if you don't have large breasts, you can be grateful that thanks to an industry full of push-up bras and low-cut tops, this is one of the easiest dress-sexy elements to fake! Overall, your full figure, gives you some curves to work with when it comes to dressing sexy.

YOUR CURSE

As an AVERAGE, FULL TRIANGLE, you have what's called a low balance. This just means that the visual line of your silhouette reaches its broadest point at your hips. For this reason, you can appear bottom-heavy if you choose the wrong clothes. Your goal will be to downplay those curves on your bottom so you're more balanced. Your other curse? Your narrow shoulders can look sloped downward, which doesn't scream "sexy." Neither does the fact that your chest is small in relation to the weight you're carrying on your hips. But with just a few subtle changes, your silhouette can be balanced in no time.

YOUR CELEBRITY BODY STAND-IN: *Kathy Bates*

WHAT TO WEAR

*Your fashion challenge is to downplay your oversized
lower half to bring out your shoulders so it balances your hips.
You also want to look slimmer overall.*

DRESSES

Wear **off-the-shoulder dresses** that widen your shoulders to
balance your hips. Choose **sweetheart necklines** that add
shape to your chest and reveal cleavage. Try **empire dresses**
with ruffles or ruching at the bustline to create more volume on
your top half. Pick dresses with **flared or fluted hems** to
balance out your hips from below.

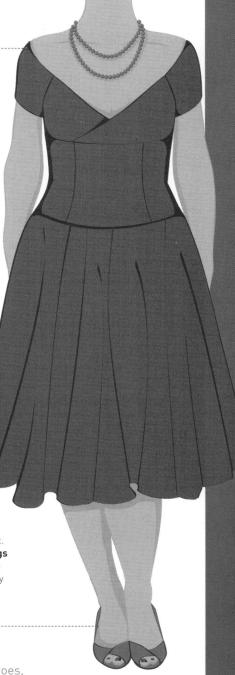

TOPS	SKIRTS
Wear **V-necks, wide scoop necks, boatnecks,** or **off-the-shoulder tops and sweaters** in fitted fabrics that reveal your narrow ribcage. Choose **military tops with epaulets** on the shoulders and breast pockets to add volume to your top half. Or choose **light, bright colors, patterns,** or **horizontal details** on top. Choose tops with **puffed sleeves** or **flutter sleeves** to add volume to your shoulders, while revealing your arms.	Wear **dark-colored, flared skirts** that drape with ease over your hips such as **full gored skirts, godet skirts,** and **wrap skirts.** Similarly, wear **A-line skirts** that taper gently over your hips without clinging and hit at, or just above, your knee. Or choose **pencil skirts** with princess seams that build a long, vertical line into the garment to help slim you.

PANTS & JEANS	COATS & JACKETS	JEWELRY & ACCESSORIES
Wear **straight-leg pants** or **boot cut pants and jeans** that balance out your wide hips by flaring slightly toward the ankles. Choose **mid-rise jeans** with a waistband that hits just above the widest part of your hips; this will make your hips seem smaller.	Choose **corseted blazers** with a narrow ribcage to show off your slim torso. Pick blazers with **puffed-sleeves, small shoulder pads,** or **wide lapels** to widen your shoulders. Choose coats with **princess seams** that have a high, one-button closure to give you a curvy, romantic silhouette.	Wear **full-sized accessories** in scale with your full-sized frame. Try **large colored beads, pearls,** or **long, necklaces with large pendants** that draw the eye up to your chest. Wear **chandelier earrings** which will draw the eye up to your face and away from your wide hips.

SHOES

Wear **pointy-toed stilettos, peep-toe heels,** or **high slingbacks**—
the taller the better—to draw the eye all the way to the tips of your toes,
which slenderizes you overall. Or for something more comfortable,
try a **substantial pump** with feminine details such as **cut-away arches.**

FIGURE 7.3.1
You, only sexier.

WHAT NOT TO WEAR

Really. I mean it.

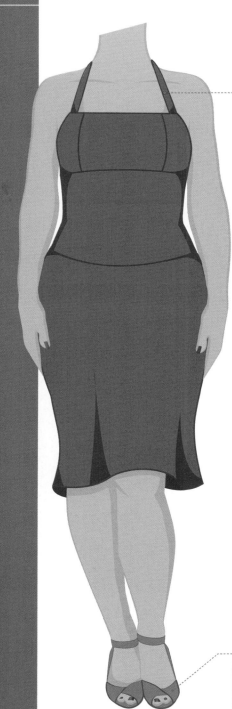

FIGURE 7.3.2
You, wearing the wrong things.

DRESSES

Avoid **wide-set halter top** dresses that, because they reveal so little skin on either side of the straps, make your shoulders seem even smaller. Don't wear tight, fitted dresses that follow the exact curve of your bottom-heavy figure. Skip tops that cut straight across your chest, flattening your cleavage. Avoid **ankle-length dresses** that weight down your bottom half.

TOPS

Steer clear of **raglan tops or sweaters** that make your shoulders seem too narrow in relation to your hips. Don't wear tops or **sweaters** that hit across your low hip—the widest point on your body. Avoid **peasant tops** or **drop-waist styles** that hide your waistline. Don't wear dainty halter tops or **dainty spaghetti straps** that aren't proportional to your full-sized frame.

SKIRTS

Steer clear of **poufy, bell-shaped skirts** such as **circle skirts** and **pleated skirts** that add unwanted volume to your hip area. At the same time, don't wear tapered **tulip skirts** that make your hips appear larger than they are. Avoid **shiny fabrics** and **busy patterns** or stripes on your bottom half at all costs—this will draw unwanted attention to your wide hips.

PANTS & JEANS

Avoid **big, baggy pockets** on the sides of your pants at all costs—**light-colored cargo pants** are your enemy! Steer clear of low-rise jeans that hit at the broadest part of your hips. Don't wear **cuffed trousers** or cuffs on your jeans, which make you look shorter and wider.

COATS & JACKET

Don't wear blazers with **small lapels** that are out of scale with your full-sized figure. Avoid jackets that hit at the mid hip—either choose a shorter jacket or a longer one, but not one that hits at the broadest point on your body. Don't wear **long, straight coats** that squeeze your hips.

JEWELRY & ACCESSORIES

Steer clear of **choker necklaces** that cut off your slender neck. Don't carry **too-small purses** that seem too small in relation to your figure; full-sized women should carry full-sized accessories. Avoid **shoulder bags** that hit at your hips, drawing attention to your broadest point.

SHOES

Don't wear shoes with **ankle straps** or **ankle ties;** the horizontal line created by the straps will make your ankles look wider and make you look shorter. Avoid **chunky heels** and **thick soles** that will weigh down your look, making you appear heavier.

THE NEW YOU

Three ways to put your dress-sexy rules into play.

CASUAL

The bright color of
the top draws instant attention to your top half, where you
want it. The off-the-shoulder
style widens your shoulders
to balance out your hips.
The dark denim helps your
bottom half recede into
the background. The straight
leg elongates your
bottom half, making you
seem slimmer overall.

CAREER

The lapels of this
blazer sit wide, adding width
up top where you need
it most. The bright top under
the blazer draws the
eye straight to your center,
slimming you. The monochromatic jacket and skirt
with matching princess seams
lengthens your whole figure.

FORMAL

The empire cut of this
dress hugs your bust line,
giving it more volume,
which makes you look taller.
The puffed sleeves make
your shoulders appear wider
to balance your bottom
half. The top flows out along
your hips to a fluted hem,
making you look like you have
a high, slim waist.

YOUR ONE FASHION MUST-HAVE: *a tailored dress shirt*

**Bright, quality, tailored shirts in sturdy fabrics will draw attention
to your top half, while holding in any lumps. Leave the top one or two
buttons undone—the V-neck shape it creates will reveal cleavage.**

AVERAGE FULL HOURGLASS

YOU

You are **AVERAGE** height.
[BETWEEN 5'3" AND 5'7"]

You are **FULL**-size.
[BETWEEN 155 AND 195 LBS.]

Your body forms an
HOURGLASS
as your shoulders are the
same width as your hips.

You have broad shoulders.
Your hips and butt are curvy.
Your waist is defined.

YOUR BLESSING

You, my friend, have a dream shape! Your biggest blessing is your hourglass silhouette. You have something the other body shapes wish they did: a perfectly balanced body. Your top and bottom half match—and that is the essence of the sexy silhouette. You have a gorgeous full bottom and broad shoulders. You have a curvy chest. All in all, your body is just like the voluptuous, womanly figure that artists have been painting for centuries. Your other blessing? Your defined waist. Because no matter how big your chest is and no matter how big your hips feel some days, with that small, defined waist of yours, you can look good in so many outfits. You don't need to make up for unbalanced areas of your body to pull off an outfit. All you need to do is keep yourself looking proportional and accentuate what you already have!

YOUR CURSE

As an AVERAGE, FULL HOURGLASS, you have an extra issue to consider when you're dressing, which is making your figure look slimmer overall. And because your curves are full-sized, you might have a hard time finding your size in the styles you want. Your other curse? You have an extra dressing element you need to pay close attention to: your undergarments. Before you can dress your curves, you need to choose bras and underwear that contain and support your full figure. Once you have those taken care of, the clothes you put on top will be able to work their sexy magic.

YOUR CELEBRITY BODY STAND-IN: *Oprah Winfrey*

WHAT TO WEAR

Your fashion challenge is to keep your broad shoulders and wide hips balanced, while defining your waist. You also want to look slimmer overall.

DRESSES

Choose **corset dresses** that cinch your defined waist, then drape into a slight flare. Wear dresses with **V-necks, sweetheart necks,** or **scoop necks** to reveal skin at your chest. Or choose **wrap dresses** that essentially duplicate your hourglass figure. Pick dresses in **sturdy, stiff fabrics** that help contain and smooth out your curves.

TOPS

Wear **open neck wrap tops** and **surplices,** which bring the eye up to your cleavage and show off your waist. Wear **fitted sweaters** that hug your curves. Wear **tailored dress shirts**—undo the top two or three buttons to reveal a flattering V-neck that points toward your smaller waist.

SKIRTS

Try **gored skirts,** in which the pleats are stitched into place up to the hip line, then release into your thighs. Wear **A-line skirts** that add steady volume over your hips. Hem your skirts just above or at your knee to show off your curvy calves. Or choose skirts with slits at the hem to make your legs look longer.

PANTS & JEANS

Wear **mid-rise jeans,** which hit just above your hips and create a smooth line from your waist to your hips without adding bulk. Opt for **straight-leg pants and jeans** with full-size back pockets, proportional to your body; if you choose **small back pockets**, your butt will look big in comparison.

COATS & JACKETS

Choose jackets with **princess seams** that clone your curves. Or wear **peplum jackets,** which cinch in at your thinnest point, then flare out toward your hips. Try a basic **trench coat** that defines your shoulders, belts at the waist, then tapers out toward your hips in an A-line silhouette.

JEWELRY & ACCESSORIES

Wear necklaces that feature a single focal point—such as a **medium pendant necklace** that falls in a V-shape. Or wear **colored beaded necklaces** or **medium-sized drop earrings** to draw the eye up toward your face. Carry sizeable purses in scale with your frame.

SHOES

Wear a **pointy-toed heel**—the taller the better—in the same color as your pants, which will elongate your look and slim you down. At the very least, try a **kitten heel;** even the slightest lift will make you look slimmer. Or wear **knee-high boots** with jeans, which help balance your curvy hips from below without making you look short.

FIGURE 7.4.1
You, only sexier.

WHAT NOT TO WEAR

Really. I mean it.

DRESSES

Don't wear **empire dresses** that completely disguise your gorgeous waist. Avoid **long, ankle-length dresses** that hit at the widest point on your calf, making your bottom look heavy. Avoid dresses with busy detailing around the hip area of your dress. Don't wear dresses in **stretch fabrics** that will bunch and wrinkle around your curves.

TOPS

Steer clear of **peasant tops** that are baggy around your middle, hiding your defined waist. Avoid **crew necks** and **turtlenecks;** turtlenecks plus large breasts instantly morph into the dreaded "uniboob" that will make you appear top-heavy. Don't wear **cardigan sweaters** buttoned to the top, which cover up the skin at your chest.

SKIRTS

Steer clear of **poufy, bell-shaped circle skirts** that add unwanted volume to your hip area. Avoid **shiny fabrics** and **busy patterns or stripes** on your bottom half, which will draw unwanted attention to your hips. If you're wearing a pattern on the bottom, you should be balancing your figure out on top as well.

PANTS & JEANS

Don't wear **low-rise jeans;** your full-size frame may spill over, making you look heavier. Avoid **pants with angled or diagonal pockets** that land at the hip and make you look bottom-heavy. Avoid **distressing, bleaching, or whiskering** on the thighs of your jeans, which will widen your hips too much.

COATS & JACKET

Steer clear of boxy jackets such as **Chanel-style jackets** that square off your curves. Avoid front or side pockets at the hip area of your jackets and that widen your hip area. Avoid **cropped jackets** that hit at your waist and interrupt the smooth line of your curves there.

JEWELRY & ACCESSORIES

Don't wear **flowers or bows and ruffles,** which adds unnecessary volume to your frame. Avoid **hip belts** that land at the broadest area of your hips. Don't cover the skin area around your neck with **scarves** or **chunky choker** necklaces that cover your skin and cleavage.

SHOES

Don't wear shoes with **ankle straps** or shoes that tie around your ankle in any way; the horizontal line created by the straps will make your ankles look wider. Avoid **ankle boots** which will make your large calves seem thick. Don't wear shoes with **thick soles** or **chunky heels,** which weigh down your look.

FIGURE 7.4.2
You, wearing the wrong things.

THE NEW YOU

Three ways to put your dress-sexy rules into play.

CASUAL	CAREER	FORMAL

The surplice top creates a flattering V-neck that draws the eye up to your chest. The shape created by the surplice also accentuates your small waist. The straight-leg jean hugs your shapely hips. The knee-high leather boots offer some lift, while balancing your hips from below.

The corseted blazer fits the curves of your torso and cinches your waist. The structured shoulders of the blazer keeps you looking tall and slim. The monochromatic blazer, skirt, and high-heel pumps create a long, slenderizing effect.

The wide scoop neck created by this corseted dress reveals skin and cleavage at your chest. The thick straps are in scale with your full-sized frame. The corset accentuates your waist. The full, pattern skirt flows out from your waist, adding slight fullness to the bottom half of your hourglass shape.

YOUR ONE FASHION MUST-HAVE: *a corset dress*

This style will accentuate the defined waist you already have without creating uncomfortable or unflattering bunching above or below the corset.

FITTING ROOM 8

If you're average height and plus-sized, you're in the right place. Just find your silhouette and prepare to get sexy.

AVERAGE
PLUS
INVERTED TRIANGLE

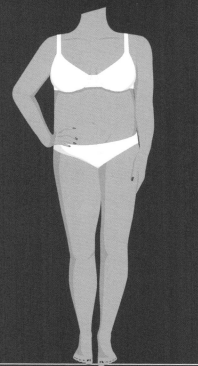

YOU

You are **AVERAGE** height.
[BETWEEN 5'3" AND 5'7"]

You are **PLUS**-sized.
[OVER 180 LBS.]

Your body forms an
INVERTED TRIANGLE
as your shoulders are wider
than your hips.

You have wide shoulders. Your
hips are smaller than your
shoulders. Your legs and bottom are
not as wide as your shoulders.

YOUR BLESSING

What's the one essential detail at the heart of the sexy silhouette? Curves. And you were born with plenty of them! But your true blessings are your hips and legs, which are slim in comparison to your top half. Because of your proportionally thinner legs, you get to play them up. I'm not saying you should be wearing short mini-skirts and hot pants, but by wearing a skirt that hits above the knee and shows off your killer legs, you have the ability to knock 'em dead instantly. Also, your proportionally smaller bottom half comes in handy when you go shopping, because your slimmer thighs and bottom fit into most styles of pants. Your other blessing? If you have a full chest, you can use it to create gorgeous cleavage—which, by the way, is a great way to draw the eyes in and away from your shoulders.

YOUR CURSE

As an AVERAGE, PLUS, INVERTED TRIANGLE, you have what's called a high balance. This means that the visual line of your silhouette reaches its broadest point at your shoulders. Thus, you can appear top-heavy if you choose the wrong clothes. Your other curse? Because your weight tends to collect on your top half, you can appear heavier than you are, even though you have small hips and legs in comparison. All you need to do is conceal some of your weight and reveal your best features.

YOUR CELEBRITY BODY STAND-IN: *Wynonna Judd*

WHAT TO WEAR

Your fashion challenge is to narrow your shoulders, widen your hips so they match your broad shoulders, and reveal more of your waist. This will turn your top-heavy frame into a perfectly balanced hourglass.

COATS & JACKETS

Wear **peplum jackets** that flare out from the waist toward the hips. Choose jackets with **three-quarter-length sleeves;** if you carry weight in your arms, you will look thinner if you partially cover them. Wear jackets that hit at the hip, ideally with horizontal details there.

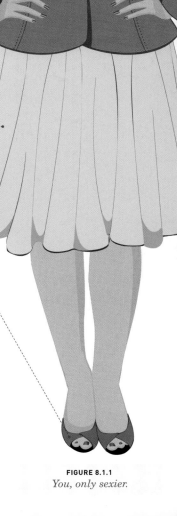

DRESSES

Wear **wrap dresses** or **surplices** with little or no detailing at the shoulders. Or opt for dresses with **three-quarter-length** or **full-length sleeves** in heavy fabrics to reveal the thinnest part of your arms. Consider **drop-waist dresses** that flare out below your hips, making you look curvier there.

TOPS

Use light layering of **V-neck** or **U-neck** tops under blazers and sweaters to soften your curves. Wear **surplice tops** and **wrap tops** to create a V-neck that draws the eye in from your shoulders. Choose shirts with horizontal detailing at the hips. Wear **dark-colored tops** to slim your top half. Try **tailored dress shirts** that reveal a similar triangle of skin.

SKIRTS

Wear **full** or **circle skirts** in **thick fabrics** such as heavy cotton or poplin. Or wear **full gored skirts, godet skirts,** or **pleated skirts** that are sewn in up to the hips in lightweight fabrics; each of these hug your small waist, then flare out, creating volume at your hips and bottom. Hem your flared skirts at the knee to reveal some of your slim legs, making you appear tall and slim.

PANTS & JEANS

Pick pants with **front or side pockets** and/or detailing around the hip area to add volume where you need it most. Choose **straight-leg pants, wide-leg pants,** or **palazzo pants** that skim your curves— not cling to them— to add volume to your bottom half.

JEWELRY & ACCESSORIES

Accent your hip area with **wide belts** that sit at the broadest point on your hips. Wear **pendant necklaces** with large ornamentation, in scale with your plus-size frame. Carry **barrel hand-bags** or **totes** that hit at your hips, adding a visual element of weight there.

SHOES

Choose heels in **bold colors, metallics,** or styles such as **cut-away arches** or **peep toes** to draw attention to your lovely legs. If wearing high heels is uncomfortable, try a **substantial pump** or a **kitten heel.**

FIGURE 8.1.1
You, only sexier.

WHAT NOT TO WEAR

Really. I mean it.

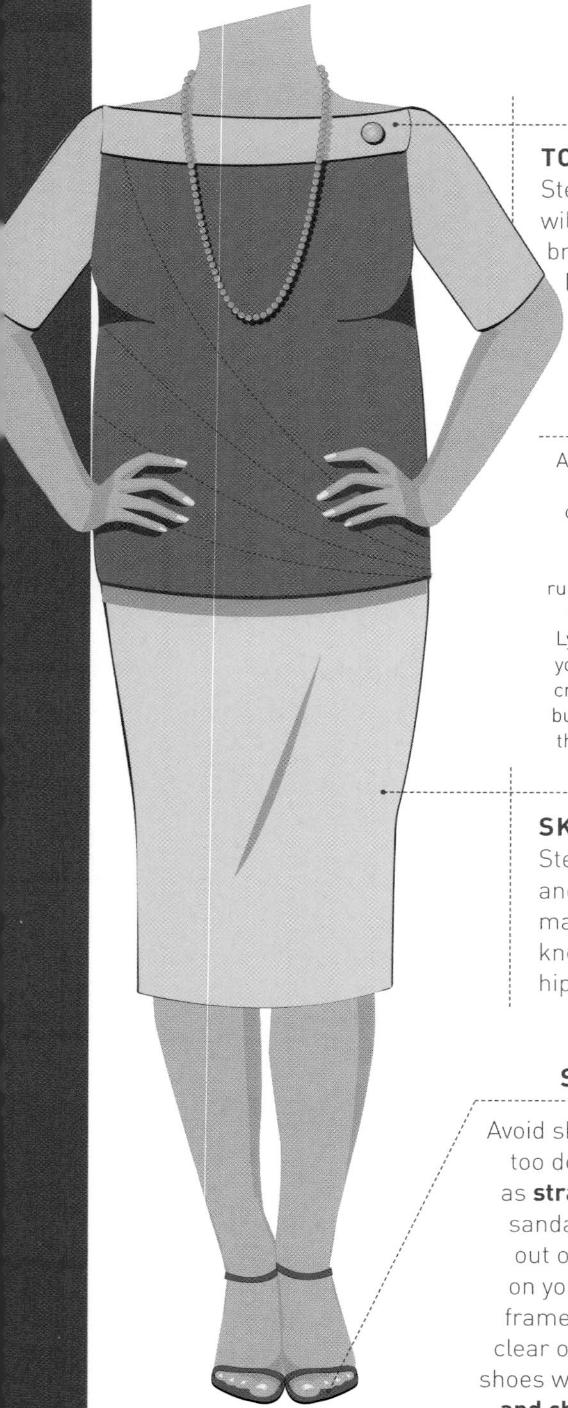

TOPS

Steer clear of **boatnecks, crew necks,** and **turtlenecks,** which will only make you appear top-heavy—and if you have large breasts, these tops create a fattening "uniboob" effect. Avoid **horizontal details** on your tops, which widen your shoulders. Avoid **short sleeves** that make your arms appear heavy. Avoid **flutter sleeves** that create unnecessary volume there.

DRESSES

Avoid **off-the-shoulder dresses** and **strapless dresses** that create a horizontal line across your shoulders. Don't wear **empire dresses** with ruching around the bust that adds volume to your top half. Avoid Lycra®-based stretch fabrics; as your body moves, stretchy fabric creates unflattering pockets and bulges that make you look larger than you are. Lumpy is not sexy.

PANTS & JEANS

Don't hide in your clothes by wearing **baggy pants** or **cropped pants** that hit at the mid calf; though you want a pant that has detailing around the hip area, you don't want to add unnecessary boxiness to your whole bottom half. On the other extreme, don't wear **leggings,** which will make you look top-heavy with Tweety Bird legs.

SKIRTS

Steer clear of **pencil skirts** that taper in from your hips and reveal how thin your bottom and thighs are; this will make you look top-heavy. Don't hem straight skirts at the knee; though it is slimming to your figure, it makes your hips look too long and thin to carry your wide shoulders.

SHOES

Avoid shoes that look too delicate such as **strappy stiletto** sandals that look out of proportion on your plus-size frame. Also, steer clear of unflattering shoes with **thick soles and chunky heels.**

COATS & JACKETS

Avoid **cap sleeve jackets** that make your shoulders appear wider, and **short-sleeve jackets** that will hit at the widest part of your arms, making them appear heavier. Don't wear boxy jackets such as **Chanel-style jackets** that will make your top have look larger than your bottom.

JEWELRY & ACCESSORIES

Avoid **long necklaces** that hit at your middle, drawing attention to the width of your torso. Don't cover up your chest area with **scarves** or **chunky chokers,** which will make your torso look thicker. Steer clear of **tiny clutches** and **dainty earrings,** which will look out of proportion on your plus-sized frame.

FIGURE 8.1.2
You, wearing the wrong things.

THE NEW YOU

Three ways to put your dress-sexy rules into play.

CASUAL

The V-neck on this top brings the eye straight to your cleavage and mimics the angle you want to create toward your waist. The horizontal detailing at the base of the top brings the eye down to your hips to add width there. The straight-leg jean creates steady volume down each leg, slimming you overall.

CAREER

The V-neck created by opening the top buttons reveals a triangle of skin that points toward your waist. The buttons running down the tailored dress shirt builds a vertical line that instantly draws the eye toward your center. The boot cut trousers add volume below your knees to balance your top half.

FORMAL

The rounded V-neck of this dress draws the eye toward your cleavage, and away from your wide shoulders. The corset belt in a contrasting fabric hold in your middle, while creating the illusion of a defined waist. The circle skirt that flares out from your waist creates volume on your bottom half to balance your shoulders.

YOUR ONE FASHION MUST-HAVE: *a structured jacket*

A shaped, structured jacket with three-quarter-length or full-length sleeves is your be-all, fix-all! Choose one in a stiff fabric, such as cotton twill, to contain your extra curves and reveal only the thinnest part of your arms.

AVERAGE **PLUS** RECTANGLE

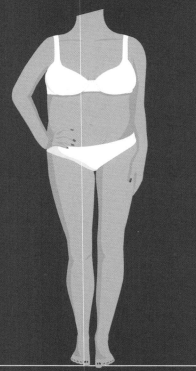

YOU

You are **AVERAGE** height.
[BETWEEN 5'3" AND 5'7"]

You are **PLUS**-sized.
[OVER 180 LBS.]

Your body forms a
RECTANGLE
as your shoulders are the
same width as your hips.

You have broad shoulders.
Your equally wide hips. Your waist
is wide and undefined.

YOUR BLESSING

Your blessing is that you were born with plenty to work with. You have broad shoulders that make you look a bit taller. At first glance, those shoulders make you look even taller than you are. You also have hips that match the width of your shoulders. What this means is that you're already balanced in the most basic way. And because of your plus-size curves, you also have another bonus: breasts that you can turn into cleavage! It doesn't have to be big cleavage; just a little will do. But since you've definitely got it, you should learn to flaunt it! Your other blessing? As an averagely tall woman, you have a little bit of height to work with. And height can do magical things to a silhouette. The taller you are, the slimmer you look. And the slimmer you look, the sexier you look! Hello and thank you high-heeled shoes!

YOUR CURSE

As an AVERAGE, PLUS RECTANGLE, you lack curves in the places that make a feminine body. Basically, without a defined waist between your wide shoulders and wide hips, your silhouette almost has a slightly male shape. That's why it's hard to find clothes that fit you—most clothes are made for women with smaller waists in mind. Your other curse? The extra weight around your middle. As a plus-sized woman, your rectangle shape turns into more of an oval, as you carry more weight in your stomach. This means you have double the work when it comes to dressing sexy: You have to work on slimming your figure overall, while you also try to invent an hourglass waist. Lucky for you, I can help you do both.

YOUR CELEBRITY BODY STAND-IN: *Mo'Nique*

WHAT TO WEAR

Your fashion challenge is to define a waist where there isn't one by widening your shoulders and hips, so that your waist looks smaller in comparison. You also want to look slimmer overall.

TOPS

Wear **wrap tops, surplice tops,** and **V-neck tops** to open up your chest area and draw the eyes in from your wide shoulders. Or widen your shoulders with **boatneck tops,** provided you wear poufy skirts to balance them. Wear dark, slimming colors on top. Choose tops with large details, such as buttons, in scale with your frame.

DRESSES

Wear **wrap dresses** that tie around the waist or top your dresses with shapely jackets that hit at the waist—both create the illusion of an hourglass. Choose full dresses that bell out from the waist in **stiff fabrics,** such as taffeta, which will add volume to your lower half; this creates the illusion of a defined waist.

PANTS & JEANS

Wear **straight-leg pants and jeans** that elongate your body. Or choose pants with a **subtle boot cut flare** from the knees to the ankles, to create a bit more volume on your lower half. Pick pants with lots of embroidery or detailing around the hip area, and choose **large, round pockets** in scale with your size to create the illusion of curves at your hips.

SKIRTS

Pick **full skirts, circle skirts, semi-circle skirts,** or **gored skirts** in lightweight fabrics with a feminine drape to invent necessary fullness around your hips and bottom. Or try **A-line skirts** in sturdy fabrics that taper out from your waist. Wear skirts in **medium-sized patterns** with a dark background on the bottom to draw the eye toward your hips.

COATS & JACKETS

Wear **princess seam** or **peplum jackets** that cinch in slightly at your waist. Or wear **rounded collar jackets** left open to create a slimming vertical line down your center. Choose **high-stance jackets** in a stiff, sturdy fabric to hold in the weight in your torso.

JEWELRY & ACCESSORIES

Wear **large beaded necklaces** in proportion to your plus-size frame to draw the eye to your chest. Or try **long, dangling chandelier earrings** to bring the eye up to your neck. Try a **large shoulder bag** that hits at your hip to add volume there.

SHOES

With a skirt, bring attention to your feet with **cut-away arches** or **peep-toe heels**—don't forget the fabulous pedicure! Wear **pointy-toed heels** to lengthen and slim your look—the taller the better.

FIGURE 8.2.1
You, only sexier.

WHAT NOT TO WEAR

Really. I mean it.

TOPS

Don't wear shirts with weak shoulder lines that make your shoulders look narrow. Avoid fitted tops that cling to your torso and accentuate your round middle. Avoid **bright-colored tops** or **big patterns** that draw attention to your middle. Steer clear of horizontal stripes on top which will widen your middle. Don't wear **crew necks,** which can turn your breasts into a "uniboob."

SKIRTS

Avoid **fitted pencil skirts** that minimize your lower half and emphasize your straight hips, making you look top-heavy. Don't wear **long, straight ankle-length skirts** or **prairie skirts** that make you look frumpy and unsexy. Avoid skirts that bell out from the waist, adding too much volume to your frame.

PANTS & JEANS

Avoid **skinny jeans** that will accentuate your straight, flat bottom half, making you look top-heavy. Don't wear **flared pants** that create too much volume at the base of your feet, dragging your look down and making you look heavy.

DRESSES

Don't wear **boxy dresses** that fall straight from under your arms down to the hem without playing up any curves. Avoid **thin fabrics** that will cling and reveal lumps in your middle, as well as shiny fabrics that add weight to your figure. Avoid **stretchy fabrics** at all costs, as they will buckle and bunch around your middle as you move, making you appear larger than you are.

SHOES

Steer clear of **square-toed shoes** that underscore your boxy frame. Avoid **chunky heels** and **thick soles** that will make your legs look equally thick.

COATS & JACKETS

Avoid jackets with weak shoulder lines, as well as jackets made from **thin fabrics** such as linen. Don't wear **double-breasted jackets** or **pea coats** that widen your torso instead of creating the illusion of cinching it.

JEWELRY & ACCESSORIES

Avoid **tiny clutches** that will look dwarfed in proportion to your plus-sized frame. Don't carry handbags that hit at your waist, making your middle seem wider. Don't force **tight belts** around your middle.

FIGURE 8.2.2
You, wearing the wrong things.

THE NEW YOU

Three ways to put your dress-sexy rules into play.

CASUAL	CAREER	FORMAL
The puffed-sleeves of this top create structured shoulders, so your waist looks smaller in comparison. The scoop neck adds soft, feminine lines to your boxy torso. The dark color of the top makes your torso look slimmer. The straight-leg jean creates a slimming effect all the way to your ankles.	The rounded neck of this blazer adds feminine curves to your shape. The open, dark jacket over the white top creates a bright, vertical line down your torso, making you look slimmer. The semi-circle skirt balances your shoulders. The pointy-toed stilettos add height to your look, which is instantly slimming.	The empire cut of this dress hugs your bustline, then flares outward, giving the illusion of a high waist tapering out to curvy hips. The wide open neckline draws the eye to the center of your body. The fabric of the dress skims along your torso instead of clinging to it, hiding any lumps and bumps along the way.

YOUR ONE FASHION MUST-HAVE: *an empire dress*

This dress hugs your bust, then flows out gently over your hips to the hem to create the illusion of a high, thin waist. It should hit just above the knee or just below it to make your legs look slim.

AVERAGE **PLUS** TRIANGLE

YOU

You are **AVERAGE** height.
[BETWEEN 5'3" AND 5'7"]

You are **PLUS**-sized.
[OVER 180 LBS.]

Your body forms a
TRIANGLE
as your hips are wider than
your shoulders.

You have a slim upper
body. Your hips are wide-set.
You have a shapely bottom.

YOUR BLESSING

You have curves, curves, and more curves! And when it comes to looking sexy, that's the name of the game; a sexy silhouette is all about having a figure rounded in the right places. You also carry your curves in a great place: your booty! Some women are famous simply for the fact that they have a booty like yours, and hit songs have even been written about just this blessing. Your other blessing? You have a torso that is slimmer than your bottom half and a beautiful collarbone that is perfect for showing off. And even though you carry some extra pounds, your proportionally smaller top half makes you look like you carry much less on your frame at first glance. You already have some fabulous curves to work with. All you need to do is learn how to reveal just the right parts.

YOUR CURSE

The main issue you have as an AVERAGE, PLUS TRIANGLE is your weight. And not just your weight in general, but the extra weight you carry on your bottom half. Basically, you have what's called a low balance. This means that the visual line of your silhouette reaches its broadest point at your hips. But as a plus-sized woman, that weight can be unwieldy when it comes to finding pants and skirts that fit. Your goal will be to downplay the curves on your hips, thighs, and butt as much as possible so you're more balanced. Your other curse? Your shoulders are narrow and may even be slightly sloped downward. And because you're plus-sized, your arms may be heavy. This can be a difficult combination to fix—but it can be done!

YOUR CELEBRITY BODY STAND-IN: *S. Epatha Merkerson*

WHAT TO WEAR

*Your fashion challenge is to downplay your wide
hips and to bring out your shoulders so they balance your hips.
You also want to look slimmer overall.*

COATS & JACKETS

Choose jackets with **horizontal detailing** at the shoulders—
stripes, patterns, epaulets, wide lapels—to widen your
shoulders so they match your hips. Wear **bolero jackets**
with detailing on the shoulders to widen your silhouette.
Choose **single-breasted coats** to create a taller
silhouette to slim your plus-size frame.

TOPS

Wear deep **U-necks, V-necks,** or
sweetheart necks that expose
your collarbone and create a good
amount of skin to draw the eye up.
Or wear **boatnecks** or **off-the-
shoulder tops** that make your top
half seem wider. Try **fluted sleeves**
or **kimono tops** that add width
to your shoulders while concealing
the thickest part of your arm.

DRESSES

Try dresses with **sweetheart
necklines** that add shapely curves
to your chest and reveal a little
cleavage, both of which will
complement your curvy hips.
Choose dresses with **handkerchief
hems, godets,** or **fluted hems**—
they're great for balancing out
extra-curvy hips and fuller thighs.

PANTS & JEANS

Wear **straight-leg pants** that create a long vertical line on your
legs, while adding volume from your knees down to balance
your hips. Choose **flat-front trousers** or **pressed-crease
trousers** for the cleanest, straightest vertical line. Try a fitted
pant in a lighter fabric that drapes gently over your hips. Aim for
pants with **large back pockets** proportional to your plus-size.

SKIRTS

Choose **A-line skirts**
that taper over your
trouble zones or **gored
skirts** that hug
your hips, then flare out
gently from there.
Or try **waterfall skirts**
that are shorter in the
front and longer in the
back or **asymmetrical
hems** in a drapey
fabric, both of which
minimize your hips.

JEWELRY & ACCESSORIES

Wear **bold, bright
earrings** or **chande-
lier earrings,** which
add volume at your
shoulders. Carry
a handbag in propor-
tion to your plus-size
frame, such as
a **saddle bag** or a **hobo
bag** that fits at your
chest or your waist
to balance your
larger bottom half.

SHOES

Wear **pointy-toed
heels** or **open-toed
heels;** both shoes
draw the eye to the
tips of your toes
so your legs appear
longer and slimmer.
Even a **kitten
heel** will give
you a helping lift.

FIGURE 8.3.1
You, only sexier.

WHAT NOT TO WEAR

Really. I mean it.

COATS & JACKETS

Avoid jackets that hit at the mid hip, the broadest point on your body. Steer clear of **horizontal details**—such as belts, pockets, or contrasting colors—on the bottoms of blazers. Don't wear **mandarin or rounded collars** that make a jacket seem small in proportion to your frame. Don't wear jackets made of **lightweight materials** such as linen, which accentuate your narrow shoulders.

TOPS	DRESSES
Avoid **raglan tops, crew neck sweaters and tops,** and **cardigan sweaters** buttoned up to your neck, all of which narrow your shoulders and make your lower half appear bottom-heavy. If you're layering a shirt under a sweater or jacket, don't let the shirt peek out beneath, which adds extra bulk to the broadest point of your body.	Don't wear dresses that fall straight, or taper in below the hips, accentuating how wide your hips are. Avoid dresses with **tiny patterns** that make your figure look larger than it is; especially avoid **dark patterns on light or white backgrounds**, which add weight to your frame.

PANTS & JEANS

Don't wear **flared jeans,** which add too many curves to your frame. Don't wear **leggings** and **skinny jeans** that taper to your ankles and make your hips look wider. Avoid **low-rise jeans** at all costs, which enhance the broadest part of your body. Skip light-colored pants, as well as jeans with **whiskering, bleaching, or fading** on the thighs that make them look heavy.

SHOES	SKIRTS	JEWELRY & ACCESSORIES
Avoid heels with **ankle straps** or ties; the horizontal line created by the straps will make your ankles look wider and you, shorter. Steer clear of **chunky heels**, which shorten your legs.	Don't wear skirts that taper in below the hips (such as **tulip styles**) that will make your hips appear, well, humongous. Avoid **busy patterns or stripes** on your bottom half at all costs—this will draw unwanted attention to your wide hips.	Don't wear **choker necklaces** that cut off your slender neck. Don't carry **too-small purses** that seem tiny in relation to your figure; plus-sized women should carry larger accessories. Avoid shoulder bags that hit at your hips, drawing attention to your broadest point.

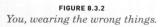

FIGURE 8.3.2
You, wearing the wrong things.

THE NEW YOU

Three ways to put your dress-sexy rules into play.

CASUAL	**CAREER**	**FORMAL**
The kimono-sleeve top draws attention outward, to your shoulders, which helps balance your bottom half. The open neckline lets you show off your slim neck and reveal a bit of cleavage. The empire cut of the top flows out from under the bust, creating the illusion of a high, slim waist.	The double-breasted jacket over the camisole adds structure to your top half to match the wideness of your hips. The belt at your waist accentuates your slim waistline. The A-line skirt fits your hips without adding unnecessary volume to it. The pump lifts you, creating a tall, lean look.	The wide-set V-neck of this dress stretches your shoulder line to match your wide hips. The lightweight material of this godet skirt falls gracefully over your hips. The knee-length hem completes the illusion of an hourglass shape.

YOUR ONE FASHION MUST-HAVE: *jackets*

Jackets, jackets, jackets! You should have a closet full of jackets and blazers with structured shoulders that hit high at the hip. They widen your torso just enough to match your curvy hips.

AVERAGE
PLUS
HOURGLASS

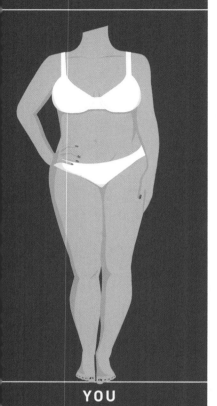

YOU

You are **AVERAGE** height.
[BETWEEN 5'3" AND 5'7"]

You are **PLUS**-sized.
[OVER 180 LBS.]

Your body forms an
HOURGLASS
as your shoulders are the
same width as your hips.

You have very broad shoulders
and a super-shapely bust.
Your hips and butt are very curvy.
Your waist is defined compared
to your hips and shoulders.

YOUR BLESSING

You have a great shape! Your greatest blessing is your perfectly balanced body. Your top and bottom half match. The hourglass silhouette is the essence of the sexy silhouette! You have a gorgeous, full bottom. You have broad shoulders. You have a curvy chest. Your body is considered voluptuous, which has been a desirable figure for centuries. Your other blessing? You have a defined waist. That means no matter how big your chest is and no matter how big your hips feel some days, your defined waist makes it easier for you to look good when you get dressed. Instead of trying to conceal one particular part of your body, all you need to do is choose clothes that keep you looking proportional so you can accentuate what you already have!

YOUR CURSE

As an AVERAGE, PLUS HOURGLASS, you have a broad upper body as well as a broad lower body. Yes, you're balanced, but because you have a full bottom on your plus-size shape, it can be difficult to find clothes that fit properly. And that leads to another issue to consider when dressing: making your figure look slimmer overall. Your other curse? In addition to focusing on the clothes that flatter your figure, you need to pay extra attention in choosing bras and underwear that hold in and support your weight. That can be time-consuming and expensive. Luckily, it's worth all the effort, as you start learning how to dress sexier.

YOUR CELEBRITY BODY STAND-IN: *Aida Turturro*

WHAT TO WEAR

*Your fashion challenge is to keep your broad
shoulders and wide hips balanced, while defining your waist.
You also want to look slimmer overall.*

TOPS

Wear **low V-necks** and **deep scoop necks** to reveal any cleavage you
have. Layer bright-colored tops under wrap shirts, sweaters, and
blazers to bring attention to the center of your body, making you
appear thinner. Wear **surplices wrap tops** that tie around your waist.
Wear **fitted sweaters** that hug your curves to your waist. Choose
tops with **three-quarter-length** sleeves to reveal only the
thinnest part of your arms.

DRESSES	SKIRTS
Aim for **fitted sheaths** that reveal your balanced curves. Wear **A-line dresses** or **wrap dresses** that cinch at the waist with a strong, wide waistline, then taper out. Or wear **tulip skirts** that fit your hips, taper in, then flare at the hem to balance you. Choose **sturdy, stiff fabrics** such as taffeta and satin to hold in your plus-size curves.	Choose **pencil skirts** with **princess seams** and **fluted hems** to reveal your figure as is. Or wear **drapey skirts** that gently graze your curves, such as **semi-circle skirts** and **gored skirts;** similarly, wear **tulip skirts** or **godet skirts** that hug your curves, then add flare at the base. Hem your skirts just above or at your knee to show off your curvy calves.

PANTS & JEANS

Wear **mid-rise jeans,** which hit just above your hips and create
a smooth line from your waist to your hips without adding bulk.
Opt for **boot cut** or **straight-leg pants,** which add volume on your
lower leg to balance your hips. Choose jeans with **large, round
back pockets** that are in scale with your size; if you choose
small back pockets, your butt will look bigger in comparison.

COATS & JACKETS	JEWELRY & ACCESSORIES	SHOES
Choose jackets with **princess seams** or wear **peplum jackets,** which cinch in at your thinnest point, then flare out toward your hips. Opt for a **basic trench coat** that further defines your shoulders, pulls tight at the waist, then tapers out.	Wear necklaces that feature a single focal point—such as a **large pendant necklace** on colored beads. Wear **big belts,** because tiny belts will be dwarfed by your size. Carry a **large purse**—in scale with your plus-size frame—that hits anywhere except the waist.	Wear a **pointy-toed heel** to make you look taller and slimmer. Or try a more comfort-able **wedge heel** with jeans.

FIGURE 8.4.1
You, only sexier.

WHAT NOT TO WEAR

Really. I mean it.

COATS & JACKETS

Don't wear jackets that button, tie, or close at the neck, such as **mandarin collars;** this narrows your shoulders and makes your hips look wider in comparison. Steer clear of jackets with **front or side pockets** at the hip. Avoid jackets that land at the hip, adding weight to your broadest point. Don't wear **straight, ankle-length coats** that hide your small waistline.

TOPS

Steer clear of tops that are baggy in the middle such as **peasant tops;** that's like drawing a line from the two widest points on your body and covering up your skinniest part! Avoid **crew necks** and **turtlenecks,** which can turn your breasts into a "uniboob" that will make you appear top-heavy. Avoid **dainty halters** or spaghetti straps that aren't in scale with your size.

DRESSES

Don't wear **boxy, shift dresses** that turn your hourglass figure into an oval. Avoid **ankle-length dresses** that make your bottom half seem heavier. Avoid dresses with **large patterns** such as huge pattern florals; this will make you seem larger than you are. Don't wear **flimsy material** such as Lycra®-based cottons or thin jersey knits that will reveal extra lumps.

PANTS & JEANS

Avoid **skinny jeans** that taper to your ankles and make your hips look larger. Don't wear **cropped pants** or **Capri pants,** which accentuate your wide thighs, and make your lower legs look heavy. Avoid **cuffed trousers,** which will make your legs look shorter and thicker. Steer clear of **distressing or whiskering** on the thighs of your jeans, which will add weight to your thighs.

SHOES

Don't wear shoes with **ankle straps;** they will make your ankles look wide. Also, avoid **strappy stilettos** that are too delicate for your weight.

SKIRTS

Steer clear of bell-shaped skirts such as **poufy circle skirts** and **pleated skirts** that add unwanted volume to your hip area. Avoid **shiny fabrics** and **busy patterns** or stripes on your bottom half, which will draw unwanted attention to your hips. Don't wear **prairie skirts** that will drag you down.

JEWELRY & ACCESSORIES

Don't wear accessories with too many flowers, bows, ribbons, and ruffles that add unwanted volume to your frame. Avoid **hip belts** that land at the largest part of your hips and add unnecessary volume there. Don't cover the skin area around your neck and cleavage with **scarves** or **chunky choker necklaces.**

FIGURE 8.4.2
You, wearing the wrong things.

THE NEW YOU

Three ways to put your dress-sexy rules into play.

CASUAL	CAREER	FORMAL

The rounded V-neck
of this top reveals skin and
cleavage, drawing the
eye in and up. The three-
quarter-sleeves conceal the
widest part of your arms.
The very subtle boot cut pant
balances your hips from below
by adding a bit of volume
below the knees; it also
lengthens your look
all the way to your ankles.

The vertical princess
seams in the tailored top meet
the princess seams in
the pencil skirt, creating two
long lines from shoulder
to knee, making you appear
slimmer. The skirt grazes
your curvy hips without adding
volume. The pointy-toed
heels in the same tone creates
a slenderizing look overall.

The surplice styling
of this dress opens up your
neck and draws the
eye toward your cleavage. The
dress grazes your hips
without adding extra volume.
The tulip skirt of the dress
shows off your hourglass hips,
as the flare balances
them from below. The knee-
length hem reveals
your shapely, sexy legs.

YOUR ONE FASHION MUST-HAVE: *a wrap dress*

This is a dress that hugs the hourglass curves you already have. It also creates
a flattering V-neck that allows you to reveal either subtle
or plunging cleavage, depending on how much you're willing to show off.

FITTING ROOM 9

If you're tall and slender, you're in the right place. Just find your silhouette and prepare to get sexy.

TALL
SLENDER
INVERTED TRIANGLE

YOU

You are **TALL**.
[5'8" OR MORE]

You are **SLENDER**.
[BETWEEN 110 AND 150 LBS.]

Your body forms an
INVERTED TRIANGLE
as your shoulders are wider
than your hips.

You have slightly broad
shoulders. Your hips are small.
Your legs and butt are slim.

YOUR BLESSING

You were born with a beautiful body type. First, you're tall and slender, that's a short way of saying that your figure could pass for that of a runway model. Your other blessing? You have beautiful, broad shoulders that are wider than your hips, which means they're the first thing people see when you walk into a room. They bring attention right up to your face where it belongs. Your broad-shouldered figure is what most clothing manufacturers have in mind when they design in the first place, which is why I sometimes call inverted triangles like you "hanger girls." Clothes fall on you the same way they fall on a clothes hanger. And trust me, that's a very good thing, because it means you can wear just about anything and look great.

YOUR CURSE

If you're on the very slender side of a TALL, SLENDER, INVERTED TRIANGLE, you have more of a straight figure than a curvy one. And since curves are the name of the game when it comes to sexy, adding curves to your lower half will help. Your other curse? Your legs are on the skinny side. If you show too much of them, your upper body may look out of balance. Also, when shopping, you may find that pants and sleeves often run short on you. While you can let out the seams a bit with trousers or blazers, it doesn't work with jeans or long-sleeve shirts. And if you're very tall, you may feel self-conscious wearing high heels, which make you stand even taller than others in the room—including your date.

YOUR CELEBRITY BODY STAND-IN: *Cameron Diaz*

WHAT TO WEAR

Your fashion challenge is to narrow your shoulders, widen your hips so they match your broad shoulders, and reveal more of your waist.

COATS & JACKETS

Wear blazers and coats with **princess seams,** which add feminine curves to your silhouette. Wear **peplum jackets** that cinch at the waist and flare out, creating the illusion of curvy hips. Choose **A-line or trench coats** with no detailing in the shoulder area and pockets at the hips to add fullness there.

TOPS

Choose **V-necks, U-necks, sweet-heart necks,** or **wrap tops** that show skin in your chest area and draw the eye in and away from your broad shoulders. Wear **tailored dress shirts** that add weight at your hips in the right place. Or color-block your look with contrasting color belts, sashes, or tops peeking out beneath blazers and sweaters; this technique works best with tall women.

DRESSES

Try a **slip dress** with wide straps that hit in the center of each of your shoulders; this balances the skin evenly on either side and makes your shoulders seem proportional to your small bottom half. Choose **medium prints** for your dresses, proportional to your tall frame. Wear **V-neck** and **U-neck** cuts on top, with flared, pleated, **gored,** or **godet skirts** on the bottom.

SKIRTS

Wear **A-line skirts, wrap skirts,** or **gored skirts** that flare from the hips to create the illusion of full hips. Pick skirts with **front or side pockets,** which instantly broaden your bottom half. Wear skirts in **heavy fabrics** such as cotton twill or wool to add more fullness to your bottom half. Choose skirts that hit at or above your knee, or even at the widest point on your calf—you're one of the few body types that can create curvier legs this way.

PANTS & JEANS

Wear **straight-leg** or **boot cut jeans** that add slight volume to your lower half. Wear **low-rise pants** with pockets at the hip to add curves to your boy-shaped hips. You can get away with cuffs on the bottoms of your trousers, which break up your tall, slender look in a balanced way.

JEWELRY & ACCESSORIES

Wear **dainty jewelry** that helps break up the line of your tall, slender frame. Try **large, colored, beaded necklaces** that bring the focus toward the center of your body and help break up your very slender neck. Wear **handbags with long straps** that fall at your hip to add some weight there.

SHOES

Wear **pointy-toed heels** for a classic look, especially if you're shorter. Or wear heels with details such as **peep toes, cutouts,** and **bows** to draw attention to your bottom half.

FIGURE 9.1.1
You, only sexier.

WHAT NOT TO WEAR

Really. I mean it.

COATS & JACKETS

Steer clear of **shawl collar blazers** or those with **wide lapels** that make your shoulders look too wide. Avoid **puffed-sleeve blazers** as well as jackets with **shoulder pads** or extra detailing on the shoulder area, include military epaulets, decorative buttons, or ruffled shoulder seams; all of these styles will make your shoulders appear top-heavy.

TOPS

Avoid **boatneck tops** or **square-neck tops,** which create horizontal lines from one shoulder to the other and make you appear wider on top. Avoid **long tunics** that drag your look down over your small hips and make your tall, slender frame look lanky. Don't wear **plunging V-necks,** which may make your slender neck look to long and lanky.

DRESSES

Avoid **off-the-shoulder dresses, halter dresses,** and dresses with **dainty straps,** all of which make your shoulders look wider. Don't wear dresses hemmed at ankle length, which will drag down your long look. Steer clear of dresses that balloon out from the waist, which will make you appear young and girly instead of sexy.

SKIRTS

Avoid **short miniskirts** that show too much of your long, slender legs, which can make you look lanky. If you're going to wear a skirt above the knee, don't match it with a short top; your tall frame will look more balanced if you wear differently proportioned clothes. Don't choose **poufy bell-shaped skirts** that hit at the knee, which will look like ballerina skirts on your tall frame.

SHOES

Steer clear of **ankle straps,** which break up your long look. Don't wear **heavy, thick soles** out of scale with your slender legs. Avoid **too-tall stilettos,** which will make you look long and lanky.

PANTS & JEANS

Avoid dark pants if you're wearing a bright, light, or bold top, as this can make you seem top heavy. Don't wear **skinny jeans, or tight leggings** that accentuate your small lower half. Avoid **pressed-crease pants** that can make your thin legs look too skinny.

JEWELRY & ACCESSORIES

Don't wear **long, drapey delicate necklace strands** that accentuate how slender you are. Avoid **chunky handbags** that rest under your arm, which add weight to your top half. Don't wear **scarves** or **choker necklaces** that make your neck area seem wide and thick.

FIGURE 9.1.2
You, wearing the wrong things.

THE NEW YOU

Three ways to put your dress-sexy rules into play.

CASUAL

The tank top under the Chanel-cut jacket draws the eye in toward your center and doesn't add bulk to your shoulders. The pockets at the hip of the jacket add weight where you need it. The stovepipe jeans hit at your lower hips to add a bit of weight there.

CAREER

The substantial, wide-set straps on this knit dress make your wide shoulders seem more balanced. The deep V-cut draws attention away from your shoulders. The belt defines your waist. The godet skirt adds curves to your hip area. The bright peep-toe shoe adds a little necessary volume to your slender frame.

FORMAL

The wide scoop of the tank top is proportional to your wide shoulders and makes them seem smaller. The poufy circle skirt adds necessary curves to your hips. The skirt hits just below the knee to cover up some of your long legs, so you don't look too young or too lanky. The sash and bow defines a waist.

YOUR ONE FASHION MUST-HAVE: *tailored jeans with hip details*

Choose a pair of blue jeans with pockets at the hips and hem them to your perfect height in heels. Since it can be hard for you to find jeans that perfectly fit your height, it's worth it to buy and tailor a pair (or two)—you'll have them for years to come.

TALL SLENDER RECTANGLE

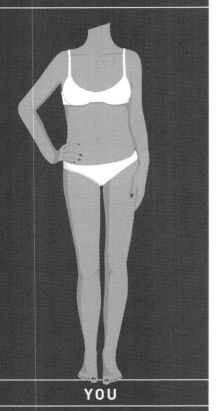

YOU

You are **TALL**.
[5'8" OR MORE]

You are **SLENDER**.
[BETWEEN 110 AND 150 LBS.]

Your body forms a
RECTANGLE
as your shoulders are the same
width as your hips.

You have slightly broad shoulders.
You have slightly wide hips to match.
Your waist is undefined.

YOUR BLESSING

You're off to a great, sexy start because you already have the body parts you need to build a sexy shape. In essence, you have broad, pronounced shoulders, and you have slightly curvy hips to match. In fact, the more you accentuate your shoulders and hips, the thinner your waist appears—which is exactly what you want to do with your silhouette. Also, because you're tall and slender, the differences on your body are proportionally small. This means you won't have to do much to create that curvy balance. Clothes fall beautifully on your figure, the same way they do on many runway models on the catwalks today. (No, you may not want to be a runway model, but doesn't it feel good to know you have a similar build?) Your other blessing? You have slim legs in perfect proportion to your frame. So you may want to consider showing them off. If you have it, flaunt it. And you certainly have a pair of sexy legs that fit the bill.

YOUR CURSE

As a TALL, SLENDER RECTANGLE, you lack a defined waist between your shoulders and hips. You also have a flatter, less-rounded butt than others. And, because you are so slender, you may not have much in the chest area to work with. Those features combined give your figure a slightly boyish shape. When it comes to looking and dressing sexy, you could do with a few feminine curves. Your other curse? As both tall and slender, your legs may run on the skinny side. And if you show too much of them, your upper body may look out of balance.

YOUR CELEBRITY BODY STAND-IN: *Charlize Theron*

WHAT TO WEAR

Your fashion challenge is to accentuate your broad shoulders and your equally wide hips, while cinching in your waist.

DRESSES

Choose **square-neck** and **scoop-neck dresses** that belt or tie at the waist and flare out at the hem. Or wear a **corset dress** that cinches your waistline or an **empire dress** that fits snugly around your chest, creating the illusion of a high waistline. Choose **medium, feminine prints** for your dresses, which soften your boxy shape.

TOPS

Pick tops with detailing at the neckline to draw the eye to your neck and chest area. Wear **wide-set V-necks, scoop necks,** and **boat-necks** which widen the appearance of your shoulders. Choose **empire tops** or shirts with ruching at the bust to create more fullness there. Try **halter tops,** which expose more skin on the outside of the straps to help widen your shoulders.

SKIRTS

Wear an **A-line skirt** that tapers out from your waist, making it appear as if you have a cinched waist. Or go the opposite direction and create a sexy silhouette with a **pencil skirt** topped with a princess seam blazer that adds to the illusion of a thin waist. Choose skirts that hit at the widest point on your calf—you're one of the few body types that can and should create curvy legs this way.

PANTS & JEANS

Wear **cropped pants** or **gauchos** that hit just above the widest point on your calves. Choose pants and jeans with pockets or detailing around the hip area so your waist looks smaller in comparison. Try **low-rise jeans, skinny jeans,** or **leggings** that make your hips look wider. Or wear **low-rise men's trousers** that add volume to your bottom half. Cuffs on your pants break up your height in a balanced way.

COATS & JACKETS

Wear **structured blazers, military jackets,** or **boleros** that help widen your shoulders. Aim for **princess seams** and darts that create a curved silhouette. Let bright shirts peek out at the hip; this color-blocking breaks up your long look and adds good volume to your hips.

JEWELRY & ACCESSORIES

Add **scarves, bows,** or other feminine accents at the neck of your shirts to add volume to the area. Round out your boxy shape with feminine jewelry that falls in a soft curve or V-shape, such as a **pendant on a chain.** Wear belts at the widest point of your hips.

SHOES

Wear moderately **high pointy-toed heels,** which will make your calves appear more shapely, giving the suggestion your figure is equally curvy. Choose shoes in bright colors or with details such as **peep-toes** and **cutouts.**

FIGURE 9.2.1
You, only sexier.

WHAT NOT TO WEAR

Really. I mean it.

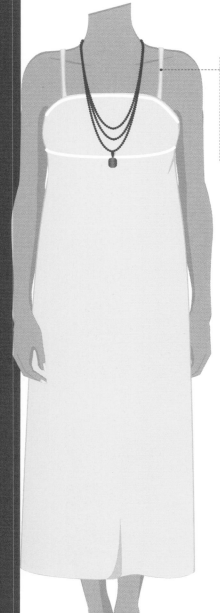

FIGURE 9.2.2
You, wearing the wrong things.

DRESSES

Avoid **long sheath dresses** that fall past your knees without implying a waistline. Don't wear **boxy dresses** that fall straight from your shoulders to your knees. Don't wear **sleeveless shell dresses** that turn the sides of your torso into straight lines.

TOPS

Avoid **horizontal patterns** on your shirts that make your square torso look boxy. Don't wear **crew necks** that make your upper body look shapeless. At the same time, avoid **plunging V-necks** that make your torso look too long. Steer clear of **too-short tops** and **cropped tanks;** showing skin between your top and your pants makes you appear wider in your stomach area.

SKIRTS

Don't wear **cold, corporate skirt suits** that make your body look too masculine. Avoid Lycra®-based straight skirts that cling snugly around your hips and butt and make your top seem larger in comparison. If you're going to wear a miniskirt, don't match it with a short top; your tall frame will look more balanced if you wear differently proportioned clothes.

PANTS & JEANS

Don't wear **Capri pants** or **leggings** with a blousy top without cinching in your waist; otherwise you'll look top-heavy instead of balanced. Don't wear trousers with **pressed seams** that will make your slender legs seem too thin and shapeless. Avoid **palazzo pants** that add too much volume to your slender figure.

COATS & JACKET

Avoid **boxy, cropped blazers, mandarin collar blazers,** or **Chanel-style jackets** that exaggerate your squared-off look. Steer clear of short coats that make your legs seem too long in proportion. Avoid **straight, ankle-length coats** that overpower your frame.

JEWELRY & ACCESSORIES

Don't choose **oversized handbags** that aren't in scale with your slender frame, and don't choose **square bags** that hit at your waist, which will add unwanted bulk to your middle. Avoid **too-long, delicate necklace** strands that accentuate how slender and uncurvy you are.

SHOES

Don't wear **clunky, thick-soled shoes** that contrast too much with your slim legs. Avoid **too-tall stilettos,** which will make you look too long and lanky because of your slender frame.

THE NEW YOU

Three ways to put your dress-sexy rules into play.

CASUAL	CAREER	FORMAL
The bold beads on the halter string draw the eye to your face, as it makes your shoulders look wider. The drop waist with the ruffle and pretty bow add volume to your hips, making your waist look smaller in comparison. The skinny jean hits at your hips to add weight there.	The fluffy blouse with puffed-sleeves adds detail to your torso and makes your boyish shape seem more feminine. The scarf tie at the neck helps break up your slender neck so you don't look lanky. The men's low-rise trouser has a wide waistband and a big button to add a bit of volume to your hip area.	The gown has a wide set V-neck that widens your shoulders and shows some cleavage to make you look more feminine. The bright, teal color adds the illusion of a fuller body. The dress fishtails out, giving you the illusion of a small waist and curvier hips.

YOUR ONE FASHION MUST-HAVE: *a belt collection*

Because you're so slender, your middle can easily be cinched to create the illusion of a defined waist. Anything that pulls the eye inward from your shoulders and your hips will give your frame gorgeous hourglass curves.

TALL SLENDER TRIANGLE

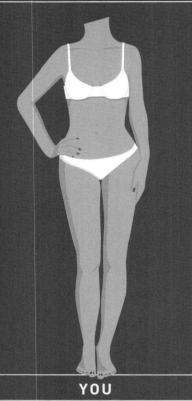

YOU

You are **TALL**.
[5'8" OR MORE]

You are **SLENDER**.
[BETWEEN 110 AND 150 LBS.]

Your body forms a
TRIANGLE
as your hips are wider than
your shoulders.

You have a slim torso
and thin shoulders. Your hips
are slightly wide-set. You
have a mildly shapely bottom.

YOUR BLESSING

You have a lot to be thankful for! You have nice curves on your hips and a slightly shapely behind. And, because of your slender weight, the difference between the size of your shoulders and the size of your hips is small. A curvy behind is one of the sexiest features you can have. Think about it: Some women are even famous for theirs! Overall, you have just enough of a feminine shape to create the sexy silhouette you're aiming for. Your other blessing? You have a slender torso and small shoulders. Again, because of your slender weight, your shoulders aren't drastically smaller than your hips, so it won't take too much to balance your figure with clothing. And, because of your small bust, you get to show off your chest and your delicate collarbone—and that's always sexy.

YOUR CURSE

As a TALL, SLENDER TRIANGLE, you have what's called a low balance. This just means that the visual line of your silhouette reaches its broadest point at your hips. For this reason, you can appear slightly bottom-heavy if you choose the wrong clothes. But since you're a slender woman, it won't take much to balance you. Also, because you have small shoulders, you tend to look slightly shorter at first glance than you may actually be. Your other curse? As a tall woman, you may find that pants, jackets, and tops run short on you. You may not have problems tailoring dress trousers and blazers to fit you, but jeans and many tops or sweaters can make it hard for you to find a style you like in the length you need.

YOUR CELEBRITY BODY STAND-IN: *Mischa Barton*

WHAT TO WEAR

Your fashion challenge is to make your shoulders appear wider to match your wide hips and to draw attention away from your hips and butt.

DRESSES

Wear **V-neck, surplice, strapless,** or **off-the-shoulder dresses** with bold jewelry at your neck to widen your shoulders and bring attention up to your neck. Pick dresses with **cap sleeves** or **three-quarter sleeves** to add volume above your waist. Choose **empire dresses** that add fullness to your bust, then grazing smoothly over your hips.

TOPS

Wear **boatnecks** and **wide scoop necks** that rest far on your shoulders, widening them to balance your hips. Try sweaters made of cashmere, mohair, or other textured fabrics, which draw the eye up to your torso. Wear tops with **flutter sleeves, fluted sleeves, kimono sleeves,** or other flouncy fabric at the arms to draw the eye out from your slender torso. For the same reason, try **turtlenecks with puffy sleeves** to add fullness around your top half.

SKIRTS

Wear **A-line skirts** with no waistband that cinch in at your waist, then flow out, to create an illusion of an hourglass figure. Or try **straight skirts** with a button-front closure to draw the eyes to the center of your skirt, away from your hips. Choose skirts that hit just below your knee, or if you're very tall, at the widest point on your calf which creates the illusion of more curves on your lower legs.

PANTS & JEANS

Wear **straight-leg** or **boot cut pants** that fall straight or flare out slightly, both of which will balance your slightly curvy hips from below. Wear **pressed-crease trousers** with a flat front and no pockets; this will create a long vertical line to your heels, making your hips look slimmer.

COATS & JACKETS

Wear blazers with **wide lapels** or with **puffed sleeves** to widen your shoulders and make your waist look slim in comparison. Wear a **cap-sleeved jacket** over a camisole to add more depth to your torso. Choose **jean, corduroy,** or **velvet jackets** to create volume that balances your hips.

JEWELRY & ACCESSORIES

Wear a colorful **pendant** or a bold **chain necklace** that falls to the top of your cleavage and attracts attention to your chest and slim upper body. Carry a small **hobo bag** or a **medium clutch** that hits under your arm and adds a bit of weight there.

SHOES

Wear shoes in **bright colors** or with interesting details, such as **peep toes, cut-away arches, cutouts,** or **bows** to add volume to your slender look. Or wear wedge heels for the same lifting effect. If you don't want the height, try classic **ballet flats** with an A-line skirt.

FIGURE 9.3.1
You, only sexier.

WHAT NOT TO WEAR

Really. I mean it.

DRESSES

Don't wear body-hugging **sheath dresses** or **slip dresses** that reveal your unbalanced wide hips. Avoid **long, floor-length dresses** that hide your legs entirely and make you seem lanky. Don't wear **high-necked halters** or **high crew neck styles** that narrow your shoulders. Steer clear of **full dresses** that bell out from the waist in stiff fabrics and make you look wider than you are.

TOPS

Don't wear **clingy tops** or **plunging V-necks** that reveal how slim and small you are on top, which will make you seem bottom-heavy. Avoid **crew neck** or **raglan sweaters** that cover up the skin on your top half and narrow your shoulders; this only makes your hips seem wider in comparison. Avoid tops or sweaters that hit at the widest point on your hips—such as a bright colored tunic over black pants.

SKIRTS

Avoid **circle skirts** or **pleated skirts** in stiff, heavy fabrics such as wool, that add too much volume to your already fuller bottom half. Also, don't choose straight **mini-skirts.** Don't wear **flared skirts** hemmed above your knee, as this will make your silhouette look like a ballerina in a tutu. Don't wear **busy patterns** or **horizontal details** on your skirts, which emphasize the wrong region of your body.

PANTS & JEANS

Don't wear **full fabrics** such as velour and terry cloth that add volume to your thighs and hips and bottom. Don't choose pants with pockets at the hip or thigh, adding unnecessary bulk at your widest point. Avoid **tapered jeans** that will make your hips look even wider in comparison.

COATS & JACKET

Steer clear of jackets in **soft fabrics** such as linen that lack strong shoulder construction and reveal how narrow they are. Avoid **long jackets** that hit at the widest point on your hips. Don't wear **long overcoats** that cover up your legs and make you look straight instead of curvy.

JEWELRY & ACCESSORIES

Don't carry **long-handled handbags** that fall at the hip and draw attention to your widest area. Avoid **tiny stud earrings** and very **delicate chain necklaces** that emphasize how much smaller you are on top and make you look bottom-heavy.

SHOES

If you're very tall, avoid **3" or higher pointy-toed stilettos** that will make you look too vampy. Don't wear **chunky heels** or **thick soles,** both of which will look too heavy for your slender frame. Avoid **knee-high boots** with skirts that will draw unwanted attention to your thighs and legs.

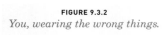

FIGURE 9.3.2
You, wearing the wrong things.

THE NEW YOU

Three ways to put your dress-sexy rules into play.

CASUAL	CAREER	FORMAL
The off-the-shoulder peasant blouse has poufy sleeves that draw the eye out. The empire waist adds fullness to your chest area. The stovepipe jean keeps your bottom half looking lean without tapering. The boots under the jeans balance your lean body. The handbag hits high on your waist, drawing the eye to the area you need it most.	The bright collared blouse underneath the skirt suit draws attention to your top half. The jacket adds structure to your shoulders, making them seem wider. The pencil skirt smoothes out your hips under the jacket. The wedge heel in the same color as your suit creates a long, slim look.	The wrap dress sits wide on your shoulders, making you seem wider on top. The three-quarter-length-sleeves are a lightweight scrunchy style that draw the eye outward and balances your hips. The tie at the waist defines your waist. The skirt flows out gently over your hips. The peep toe heel breaks up your vertical look to keep you balanced.

YOUR ONE FASHION MUST-HAVE: *a structured jacket*

Choose a jacket with small shoulder pads or a blazer with puffed sleeves that you can wear with dresses, skirts, and jeans. Make sure it hits just above the widest point on your hips to smooth the transition from your torso to your lower half.

TALL
SLENDER
HOURGLASS

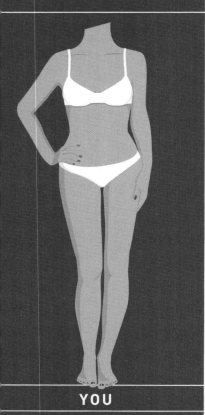

YOU

You are **TALL**.
[5'8" OR MORE]

You are **SLENDER**.
[BETWEEN 110 AND 150 LBS.]

Your body forms an
HOURGLASS
as your shoulders are the
same width as your hips.

You have broad shoulders
and a slightly shapely bust. Your
hips and butt are mildly curvy.
Your waist is small and defined.

YOUR BLESSING

You've hit the jackpot! You have slightly broad shoulders, you have mildly curvy hips, you have a shapely bottom, and you have a very defined waist. Also, because you're slender, the difference between your curvy hips and your tiny waist isn't large, which means you don't have to do much to keep yourself looking proportional. Overall, your figure is already very well-balanced—and, as you already know, that's the basic goal behind dressing sexy. Your other blessing? You're tall. Which means that underneath that great upper body of yours, you also have a pair of slender legs that probably look a mile long on a good day. You have the same body as some of the most famous supermodels today. The truth is, you could wear nothing but a knapsack and still look sexy. So if you can just keep the balance of your body in check when you dress, you've got it made.

YOUR CURSE

As a TALL, SLENDER HOURGLASS, the main thing you might have to cry about is that other women turn green with envy over your great figure! That said, being very tall can be a curse. Jackets and pants you choose off the rack may be too short for you. While trousers and blazers usually allow for extra fabric that can be let out, buying jeans, tops, or sweaters that fit your tall frame may be harder. Also, you may feel self-conscious wearing high heels, because they often make you the tallest one in the room—and sometimes taller than your date!

YOUR CELEBRITY BODY STAND-IN: *Cindy Crawford*

WHAT TO WEAR

Your fashion challenge is to keep your broad shoulders and curvy hips balanced, while defining your waist.

TOPS

Wear shirts with **princess seams** that hug your hourglass curves. Choose tops with ruching around the bust to highlight your chest area. Wear **V-necks, wide scoop necks,** and **halter tops with dainty straps** in scale with your slender size. Wear **tailored shirts** with the top one or two buttons undone to create a V-area of skin that points toward your small, defined waist.

DRESSES

Wear **wrap dresses** in light to mid-weight fabrics that cinch your small waist and drape lightly over your hips. Wear **body-hugging sheath dresses**. Or try fitted **halter dresses** that flare out at the hem, balancing your hourglass from below. Choose **medium, pretty prints** for your dresses, which are in scale to your tall size.

SKIRTS

Wear **A-line skirts** with wide waistlines to accentuate your tiny waist. Wear **three-quarter-length skirts** that hit just below your knee, or, as with dresses, choose skirts that hit at the widest point on your calf to create more curves on your lower legs. Wear **godet skirts, tulip skirts, fluted hems,** and **ruffles** to add feminine volume to your slender figure.

PANTS

Try **straight-leg** or **boot cut pants** as well as **men's trousers** that add volume below your knees to balance your curves from below. Choose **pressed-crease pants** that fit snugly at your hips, then fall straight to your ankles. Also, with your height, you can get away with **cuffs on your trousers** and still look tall and shapely.

COATS & JACKETS

Wear **peplum jackets,** which cut in at your thinnest point, then follow your natural curves out toward your hips. Try a **basic trench coat** that has subtly structured shoulders. It pulls tight at the waist and tapers out toward your hips.

JEWELRY & ACCESSORIES

Wear simple necklaces—such as a **pendant, charm, or locket necklace—** that don't distract from your figure. Choose **scarves** that tie around your neck and hang down your torso a bit to add volume to your slender neck, but still match your lean look.

SHOES

Wear **pointy-toed heels** in bright colors or with interesting details such as **peep toes, cutouts, bows,** or **cut-away arches,** all of which add to an outfit without distracting from your height.

FIGURE 9.4.1
You, only sexier.

WHAT NOT TO WEAR

Really. I mean it.

TOPS

Don't wear **peasant tops, baggy tops,** or **long tunics** that bunch up or cover up your sexy, defined waist. Avoid **off-the-shoulder** tops if you're not balancing your wider-looking shoulders with a **poufy skirt.** If you're very tall, don't wear plunging **V-necks** that may make your neck seem too lanky. Avoid **thin, clingy tops** unless you balance them with stovepipe or skinny jeans.

DRESSES	SKIRTS
Steer clear of **empire dresses** that flow too loosely over your small waist, covering up your perfectly sexy silhouette. Steer clear of **boxy cut dresses** that cover up your waist. Don't wear **tiny prints** that are proportionally too small compared to your tall frame.	Avoid skirts with overly ornamental detailing in the hip area, which draws the eyes straight to your hips. Don't wear **circle or pleated skirts** in stiff fabrics that add too much volume to your bottom half, without balancing it on top. Skip **masculine skirt suits** that flatten out your curves and take away the sexy.

PANTS & JEANS

Don't wear light-colored pants if you're wearing a dark shirt up top, as this can make you appear bottom-heavy. Don't wear pants with **big pockets or detailing** at the hips without balancing out the volume you're creating on the bottom with equal volume on top. Avoid **loose wide leg pants** or **palazzo pants** that completely cover up the shape of your killer thighs and legs.

SHOES	COATS & JACKETS	JEWELRY & ACCESSORIES
Don't wear **chunky heels,** which will look out of proportion with your slender frame. If you're very tall, avoid **pointy-toed 3" stilettos,** which will make you seem too tall and vampy.	Stay away from boxy **Chanel-style blazers, collarless square jackets,** and **double-breasted jackets** that hide your curvy waist-line. Don't choose jackets that hit at your hip, or mid thigh, unless they are built with a waist-defining shape. Don't wear **ankle-length coats** that cover you up.	Avoid choosing wide **hip belts,** which will make you seem bottom-heavy. Don't wear **too-small accessories** such as tiny stud earrings, dainty necklaces, or tiny clutches that will seem out of proportion to your tall frame. Avoid handbags that hit at your waist and widen the area you're trying to make smaller.

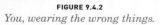

FIGURE 9.4.2
You, wearing the wrong things.

THE NEW YOU

Three ways to put your dress-sexy rules into play.

CASUAL	CAREER	FORMAL
The voluminous sleeve adds curves to your top half to make your waist look smaller in comparison. The subtle gathering on the front of the shirt adds sexy there. The stovepipe jean hits at mid waist to define your waist. The different-color open toed shoe breaks up your vertical line so you don't look too long.	The bright blouse underneath the suit jacket breaks up your long frame a bit, drawing attention to your face. The structured jacket keeps your shoulders broad, while cutting in at your small waist. The trouser cut of the pants adds a bit of shape to your bottom half to balance your layered torso.	The halter top of this gown crisscrosses at the center of your chest to break up the long line of your neck. The super clingy cut shows off your curves along your defined waist. The slight flare on the bottom grazes over your hips. The stiletto sandal adds interest at your feet to keep your look balanced overall.

YOUR ONE FASHION MUST-HAVE: *a good tailor*

Honestly, what you could use most is a wardrobe tailored to the exact lengths of your legs and arms. Ideally, you should own a perfect pair of jeans hemmed to your height in heels and match them with tops that keep your hourglass curves in full view.

FITTING ROOM 10

If you're tall and
medium weight, you're
in the right place.
Just find your silhouette
and prepare to get sexy.

TALL
MEDIUM
INVERTED TRIANGLE

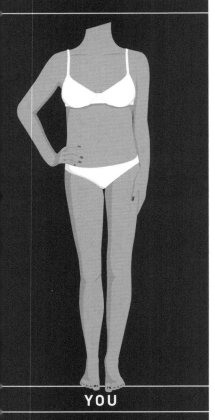

YOU

You are **TALL**.
[5'8" OR MORE]

You are **MEDIUM** weight.
[BETWEEN 135 AND 195 LBS.]

Your body forms an
INVERTED TRIANGLE
as your shoulders are wider
than your hips.

You have broad shoulders.
Your hips and bottom are slim.
Your undefined waist is
similar in size to your hips.

YOUR BLESSING

You have a beautiful shape. First, you're a tall woman. You're off to a great start, because a long, slender look is part of building a sexy silhouette. You also have gorgeous, broad shoulders. In fact, those shoulders make you appear taller than you are when people first see you. Because you're of medium weight, your chest and shoulders aren't proportionally that much larger than your hips, so it won't take much to balance your body with the right clothes. Your other blessing? If you have a shapely chest, you may have the ability to create a little cleavage—which is one of the most sexy elements you can have. Finally, you have nice, slim legs that also deserve a little attention. You don't want to be prancing around in miniskirts, but showing those legs will add to the sexy and help balance your overall shape.

YOUR CURSE

As a TALL, MEDIUM, INVERTED TRIANGLE, you have what's called a high balance, which means that you carry more of your weight in your shoulders. For this reason, you can sometimes appear top-heavy if you wear the wrong clothes. Your other curse? As a tall woman, you may find that pants and sleeves often run short on you. That can be a problem with jeans, casual shirts, and sweaters that don't allow extra fabric to be let out for your height. Also, putting on heels can make you tower over others, which can be a curse if it makes you self-conscious.

YOUR CELEBRITY BODY STAND-IN: *Gabrielle Reece*

WHAT TO WEAR

Your fashion challenge is to play down your wide shoulders and add some curves to your hips to balance them.

TOPS

Pick **button-down shirts** that create a long vertical line down the center of your body and **V-neck tops** that draw the eye in and away from your wide shoulders. Wear tops with **thick, wide straps** that break up your wide shoulders and are in proportion to your tall frame. Wear **monochromatic outfits** that elongate your entire silhouette and make you appear slimmer.

DRESSES	SKIRTS
Try dresses with **scoop necks** or **deep U-necks** on top, to draw the eyes in from your shoulders, and flare from the hips. Wear **halter dresses** with wide fabric straps that are proportional with your broad shoulders (this makes them appear smaller). Create volume on your bottom half with **corset dresses** that cinch in at the waist then taper out to widen your hips.	Wear **full skirts, A-line skirts,** or **semi-circle skirts** that create volume around your slimmer hips. Or try skirts with **horizontal details,** such as ruching, contrasting fabric, or a **wide belt** to add volume at your hips. Choose skirts in **thick fabrics** that hold their shape on your hips, where you want it. Hem your skirts at or below your knee, which works best with your height.

PANTS & JEANS

Wear **straight-leg pants** or pants with a slight **boot cut** to add a bit of volume on your bottom half; with your height, the flare won't shorten you. Pick pants with **diagonal pockets at the hip** to create the illusion of more curves there. Or choose jeans with **distressing, whiskering,** or **fading** on the hip area, which draws attention toward your bottom half. Consider **low-rise pants** with a wide waistband that add curves to your narrow-looking hips.

COATS & JACKETS	JEWELRY & ACCESSORIES	SHOES
Choose a **short, peplum jacket** that flares out from your waist. Wear **low-stance blazers** over a camisole top. Or layer fitted jackets—such as a **Chanel-style jacket** left open—over camisoles or dress shirts that hit at the waist and add volume there.	Wear beautiful **bangles** or **cuffs** that hit at your hips when your arms are resting, drawing attention there. Wear bold jewelry, such as colorful **beaded necklaces,** or eye-catching **charm necklaces** that help break up the line of your tall frame.	Wear **pointy-toed heels, peep-toed heels, heels with cutaway arches,** or other interesting details; your tall frame works well with bright, bold shoes. Try **knee-high boots** to balance your top half.

FIGURE 10.1.1
You, only sexier.

WHAT NOT TO WEAR

Really. I mean it.

TOPS

Don't wear **puffed-sleeve tops, off-the-shoulder tops, boatnecks, cowl neck sweaters,** and **turtlenecks** that show just how wide your shoulders are. Avoid **scarves, bows,** and **horizontal detailing** around the neck of your tops, which makes you appear top-heavy. Don't wear **plunging V-necks,** which may make your neck look too long and reveal too much cleavage.

DRESSES	SKIRTS
Steer clear of **narrow-set halter dresses** with dainty straps that make your broad shoulders look wider than they are. Avoid **long, ankle-length dresses** that reveal your straight hips and cover up the curves you have, while weighing your look down. Don't wear dresses that balloon out from the waist, which will make you look girly instead of sexy.	Don't wear fitted **pencil skirts** that minimize your lower half and emphasize your straight hips. Don't wear **miniskirts** that show too much of your long, slender legs, which can make you look lanky; if you're going to wear one don't match it with a short top; your tall frame will look more balanced if you wear differently proportioned clothes.

PANTS & JEANS

Don't wear jeans with **flat fronts** or **no pockets,** which will make your bottom half too small to balance your top. Steer clear of **dark-colored skinny jeans** or **leggings** that emphasize how much slimmer your legs are in relation to your top. Avoid pants with **small back pockets** that aren't in scale with your tall frame.

SHOES	COATS & JACKETS	JEWELRY & ACCESSORIES
Don't wear **heavy, thick soles,** which is out of proportion with your slender legs. Avoid **too-tall stilettos,** which will make you look too long and lanky because of your slender frame.	Avoid **military jackets, denim jackets** with lots of pockets, or trench coats with heavy detailing on the shoulders; these will all make you appear top-heavy. Don't wear **long, ankle-length coats** that cover your legs and make you seem like you're swimming in your coat.	Avoid **drapey, delicate necklace** strands that emphasize your straight look. Avoid **chunky handbags** that rest under your arm, which add weight to your top half. Don't add **scarves** or **brooches** to the neck of your shirts, as this covers up the skin you need to show at your neck.

FIGURE 10.1.2
You, wearing the wrong things.

THE NEW YOU

Three ways to put your dress-sexy rules into play.

CASUAL

The slightly flowy blouse adds a feminine touch to your broad-shouldered torso. The scoop neck draws the eye in and away from your shoulders. The pretty ruffle and tie at your hips adds volume there, where you need it. The straight-leg jean adds weight below your hips, to balance you. The boots help add some volume to your thin legs.

CAREER

The wide straps of this textured top are proportional to your tall frame and balance your wide shoulders. The pattern is in scale with your medium frame. The top hits at mid-hip with pockets at the front to add volume to the hip area. The knee-length gored skirt helps balance your shoulders.

FORMAL

The wide set straps on this dress are in proportion with your tall frame and help balance your wide shoulders. The dress is fitted through the waist to define your silhouette. The flouncy circle skirt adds volume around your hips where you need it. The bright beaded necklace, in scale with your frame, draws the eye toward your chest.

YOUR ONE FASHION MUST-HAVE: *a full skirt*

Choose a skirt that cinches at your waist, then flows out adding volume to your hips to balance your broad shoulders. Hem the skirt just below your knee to show off your great legs and sexy height.

TALL
MEDIUM
RECTANGLE

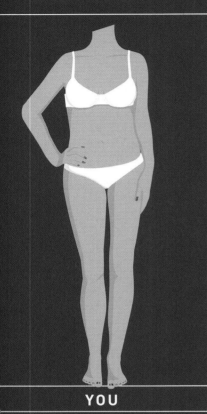

YOU

You are **TALL**.
[5'8" OR MORE]

You are **MEDIUM** weight.
[BETWEEN 135 AND 195 LBS.]

Your body forms a
RECTANGLE
as your shoulders are the
same width as your hips.

You have broad shoulders.
You have equally wide hips.
Your waist is wide and undefined.

YOUR BLESSING

With your figure, you have many blessings. First, you're tall. Looking lean and long is part of building a sexy silhouette. You have wide, strong shoulders. You have a pronounced collarbone. And you even have some curves around your chest to play with. Without even doing a thing, your hips and shoulders are already balanced by one another. Your other blessing? Because you're of medium weight, you're not carrying very much weight around your waist and belly area. That makes it easy to cinch you in around the middle with structured clothes. As long as you keep your top and bottom proportional to one another, you can pull in your waist and create the illusion that you have a defined waist as well as a perfectly balanced body. In one word: sexy.

YOUR CURSE

As a TALL, MEDIUM RECTANGLE, you lack the defined waist of an hourglass. Without that lack of curves in the center of your figure, you can sometimes appear to have a boyish body. So you have to pay extra attention when it comes to dressing. If you just throw on loose, comfortable clothes, they'll hang from your shoulders straight to your hips and make you look shapeless. Your other curse? Your height can make it hard to find clothes that fit you off the rack because they run short in the legs and arms. Tailored dress trousers and blazers usually allow for more length with extra fabric that can be let out. But buying jeans that fit you in the legs, tops or sweaters that fit you sleeves may be harder.

YOUR CELEBRITY BODY STAND-IN: *Liv Tyler*

WHAT TO WEAR

Your fashion challenge is to accentuate your broad shoulders and your wide hips while defining your waist.

DRESSES

Wear dresses with **V-necks, U-necks, scoop necks,** and **boat-necks** to create soft curves on your square frame. Choose **wrap dresses** or **surplice dresses** that cinch in your waist with a tie or flattering ruching. Try **corset dresses** that cinch in your waist. Or try a **strapless sweetheart neck** that elongates your shoulders and hugs your waist.

TOPS

Choose **wrap tops** or **surplices with camisoles underneath** that cinch around your waist. Wear **boatneck tops** and **square neck tops** balanced on the bottom with full skirts. Wear **wide-set scoop neck tops with detailing** at the the hips—such as sequins, ribbon, wide fabric bands, ties— which makes your waist look smaller in between. Pick tops with **pretty prints** and details to add a feminine element.

SKIRTS

Wear **A-line skirts, gored skirts, godet skirts,** or **pleated skirts** sewn in to the hips, all of which create imaginary curves at your hips so your waist looks smaller. Choose skirts in **mid- to heavy-weight fabrics** such as thick cotton to add volume on the bottom half. Wear a sexy, **corset dress** that pulls in your waistline. Hem skirts at the knee, or even at the widest point on your calf—your tall thin calves could use the curves this creates.

PANTS & JEANS

Wear **straight-leg pants** or **subtle boot cut pants** and jeans that elongate your body and make you appear taller. Pick pants with detailing around the hip area, such as **angled pockets,** to create the illusion you have curves at your hips. Consider **cuffed-trousers** which break up your tall frame in a balanced way.

COATS & JACKETS

Make use of **light layering:** wear a bright dress shirt under a sweater or blazer so the shirt hits at the hip and creates volume where you need it. Because you're tall, this "color blocking" won't add weight to you. Choose jackets with **princess seams** that turn your torso into an hourglass.

JEWELRY & ACCESSORIES

Wear a **hip belt** that sits at the broadest part of your hip. Soften your shape with **medium-sized purses,** in scale with your tall frame, that fall either at your bust line or at your hips to add a bit of volume there.

SHOES

Try **moderately high heels** or **kitten heels,** which will make your calves appear more shapely. Choose shoes in bright colors or with interesting details such as **peep toes, cutouts, or bows** to help draw attention to your bottom half and break up your tall look a bit.

FIGURE 10.2.1
You, only sexier.

WHAT NOT TO WEAR

Really. I mean it.

DRESSES

Avoid **halter dresses** that pull from the far sides of your shoulders, widening them too much. Don't wear dresses that fall straight from under your arms down to the hem. Avoid **square neck** or **boatneck dresses** that accentuate your boxy shape. Avoid thin or stretchy fabrics that cling to your middle. Don't wear dresses with waist detailing that don't cinch you in.

TOPS

Avoid **high-necked crew necks** and **square necks** that cling to your boxy torso. Don't wear **peasant tops or baggy tops** to cover up your middle, as this will make you seem wider. Avoid **cropped tanks;** even though you're tall, showing off skin between your top and your pants breaks up the vertical flow of your figure and makes you appear wider in your stomach area.

SKIRTS

Don't wear **cold, corporate skirt suits** that make your figure look too masculine. Don't wear **pencil skirts** that emphasize your lack of curves. Avoid **straight, ankle-length skirts** that flatten your bottom and cover your legs, making you look too tall and big. On the other hand, don't wear short **miniskirts** that show too much of your long, slender legs and make you look top-heavy.

PANTS & JEANS

Don't wear **thigh-hugging or Lycra®-based pants** that reveal your flat bottom and small hips. Avoid baggy, wide leg pants or **palazzo pants** and **drawstring straight-leg pants** that accentuate your body's already boxy look.

COATS & JACKET

Avoid **short coats** that make your legs seem too long in proportion. Don't wear **double-breasted blazers** or **pea coats** that mimic your rectangular shape. Steer clear of **straight coats** that button from the neck to your knees without tapering at your waist, which will accentuate a lack of curves.

JEWELRY & ACCESSORIES

Don't choose handbags that hit at your waist, which will add unwanted bulk to your middle. Avoid **long, delicate necklace** strands that accentuate your straightness. Don't wear **chokers** that make your neck look square.

FIGURE 10.2.2
You, wearing the wrong things.

SHOES

Don't wear **thick-soled shoes** that seem out of proportion to your petite legs. Steer clear of **square-toed shoes** that underscore your boxy frame. And if you're very tall, don't wear **pointy-toed stilettos** that are 3" or higher, as they will make you seem a bit too tall.

THE NEW YOU

Three ways to put your dress-sexy rules into play.

CASUAL	CAREER	FORMAL
The boatneck cut on the blouse, highlighted by the satin band, helps widen your shoulders to balance your hips. The bows on the wrists add a feminine element. The lightweight, drapey fabric adds a feminine touch to your torso. The boot cut jean adds weight to the bottom of your legs to balance your hips.	The princess seam chocolate blazer adds shape to your square torso. The bright tailored shirt peeks out from the blazer, hitting at the waist, to make it look like you have hips. The flowing circle skirt adds more volume at your hips. The matching color and seams of the skirt keep your look long and lean.	The square-neck of this dress widens your shoulders. The medium-sized straps are in scale with your height and weight. The belt cinches in the top and gathered bottom, making it look as if you have a defined waist. The flared style at the hem of the dress adds necessary fullness to your bottom half.

YOUR ONE FASHION MUST-HAVE: *a corset*

A corseted dress, top, or blazer helps you create a waist where there isn't one. Because you're of medium weight, you're still slender enough around the middle for a corset to work its magic without sucking you in too much.

TALL
MEDIUM
TRIANGLE

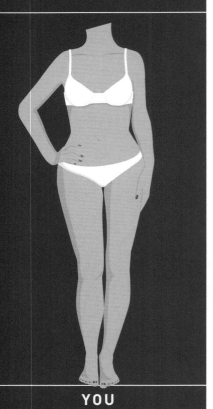

YOU

You are **TALL**.
[5'8" OR MORE]

You are **MEDIUM** weight.
[BETWEEN 135 AND 195 LBS.]

Your body forms a
TRIANGLE
as your hips are broader
than your shoulders.

You have a defined waist.
Your hips are full and curvy.
Your bottom is round.

YOUR BLESSING

Your shape is already halfway to sexy. You have beautiful, rounded hips. You have a rounded bottom. And you have shapely thighs. Your curvy bottom half is one of the most womanly attributes you can have. Even if you have more on your bottom than you wish, you can easily balance it with the right tops, to make your body appear perfectly balanced. The other aspect of your figure that helps? Your height. As a tall woman, your medium-weight figure looks long, lean, and very healthy, which is an important part of looking sexy. Your other blessing? You have a narrow waist and a small ribcage. In fact, at first glance, your small shoulders and pretty collarbone makes you look even slimmer than you actually are. This makes it easy for you to flatter your upper body, work it with your waist, and turn your figure into a perfect hourglass.

YOUR CURSE

As a TALL, MEDIUM TRIANGLE, you have what's called a low balance. This just means that the visual line of your silhouette reaches its broadest point at your hips. For this reason, you can appear bottom-heavy if you choose the wrong clothes. If you also happen to have small breasts and narrow, sloped shoulders, these can both make you look shorter than you are. Your other curse? As a tall woman, you may find that pants, jackets, and tops run short on you. You may not have problems with tailored dress trousers and blazers, which usually allow for extra height, but it's sometimes harder for you to find jeans in the length you need.

YOUR CELEBRITY BODY STAND-IN: *Julia Roberts*

WHAT TO WEAR

Your fashion challenge is to make your shoulders appear wider, to match your hips. You also need to draw attention away from your hips and butt.

TOPS

Wear **deep scoop necks, boatnecks** or **off-the-shoulder tops** in shiny or textured fabrics such as velvet, silk, satin, merino or cashmere to add volume to your torso. Tops with ruching or gathers also work. Try **light layering on top:** Wear light-colored wrap sweaters and blazers over bright tops to draw attention to your torso.

DRESSES	PANTS & JEANS
Choose little black dresses with **boat necks** or **square necks** to widen your shoulders, paired with a full skirt bottom. Try **sheaths with fluted sleeves, flutter sleeves, or kimono sleeves** to balance your hips. Wear **empire waist dresses** with ruching at the bust or **halter dresses** in fluid, mid-weight fabrics that graze over your hips.	Wear **dark colored bottoms**— don't underestimate the slimming properties of black, charcoal, dark brown, navy, and dark green. Choose **straight-leg** or **boot cut jeans** that subtly balance your hips from below. On casual days, try **drawstring straight-leg pants,** such as yoga pants in heavy matte jersey, which fall with ease over your hips without adding volume to your butt.

SKIRTS

Choose **simple flared skirts** hemmed at knee length that drape with ease over your hips and show off your legs. Or choose **A-line cuts** with small or no waistband that flow easily over your hips and keep your silhouette looking defined. Or consider **straight skirts** with a button-front closure to draw the eyes to the center of your skirt and away from your hips.

COATS & JACKETS	JEWELRY & ACCESSORIES	SHOES
Wear a **cap-sleeved jacket** over a feminine camisole or a cardigan sweater over a tailored shirt to add more depth to your torso. Wear blazers in **structured fabrics** such as leather, denim, suede, tweed, or velvet to form a strong shoulder and add texture.	Wear **colorful beads** or a **medium pendant** that falls to the top of your cleavage and attracts attention to your upper body. Carry a **medium-sized purse** or **clutch** that hits under your arm and adds volume where you need it.	Wear shoes in bright colors and patterns, or with interesting details such as **peep toes, cutouts,** and **bows,** which don't distract from your height. Or wear classic **ballet flats** with flared or circle skirts.

FIGURE 10.3.1
You, only sexier.

WHAT NOT TO WEAR

Really. I mean it.

TOPS

Steer clear of **high crew neck tops** or **raglan styles,** which narrow your shoulders and make you look bottom heavy. Don't wear **wide-set halter tops** that cover your chest area, as they'll accentuate your bottom half. Avoid tops or sweaters that hit at your hips. Avoid **clingy tops** or **plunging V-necks** paired with dainty strap tops, that reveal how much smaller you are on top.

DRESSES

Don't wear dresses that balloon out from the waist in stiff, heavy fabrics and make you look like a tall woman in a tiny tutu. Avoid **long, floor-length dresses** that hide your legs entirely and make you seem big on the bottom. Don't wear **boxy, loose-fitting shift dresses** with no defined waist, as this will make you appear shapeless instead of sexy.

PANTS & JEANS

Avoid **khaki-colored cargo pants** with big pockets at the hips and thighs, adding unwanted weight there. Avoid prints, stripes, and shiny or textured fabric such as velour or terry cloth, all of which add unwanted volume to your hips, thighs, and bottom. Don't wear **tapered skinny jeans** or **Capris** that make your hips look wider.

SKIRTS

Avoid **bold patterns** or **horizontal details** on your skirts, which bring the eye down to your hips. Don't wear fitted miniskirts that accentuate your hips without balancing them from below. On the other hand, avoid **ankle-length skirts** that pull the eye down, making you look heavy. Avoid **full circle skirts** in thick fabrics that bell out, adding unwanted volume at your hips.

SHOES

Don't wear **chunky heels,** which will look too big for your medium frame. If you're on the tall end of the scale, avoid **pointy-toed stilettos** that will make you look too tall and vampy.

COATS & JACKETS

Avoid **flap pockets** at the hip of your blazers that add unwanted volume there. Also, don't choose jackets that hit at the mid-hip. Avoid **soft, flimsy fabrics** such as linen or jersey that don't hold up structure on your shoulders, making them seem narrow compared to your hips.

JEWELRY & ACCESSORIES

Avoid **tiny or dainty earrings** and very **delicate chain necklaces;** these will only emphasize how much smaller you are on top than you are on the bottom. Don't carry long-handled handbags that fall at the hip and draw attention to your widest area.

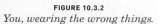

FIGURE 10.3.2
You, wearing the wrong things.

THE NEW YOU

Three ways to put your dress-sexy rules into play.

CASUAL	CAREER	FORMAL

The empire cut of the coral blouse adds volume at the bust area. The contrasting fabric along the wide-set scoop neck makes your shoulders look wider; the puffed sleeves do the same. The boot cut jean adds subtle volume below the knees, balancing your hips from below. The peep-toe coral heels help add depth to your tall frame.

The bow at the neck of this blouse adds volume to your torso, balancing your wide hips. The shawl collar jacket widens your shoulders. The layering and light colors at the torso both work to add volume to your top half. The flowing semi-circle skirt emphasizes your small waist and grazes your hips.

The high neck and kimono sleeve on this black dress adds volume to your shoulders and arms, to balance your wider hips. But the V-shape allows for some skin to show, drawing the eye up to your face. The flared skirt of the dress grazes your hips, enhancing your small waist.

YOUR ONE FASHION MUST-HAVE: *a scoop neck top*

A wide-set scoop neck top that hits far on each shoulder while showing off your collarbone will perfectly balance your curvy hips. Choose one in a textured pattern or bright fabric to bring more attention to your torso, where you want it.

TALL
MEDIUM
HOURGLASS

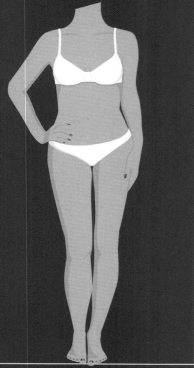

YOU

You are **TALL**.
[5'8" OR MORE]

You are **MEDIUM** weight.
[BETWEEN 135 AND 190 LBS.]

Your body forms an
HOURGLASS
as your shoulders are the
same width as your hips, with
a tiny waist in between.

You have broad shoulders
and a shapely bust. Your
hips and butt are curvy. Your
waist is small and defined.

YOUR BLESSING

You were born with a great body with curves in all the right places. You have beautiful, broad shoulders. If you have a shapely bust, you can use it to show some cleavage if you want. You also have shapely hips, a round butt, and womanly thighs. Overall, you have all the curves of a sexy silhouette. I think of you as a tall Playboy bunny. Don't worry, that doesn't mean you have to (or should) dress like one! Still, I hope you feel good knowing that your figure is similar to the most iconically sexy women of recent years. Your other blessing? You're tall. That means that the medium-sized curves you have look just right on your frame. Those broad shoulders and long legs of yours keep your shape looking long, lean, and perfectly proportional. Your only job is to keep your body balanced and show off the figure you already have.

YOUR CURSE

As a TALL, MEDIUM HOURGLASS, you already possess a balanced, curvy body, which is the definition of sexy. Still, if you're not careful to accentuate your waistline or wear the right types of clothes, it's easy for you to tip the balance and make your silhouette seem larger on top or larger on the bottom. You need to focus on that balance every single day. Your other curse? If you're a very tall woman, you may feel self-conscious wearing heels because they will make you even taller than everyone else—including your date. Also, because of your height, you may find that pants and sleeves run short on you, which can make for a frustrating shopping experience.

YOUR CELEBRITY BODY STAND-IN: *Kate Winslet*

WHAT TO WEAR

*Your fashion challenge is to keep your broad shoulders
and wide hips balanced, while defining your waist.*

TOPS

Pick **scoop neck** and **V-neck tops** with straps that sit in the center
of each shoulder. Try **wrap tops, surplice tops,** or **fitted sweaters**
which hug your slim waist. Wear dress shirts, and unbutton the
top two or three buttons to create a flattering V-neck. If you're
very tall, let a contrasting colored shirt peek out of a sweater or
blazer to "color block" and break up your height.

DRESSES

Wear **fitted sheaths** or **corset
dresses** in gorgeous colors to
show off your hourglass curves.
Wear **wrap dresses** that tie in
at your small waist; if you're very
tall with a slender neck, layer
a camisole underneath to break
up your vertical line. Hem
dresses just above your knee to
show a little leg, but not too much.

SKIRTS

Wear **pencil skirts, tulip skirts,
trumpet skirts,** or **godet
skirts** with just a slight flare at
the bottom, all of which allow
you to show off your hourglass figure
without adding pouf to your hips.
Wear **A-line skirts** that smooth over
your hips steadily. Hem your
skirts at or below your knee; any
shorter and you might look
top-heavy on your long legs.

PANTS & JEANS

Choose **mid-rise jeans,** rather than low-rise jeans, which
will create a smoother line from your waist through your
hips. Wear **straight-leg pants** and **men's cut trousers;** the
straight cut below the knee will balance your hips. Or
wear **boot cuts with a slight flare;** with your height, you can
handle widening the base of your legs a bit for added curves.

COATS & JACKETS

Wear blazers with
princess seams that
mimic your hourglass
shape. Or wear
peplum jackets,
which cinch in at your
waist then flare out
toward your hips.
Try a **basic trench** that
defines your strong
shoulders, belts at the
waist, then tapers
out in a flattering A-line.

JEWELRY & ACCESSORIES

Wear **bold neck-
laces** with a single
focal point—such as
a charm, a colored
stone, a diamond, or
a locket—to bring the
eyes up to your face.
Try **feminine scarves**
with an open-neck top
that hangs down your
torso to draw the
eye toward your face.

SHOES

Wear **knee-high boots**
over skinny jeans,
paired with fitted tops,
for a balanced
look. Choose **wedges,
round-toed heels,
peep-toes,** or shoes
with **ankle straps,**
as your tall, thin legs
can handle the detail.

FIGURE 10.4.1
You, only sexier.

WHAT NOT TO WEAR

Really. I mean it.

TOPS

Don't wear **long tunics** that cover up your sexy, defined waist. Avoid tops with pockets or gathers at the bustline, or with detailing at the shoulders unless you balance the added volume on the bottom with a flared skirt. Don't wear **crew necks** or **raglan shirts,** and don't button your dress shirts all the way up without showing a bit of skin there to match your long look.

DRESSES

Avoid **empire dresses** that flow right over your waist without defining it. Don't cover your shape with **boxy shift dresses.** Avoid bunchy fabric or ruching at the waist of your dress. Also, avoid detailing around the hip of your dress unless you're balancing it with poufy or flouncy sleeves. Don't wear dresses in thick, ungiving fabric.

SKIRTS

Steer clear of **horizontal stripes** on your skirts, which will make your hips look disproportionately bigger. Avoid **circle skirts** and **pleated skirts** that add too much volume to your bottom half. Don't wear large prints without widening your top half in balance. Don't wear skirts in **thick fabrics** that disguise your hourglass curves.

PANTS & JEANS

Skip the **low-rise jeans,** which hit at the widest point on your hips, unless you're balancing them with more volume on your top half. Don't wear **flared pants, wide-leg pants,** and **palazzo pants** that disguise your curvy figure. Avoid **distressing or whiskering** on the thighs of your jeans, which will make your thighs and hip area appear wider than they are.

SHOES

If you're very tall, avoid **pointy-toed 3" stilettos,** which will make you look too tall. Don't wear **chunky heels** or **square toed-shoes,** which will look heavy on your slender legs.

COATS & JACKETS

Don't wear **boxy blazers** with pockets at your waist or hips widening those areas. Avoid **long, hip-length jackets** that ignore your waistline. Don't wear **ankle-length coats.** Equally, don't wear **cropped jackets** or **boleros** that seem out of proportion with your long frame.

JEWELRY & ACCESSORIES

Don't wear **hip belts** that will make you seem bottom-heavy. Avoid **small accessories,** such as tiny stud earrings, dainty necklaces, and tiny clutches that will seem out of proportion to your tall frame. Don't carry handbags that hit at your waist and widen the area you're trying to reveal.

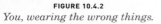

FIGURE 10.4.2
You, wearing the wrong things.

THE NEW YOU

Three ways to put your dress-sexy rules into play.

CASUAL

The low neck on this bright T-shirt draws attention to your chest and upper body. The cap sleeve helps broaden your shoulders so that your waist looks smaller in comparison. The dark stovepipe jeans hug your curvy hips and thighs. The open-toed heels add to your look without taking away from your height.

CAREER

The tailored dress shirt under the skirt suit fit your feminine, curvy silhouette. The monochromatic gray skirt suit keep your look long. The belt reveals your sexy waist. The pretty red wedge heel helps break up your tall look just enough to keep you balanced and feminine overall.

FORMAL

The wide-set halter dress shows off skin at your shoulders to bring the eye up. The slightly clingy fabric shows off your gorgeous curves. The ankle straps on the heels add a bit of volume at the base of your frame, so your legs don't seem too long and thin.

YOUR ONE FASHION MUST-HAVE: *a black dress*

Find a form-fitting black dress that hugs your curves and emphasizes the best feature of your hourglass shape: your waist. Have it perfectly tailored for your tall figure, then dress it up or own with different jewelry, accessories, and shoes.

FITTING ROOM
11

If you're tall and
full-sized, you're in the
right place. Just
find your silhouette and
prepare to get sexy.

TALL
FULL
INVERTED TRIANGLE

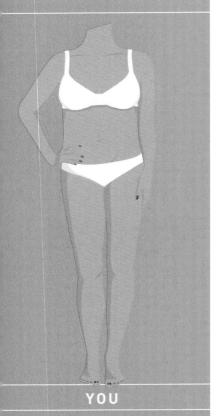

YOU

You are **TALL**.
[5'8" OR MORE]

You are **FULL**-sized.
[BETWEEN 175 AND 230 LBS.]

Your body forms an
INVERTED TRIANGLE
as your shoulders are
wider than your hips.

You have wide shoulders. Your hips
are not as wide as your shoulders.
Your legs and butt, though full,
are not as wide as your shoulders.

YOUR BLESSING

You have a lot to be proud of! First, you're tall. And your height also makes you appear slimmer, so your curves look even better on you. You have broad shoulders that make you seem tall and confident at first glance, as they draw all eyes up toward your face. And if you also have curves in your chest, you can create as much as cleavage as you want, when you want. Your other blessing? You have smaller hips and a smaller butt compared to the width of your shoulders. That means you can play up your bottom half with interesting colors, patterns, and styles. Finally, you're lucky because beneath those narrow hips of yours are a pair of terrific legs! And though you have a full-size frame, showing off those legs is a fabulous tool you can use to make your figure appear even longer and leaner.

YOUR CURSE

As a TALL, FULL, INVERTED TRIANGLE, you have what's called a high balance, which means the visual line of your silhouette reaches its broadest point at your shoulders. Also, your hips and butt lack the curves that are essential in creating a sexy silhouette. Overall, your full-sized figure can appear top-heavy if you choose the wrong clothes. You also need to be careful in choosing clothes that keep you looking long and lean. Your other curse? It can be hard to shop for your figure. First, because your top and bottom half are different widths, that can translate into needing different sizes. And, because you're so tall, pants and sleeves can run short on you. Ill-fitting, too-short pants and sleeves aren't sexy.

YOUR CELEBRITY BODY STAND-IN: *Aretha Franklin*

WHAT TO WEAR

Your fashion challenge is to narrow your shoulders, to widen your hips so they match your broad shoulders, and to reveal more of your waist. This will turn your top-heavy frame into a perfectly balanced hourglass.

COATS & JACKETS

Wear jackets with minimal shoulder detailing that button quite close to the neck, such as a **mandarin collar** or a **boxy Chanel-cut jacket.** Pick jackets that hit at the hip, or with horizontal details there to add necessary volume. Consider **peplum jackets** or **corseted blazers,** both of which create the illusion of curvier hips.

TOPS

Choose **shallow V-necks, U-necks,** or **wrap tops** that reveal some skin in your chest area—not too much skin, as you have a good deal up top. Layer camisoles underneath cardigans and blazers to draw attention to the center of your body and make you appear slimmer. Wear **similar tonal colors** on your top and your bottom to elongate your look and make you appear slimmer.

DRESSES

Choose dresses with **wide straps** that are proportional to your wide shoulders; thin, dainty straps will make your shoulders look bulky in comparison. Wear **A-line** or **corseted dresses** that curve in at the waist, then gently taper out over your bottom half. Choose **medium prints** for your dresses, proportional to your tall frame.

PANTS & JEANS

Choose **straight-leg** or subtle **boot cut jeans** to keep your figure looking tall and slim. Pick jeans with **full-size back pockets** that are proportional to your full frame; they will make your bottom look curvier to balance your top half. Choose pants that add volume to your hips, such as **palazzo pants** or **men's trousers** with side pockets at the hips.

SKIRTS

Wear **full gored skirts, semi-circle skirts,** or other **flared skirts** that add volume at the hips. Choose skirts in **feminine patterns** or **lighter tones** to bring up your bottom half. Hem your skirts at or just below your knee; showing too much of your long legs will make your body look top-heavy.

JEWELRY & ACCESSORIES

Choose necklaces with **full-size pendants or charms,** in scale with your full-size frame, that bring the focus toward your chest. Pick handbags that fall at your hip to add weight there. Wear **belts, sashes,** and **ties** at your waist to draw the eye to your center.

SHOES

Choose **pointy-toed heels** in the same tone or color as your outfit. Even a small **kitten heel** will help lengthen your overall figure.

FIGURE 11.1.1
You, only sexier.

WHAT NOT TO WEAR

Really. I mean it.

COATS & JACKETS

Avoid **horizontal details** at the tops of your jackets and blazers, including stripes, pockets, epaulets, shoulder pads, and wide portrait collars that accentuate your shoulders. On the other hand, avoid jackets with **tiny lapels,** making your shoulders seem larger in comparison. Steer clear of **double-breasted blazers** and **pea coats,** which make you look top-heavy.

TOPS

Don't cover up your top half with **baggy tops, crew necks,** or **boatnecks,** which will make your shoulders seem wider; if you have big breasts, they can also create a "uniboob" effect. Avoid too-tight tops, which will cling to your large breasts and make you appear heavier. Also avoid **dainty, spaghetti straps,** which will make your shoulders seem disproportionately larger.

DRESSES

Don't wear **tiny halters, sleeveless dresses,** and **strapless dresses** that will make you look thicker on top. Avoid ankle-length dresses that cover up your thin legs entirely. Don't wear **boxy shift dresses** unless they cinch in at the waist in some way. Steer clear of dresses with **puffed sleeves** or **kimono sleeves** that add too much volume on top.

PANTS & JEANS

Though you want to add volume at your hips, avoid **low-rise jeans,** which at your full-size weight, will reveal too many curves. Don't wear **stretchy, tight,** or **tapered pants** that accentuate how small you are on the bottom; this will make your top look larger in comparison.

SHOES

Don't wear **dainty, strappy stilettos** that will look out of scale with your tall, full-sized body. Avoid **chunky heels** or **slip-on mules** that will make your legs seem wide.

SKIRTS

Avoid **fitted pencil skirts** that accentuate your small hips. Don't wear **ankle-length skirts,** which cover up your calves and will make you look heavier. Don't wear **stiff or poufy skirts** that bell out from your waist, adding too much weight there.

JEWELRY & ACCESSORIES

Avoid **long, delicate necklace** strands that aren't in scale with your tall, full-sized body. Don't carry a purse that sits under your arm and adds more width to your top half. Avoid **bows** or **scarves around your neck** that add too much volume to your top half.

FIGURE 11.1.2
You, wearing the wrong things.

THE NEW YOU

Three ways to put your dress-sexy rules into play.

CASUAL	**CAREER**	**FORMAL**
The square neck with a V at the base draws the eye in toward your chest and away from your shoulders. The belt pulls in your true waist. The strong boot cut jean adds volume to the bottom of your legs, making your hips seem wider, to match your shoulders.	The layering of the corseted blazer over the dress helps draw the eye in and way from your wide shoulders. The pockets at the bottom of the blazer add a touch of volume where you need it. The flowing gored skirt adds fullness to your hips.	The rounded V-neck draws the eye in toward your chest. The pretty bow at the waist of the dress cinches your natural waist, while the ribbon falls toward the ground, creating a vertical element to slim you. The semi-circle skirt in a soft, flowing fabric, adds volume at your hips.

YOUR ONE FASHION MUST-HAVE: *a full skirt*

**Choose a full, pretty skirt with feminine details, such as subtle chiffon
ruffles, a fluted hem, or a pretty floral pattern. It will create volume at your hips
where you need it and soften up your overall look.**

TALL
FULL
RECTANGLE

YOU

You are **TALL**.
[5'8" OR MORE]

You are **FULL**-sized.
[BETWEEN 175 AND 230 LBS.]

Your body forms a
RECTANGLE
as your shoulders are the
same width as your hips.

You have broad shoulders.
You have equally wide hips.
Your waist is wide and undefined.

YOUR BLESSING

You were born with everything you need to create a sexy silhouette. Your full figure offers plenty to work with when it comes to looking sexy. First, you're tall, which means that many imperfections on your body can be smoothed out by your long look. And the longer you keep yourself when you dress, the leaner you'll look. Your other blessing? You have nice legs in proportion to your body. Because you're tall, those legs of yours can really make an entrance if you show them off a bit. (But remember, a little goes a long way.) Finally, your figure is very nicely balanced, because the weight you carry on top is matched by the width of the curves in your hips. Your goal when getting dressed is to keep balanced, and your stunning height will help you do the rest.

YOUR CURSE

As a TALL, FULL RECTANGLE, your figure is missing a small, defined waist. That gives your silhouette a slightly boxy and masculine shape if you don't wear clothes that show off your curves in the right way. You also carry more weight in your shoulders and middle than you do in your legs and bottom. For this reason, it may be hard to find clothes that fit you, as most clothes are made for women with curvier hips and butts, and smaller waists. Your other curse? You may find that pants and sleeves often run short on your tall frame. While this may be okay with trousers or blazer jackets, which usually allow you to take out the seam a bit, you may have trouble finding jeans that fit your long, full frame.

YOUR CELEBRITY BODY STAND-IN: *Queen Latifah*

WHAT TO WEAR

Your fashion challenge is to define a waist where there isn't one by widening your shoulders and hips so your waist looks smaller in comparison. You also want to look slimmer overall.

DRESSES

Wear **empire dresses** that hug your bust and flow out, creating the illusion of a high, small waist. Pick dresses with **gored or flared skirts** that make your waist look smaller. Or choose **wrap dresses** or **surplice dresses** that tie in at the waist. Hem your dresses at the knee to reveal your gorgeous legs, which slims your figure.

TOPS

Wear **wrap tops, surplices, and V-neck tops and sweaters** to create a sexy triangle line at your chest, making you seem slimmer. Try **light layering:** Slip on camisole tops under jackets to bring attention to your chest area while still holding in your assets; the layering will also help smooth out any lumps and bulges on your torso.

SKIRTS

Wear **flared skirts** or **gored skirts** that hug your waist, then flow out slightly to create the illusion of curvy hips and a curvy bottom. Or wear an **A-line skirt** in a soft, forgiving fabric that tapers out from your waist. Aim for **mono-chromatic skirts and tops.** Top skirts with a cute cropped jacket to break up your height and create the illusion of a waist.

PANTS & JEANS

Wear **straight-leg** or **subtle boot cut pants** and jeans that elongate and slim your frame. Pick pants with detailing around the hip area, and **angled or diagonal pockets** that create the illusion of curves at your hips. Also, consider **cuffed trousers,** which your tall height can carry well.

COATS & JACKETS

If you have large arms, wear light jackets to cover them; be sure they have subtle structure in the shoulders to make your waist seem smaller in comparison. Try **princess seam jackets** that curve in at the waist or **peplum jackets** that flare out toward your hips.

JEWELRY & ACCESSORIES

Carry a handbag that hits at the hips to add a bit of volume there. Wear **beaded necklaces** or **large, dangling earrings** that are in scale with your full-sized figure and draw attention to your chest and face. Put on **wide, dark corsets** or belts that create the illusion that you have a waist.

SHOES

Wear **moderately high to high heels,** which will make your thin calves appear more shapely. Choose shoes with interesting details such as **peep toes, cut-away arches, and bows** to add a feminine touch to your figure; these shoes look especially good under flared skirts.

FIGURE 11.2.1
You, only sexier.

257

WHAT NOT TO WEAR

Really. I mean it.

DRESSES

Avoid **long, ankle-length dresses** that pull down the curves you do have and make you look heavier overall. Don't wear **halters** that will make your shoulders appear to bulge around the fabric. Avoid thin fabrics that can be light and clingy around your middle. Don't wear **boxy shift dresses** that fall straight to the hem without implying a waistline.

TOPS

Avoid **sleeveless tops** that cut off at the edge of your shoulder and make your arms seem thicker. Don't wear **baggy tops, peasant tops,** or **thick sweaters** to cover up your torso, which will only make you look heavier. Avoid **crew necks, high boatnecks,** and **raglan tops** that cover up the skin at your chest and make you look boxy.

SKIRTS

Avoid fitted **pencil skirts** that minimize your lower half and emphasize your straight hips. Don't wear **tiny print patterns** on your skirts, which will seem out of scale on your full-sized frame. Avoid **prairie skirts** or skirts with lots of tiers and ruffles that add unnecessary weight to your frame.

PANTS & JEANS

Don't wear **leggings, stovepipe pants,** or **Capris** that follow the line of your smaller legs and will make you appear top-heavy. On the other hand, avoid **light-colored pants** or **cargo pants** that make your figure look heavier overall.

COATS & JACKET

Avoid **double-breasted blazers** and **pea coats,** which will make your torso look wider. Steer clear of **cropped jackets** that make your legs seem too long in comparison. Also, steer clear of **long, straight coats** that don't reveal your waist.

JEWELRY & ACCESSORIES

Don't wear **small, dainty jewelry** such as tiny diamond studs that will be dwarfed by your full-size frame. Avoid belts at your waist, which only accentuate your undefined middle. Don't carry **boxy handbags** that hit at your waist, widening your torso there.

SHOES

Steer clear of **square-toed shoes, slip-on mules,** and **chunky heels** that underscore your boxy frame. Avoid too-tall stilettos which will make you look a bit too tall.

FIGURE 11.2.2
You, wearing the wrong things.

THE NEW YOU

Three ways to put your dress-sexy rules into play.

CASUAL

The feminine white dress shirt creates a flattering V-neck at your chest. The beaded necklace draws the eye to the center of your body. The three-quarter-length sleeve reveals only the thinnest part of your arms. The straight-leg, trouser-cut jean adds volume on your bottom half so that your legs don't seem to thin beneath your body.

CAREER

The surplice top creates a V-neck shape that points toward your waist. The pretty detailing on the shoulders and puffed sleeves widen your top half, making your waist look smaller. The flowing semi-circle skirt adds volume to your hips and thighs. The skirt is hemmed to show a bit of your sexy legs.

FORMAL

The wide-set V-neck of this dress helps stretch your shoulder line and show more skin at your chest. The feminine detailing at the neck combined with the necklace soften your look overall. The subtle flare of the skirt adds the illusion of curvy hips on your frame.

YOUR ONE FASHION MUST-HAVE: *an empire dress*

Choose one with feminine details such as beading, ruching, or pretty patterns around the bust, neck, and shoulders. This dress creates the illusion that you have a high, slim waist, then flows out over your hips in a pretty flare.

TALL
FULL
TRIANGLE

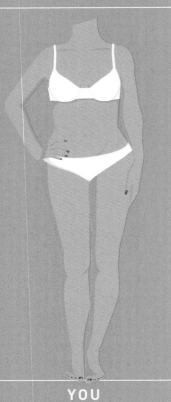

YOU

You are **TALL**.
[5'8" OR MORE]

You are **FULL**-sized.
[BETWEEN 175 AND 230 LBS.]

Your body forms a
TRIANGLE
as your hips are broader
than your shoulders.

You have a smaller upper
body than lower body. Your hips
are wide-set and curvy.
You have a super shapely bottom.

YOUR BLESSING

Lucky you. You have a lots of gorgeous features on your figure! You have a nice, round bottom. You also have a gorgeous neck and collarbone. Initially, when people meet you, your small upper body makes you appear slimmer. Your small torso also makes it easier for you to find shirts and dresses that fit your top half. Your other blessing? You're tall. Even though you have some full-size pounds on your frame, your height is always there to pull you up and make you seem long and lean. When you walk down the street, your stunning stature combined with your feminine curves send off a seriously sexy vibe. All you need to do is learn how to dress to flatter your figure so that people will notice you, not just your curves.

YOUR CURSE

As a TALL, FULL TRIANGLE, you have what's called a low balance. This just means that the visual line of your silhouette reaches its broadest point at your hips. For this reason, you can appear bottom-heavy if you choose the wrong clothes. Yes, your height does help lift and lengthen your figure, but it is vital you find pants that downplay your full-sized lower half so that you look more balanced overall. Your other curse? Your tall frame means that pants and jacket sleeves often come up short on you. This isn't as big an issue when it comes to tailored trousers and blazers, which usually have extra fabric at the hems. But you can't make jeans or pretty tops longer. So it will take you extra effort to find styles you like in the lengths you need.

YOUR CELEBRITY BODY STAND-IN: *Trisha Yearwood*

WHAT TO WEAR

*Your fashion challenge is to downplay your oversized lower
half and bring out your shoulders so it balances
with your bottom. You also want to look slimmer overall.*

TOPS

Tailored dress shirts with clean vertical seams will help
diminish the fullness of your figure. Wear shirts with
horizontal details such as **puffed sleeves, kimono sleeves,**
or **flutter sleeves** that will add pretty volume to your torso.
Choose **V-neck, U-neck,** and **boatneck tops** that reveal
your collarbone and show some skin at your neck.

DRESSES

Wear **monochromatic dresses**
in dark colors such as charcoal, navy,
black, and brown to create a long,
lean vertical line. Choose dresses with
cap sleeves or **kimono sleeves** to
add volume at your shoulders. Wear
dresses topped with **cropped jackets**
or **boleros** that add structure to
your shoulders while disguising
the thickest part of your arms.

SKIRTS

Wear **dark-colored skirts**—
again, think charcoal, navy, black,
and brown—to help diminish your
hips. Choose **lightly flared gored
skirts, godet skirts,** or **A-line skirts**
that flow easily over your hips
without clinging. Try skirts detailed
with a button-front closure to create
a vertical effect on your bottom
half and make you seem thinner.

PANTS & JEANS

Wear **flat-front, straight-leg trousers** with a generous,
fluid fit through the hips and thighs. Or wear **subtly flared
boot cut pants** to balance out your shapely thighs and hips
from below. Choose mid-rise jeans that start just above the
widest part of your hips. Stick with **dark-colored pants**
and **dark washed denims** to minimize your lower half.

COATS & JACKETS

Choose **princess
seams** or **peplum
jackets** with shawl
collars or wide lapels;
wear these over
dresses for a
flattering layering
effect that balances
out your bottom half.
Try **A-line coats**
in bright colors with
slim, flared hems.

JEWELRY & ACCESSORIES

Wear a **colorful
pendant** or a bold
necklace that attracts
attention to your chest.
Or choose **bold
chandelier earrings**
to draw the eye up
from your bottom
half. Carry a **medium-
sized hobo bag**—in
scale with your full-
sized frame—that
rests under your arm.

SHOES

Wear a **substantial
pump** or a **wedge
heel** with pants
and jeans. At the very
least, try a **small
kitten heel;** even
the slightest lift
will help make you
look slimmer.

FIGURE 11.3.1
You, only sexier.

WHAT NOT TO WEAR

Really. I mean it.

TOPS

Avoid **sleeveless tops** or **halter tops** that make your top half look smaller in relation to your hips. Steer clear of tops that have **horizontal detailing** at your hips, or hit at the hips, accentuating the widest part of your figure. Don't wear **baggy tunic tops** that hide your waist and make your torso look heavy.

DRESSES

Don't wear **boxy, drop-waist dresses** that lack a defined waist. Avoid **long, ankle-length dresses** that make you look bottom-heavy. Don't wear **full circle dresses** that balloon out from the waist and hit above the knee. Steer clear of **shiny, stiff fabrics** such as taffeta and iridescent fabrics that add too much volume to your hips.

PANTS & JEANS

Don't wear **wide-leg** or **flared pants,** which bring the eye to the ground and make your tall frame look wider. At the same time, steer clear of **tapered jeans** that will make your hips look even wider in comparison. Avoid **big, baggy pockets** on the sides of pants at all costs—**light-colored cargo pants** are your enemy!

SKIRTS

Steer clear of **miniskirts** that reveal too much of your full legs. Don't wear **prairie skirts** or **poufy circle skirts** that add unwanted volume to your hip area. At the same time, don't wear **tulip skirts** that taper in below the hips before flaring out. Avoid **shiny fabrics, busy patterns, stripes,** or **ruffles** on your bottom half that will draw unwanted attention to your wide hips.

SHOES

Don't wear **ankle straps** or **ankle boots** that will make your legs look wide and heavy. Avoid **too-tall, too-pointy stilettos** that will make you look too tall.

COATS & JACKETS

Don't wear jackets that hit at the mid-hip, at the broadest point on your body. Avoid blazers with **narrow, weak shoulders.** Steer clear of long coats in **bright fabrics** or **shiny leathers** that appear to add volume to your hips.

JEWELRY & ACCESSORIES

Don't carry purses that are too small in relation to your figure. Avoid **long-handled handbags** that fall at the hip and draw attention to your widest area. Avoid **tiny stud earrings** and delicate chain necklaces that emphasize your small torso.

FIGURE 11.3.2
You, wearing the wrong things.

THE NEW YOU

Three ways to put your dress-sexy rules into play.

CASUAL	CAREER	FORMAL

CASUAL

The boatneck top broadens your shoulder line. The short-sleeve top hitting at your bustline makes your torso look a bit wider to match your hips. The large pendant attracts attention to your chest. The straight-leg jean adds volume to the bottom half of your legs, to balance your hips.

CAREER

The shawl collar jacket draws the eye out to your shoulders. The peplum seams in the jacket curve in at your waist, then smooth the transition to your curvy hips. The flared skirt balances your hips from below.

FORMAL

The cap-sleeved bolero jacket over the dress adds volume to your torso, to match your hips. The wide, low V-neck helps widen your shoulders, while revealing skin at your chest, making you look slimmer. The skirt of the dress flows fully over your full hips and butt.

YOUR ONE FASHION MUST-HAVE: *a jacket*

A jacket or blazer with small shoulder pads, puffed-shoulders, or even military-style epaulets will broaden your shoulders to balance out your hips. Choose one that hits above the widest point on your hips so you don't add too much volume there.

TALL
FULL
HOURGLASS

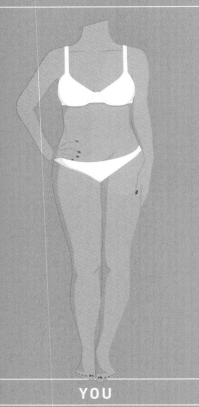

YOU

You are **TALL**.
[5'8" OR MORE]

You are **FULL**-sized.
[BETWEEN 175 AND 230 LBS.]

Your body forms an
HOURGLASS
as your shoulders are the
same width as your hips, with
a defined waist in between.

You have broad shoulders and a
shapely bust. Your hips and butt are
curvy. Your waist is defined.

YOUR BLESSING

Lucky you. You were born with great curves shaped in an hourglass silhouette! It's the ultimate essence of sexy. You have a gorgeous, full bottom. You have beautiful, broad shoulders. And if you have a shapely bust, you can also show off some cleavage (when you want to, of course). Basically, you have a perfectly balanced body. Your other blessing? You also have a defined waist. What that means is that no matter how big your chest is and no matter how big your hips feel, that curved, defined waist is always your fallback to looking sexy. With a silhouette as balanced as yours, you actually look smaller than the numbers on your clothing say you are. You also have your height to thank for that. Because of your tall, stunning stature, you have the power to dress in clothes that will make you look longer—and longer means leaner.

YOUR CURSE

As a TALL, FULL HOURGLASS, your biggest curse is trying to find clothes that fit your body properly. First, because you're full-sized, you may have to hit specialty stores or special sections in department stores to find the styles you want in the sizes you need. Your other curse? Because you're so tall, many pants and sleeves fall short on you. Tailored dress trousers and blazers usually allow for more height with extra fabric that can be let out, but buying jeans, tops, or sweaters that fit your tall frame may be harder. Finally, you may feel self-conscious wearing high heels—especially when they make you taller than everyone else in the room.

YOUR CELEBRITY BODY STAND-IN: *Emme*

WHAT TO WEAR

Your fashion challenge is to keep your broad shoulders and wide hips balanced, while defining your waist. You also want to look slimmer overall.

DRESSES

Choose **V-neck** or **scoop neck dresses,** or **shirt-dresses** that reveal a triangle of skin at your chest. Pick **wrap dresses** or **surplices** that cinch at your waist or **A-line dresses** with a belt that do the same. Wear **single-color, dark dresses** that create one long vertical line from head to toe, making you look leaner. Choose **flowing fabrics** that graze easily over your curves.

TOPS

Wear **wrap tops** and **surplice tops,** which follow your hourglass curves and reveal your waist. Try light layering by wearing **camisole tops** under wrap sweaters and jackets; this draws attention there while still holding in your full-sized assets. Wear **tailored shirts** with vertical seams, which will help diminish the fullness of your figure; the V-neck created by opening two buttons will point toward your defined waist.

SKIRTS

Wear **A-line skirts, gored skirts, godet skirts, tulip skirts,** or **semi-circle skirts** that add flow over your curvy hips with steady volume. Choose **drapey fabrics** that gently flow over your curves. Hem your skirts at or just below your knee to show off a bit of your long legs (just keep in mind that showing too much leg can make you seem larger).

PANTS & JEANS

Wear **mid-rise jeans,** which hit just above your hips and create a smooth line from your waist to your hips without adding bulk. Choose **dark-colored straight-leg pants** to slim you down. Pick pants with **full-sized back pockets,** proportional to your body.

COATS & JACKETS

Choose jackets with **princess seams** or **peplum jackets** that curve in at your waist. Pick a **basic trench coat** that follows your hourglass curves, then tapers out in an A-line silhouette. Choose coats that hit at your knee or below; shorter or longer coats will look out of proportion on your frame.

JEWELRY & ACCESSORIES

Wear **bold, large necklaces** that feature a single focal point— such as a **pendant necklace** that falls in a V-shape. Consider **scarves** that tie around your neck and hang down your torso a bit to draw the eye up your face, but still showing a peek of skin at your chest.

SHOES

Wear a **pointy-toed, mid- or high-heeled shoe** to keep you looking slim. For something more comfortable, try a **wedge heel** with jeans. At the very least, try a **kitten heel** for a slight, slimming lift.

FIGURE 11.4.1
You, only sexier.

WHAT NOT TO WEAR

Really. I mean it.

DRESSES

Avoid **drop-waist dresses,** or dresses with horizontal details or belts at the hip, instead of your natural waist. Don't wear stretchy **Lycra®-based fabrics** that will buckle and gather in unflattering places, making you look heavier. Avoid **boxy, shift dresses** that turn your hourglass figure into in oval. Don't wear **long, ankle-length dresses** that drag your curves down.

TOPS

Don't wear **oversized tunics and baggy tops** to try and cover up your figure; this will actually make you look larger. If you have large breasts, avoid **crew necks, raglan tops,** and **turtlenecks,** which can create a dreaded "uniboob" and make you appear top-heavy. Don't wear long tops that hit at your hips or thighs without implying a defined waistline.

SKIRTS

Avoid skirts that bell out from your hips and add unwanted volume to your hip area. Don't wear **straight pencil skirts** that flatten the sexy curve from your waist to your hips. Steer clear of **shiny fabrics and busy patterns or stripes** on your bottom half, which will draw unwanted attention to your hips.

PANTS & JEANS

Steer clear of **low-rise jeans** as a full-sized woman. Avoid **light-colored pants,** as this can make you appear bottom-heavy. Avoid **distressing or whiskering** on the thighs of your jeans, which will make both areas look wider. Don't wear **Capris** that make your hips look larger than they are.

COATS & JACKET

Don't wear **double-breasted jackets** and **pea coats** that square off your curved torso and cover up your defined waist. Avoid jackets with **front or bulky side pockets** that widen your hip area. Don't wear **flimsy fabric blazers** that lack a structure around your shoulders and waist.

JEWELRY & ACCESSORIES

Avoid **hip belts,** which will make you seem bottom-heavy. Don't wear **small accessories,** such as tiny stud earrings, dainty necklaces, and tiny clutches that will seem out of proportion to your tall frame. Avoid **flowers, bows, and ruffles** that add unnecessary weight to your silhouette.

SHOES

Don't wear shoes with **ankle straps** or **wedge heels that tie** around your ankle Don't wear **square-toed shoes** that will shorten the long line of your body and make you seem shorter. Don't wear **too-tall stilettos** that will look too small for your full-size frame.

FIGURE 11.4.2
You, wearing the wrong things.

THE NEW YOU

Three ways to put your dress-sexy rules into play.

CASUAL

The V-neck of this short-sleeved top creates a flattering triangle of skin at your chest. The fabric grazes along your natural waist. The mid-rise dark denim jean hits at the low waist and hugs your curves. The straight-leg cut adds subtle volume below the knee to balance your hips.

CAREER

The monochromatic skirt suit creates a long, lean silhouette. The blazer has princess seams and a corset, emphasizing what you already have. The hem at the knee allows you to show just enough leg to keep a tall impression.

FORMAL

The top to this gown helps push up your chest while cinching your waist, emphasizing your hourglass curves. The wide straps ever-so-slightly broaden your shoulders. The skirt of the dress flows over your hips with a little bit of flare to balance your figure overall.

YOUR ONE FASHION MUST-HAVE: *a wrap dress*

A wrap dress is one of the most flattering choices for your figure. It hugs your curves from shoulders to knees, and it cinches in your natural waist—the best feature of your hourglass shape.

FITTING ROOM 12

If you're tall and plus-sized, you're in the right place. Just find your silhouette and prepare to get sexy.

TALL
PLUS
INVERTED TRIANGLE

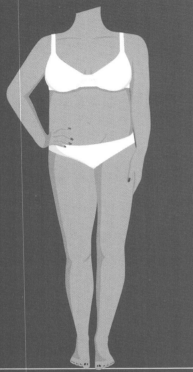

YOU

You are **TALL**.
[5'8" OR MORE]

You are **PLUS**-sized.
[OVER 205 LBS.]

Your body forms an
INVERTED TRIANGLE
as your shoulders are wider
than your hips.

You have wide shoulders.
Your hips are not as wide as your
shoulders. Your legs and butt
are not as wide as your shoulders.

YOUR BLESSING

You were born with curves galore! Your first blessing is that you're tall. Since your weight is distributed on a longer frame, you have a lot to work with when it comes to balancing your body. Your broad shoulders also make you look taller—and looking taller is your key to looking slimmer. Another blessing is that if you have breasts to play up, you can create cleavage to help create a sexy look. Your other blessing? In comparison to your top half, your legs and hips are slimmer. Though you're in the plus-size range, your smaller bottom half means you can get more creative with pants and skirts. You can also show off your legs a bit, which is always sexy. What a hot body you can have if you learn to play it up!

YOUR CURSE

As a TALL, PLUS, INVERTED TRIANGLE, you have what's called a high balance. This means that the visual line of your silhouette reaches its broadest point at your shoulders. You can appear especially top-heavy if you choose the wrong clothes. Also, if you don't dress to flatter your feminine curves, you can appear to have a masculine build. Your other curse? Because you're carrying a lot on your top half, you have a really serious bra issue. For you to look sexy, you must first find bras that support you, lift you up, and don't create extra bulges around your upper half. Finally, you might have issues when it comes to shopping for your size. You're not likely to find everything you're looking for in a department store, which means you need to shop at plus-size or custom stores. That can be limiting to your personal style.

YOUR CELEBRITY BODY STAND-IN: *Camryn Manheim*

WHAT TO WEAR

Your fashion challenge is to narrow your shoulders, to widen your hips so they match your broad shoulders, and to reveal more of your waist. You also want to look slimmer overall.

DRESSES

Wear **wrap dresses** or **surplice dresses** in mid-weight fabrics that aren't too clingy, such as matte jerseys, fine-gauge knits, and soft cottons that flow easily over your curves. Choose dresses with **short sleeves** or **three-quarter-length sleeves** with no detailing at the shoulders. Hem your dresses just below your knee to show off some leg and draw the eye to the smaller half of your body.

TOPS

Choose tops in **structured or thick fabrics** to smooth out bulges or imperfections in your middle. Wear **tailored, button-up dress shirts** with three-quarter-length sleeves; the triangle it creates will slim your torso. Wear **V-neck tops and sweaters** that show skin at your chest, which is slimming. Use light layering on top—such as a lightweight U-neck sweater over a **camisole**—to smooth out your figure.

SKIRTS

Wear **circle skirts, gored skirts,** or **godet skirts** in flowing fabrics that create subtle volume at your hips and bottom. Choose skirts with **feminine details** at the waist, such as ribbons, ruffles, beading, or colored sashes; this will help add volume where you need it, and make your figure seem softer. Choose **medium-size patterns** in scale with your plus-size frame.

PANTS & JEANS

Stick with **dark-colored pants** to help slim your figure overall. Pick pants with **front or side pockets** to add subtle volume where you need it most. Choose **straight-leg pants** to elongate your look and make you seem taller and slimmer.

COATS & JACKETS

Pick **high-stance blazers** to hold in your upper torso and chest; the V-shape formed at the first button on your chest is slimming. Wear **peplum jackets** that flare out from the waist. Choose jackets with **three-quarter-length-sleeves,** revealing the thinnest part of your arms.

JEWELRY & ACCESSORIES

Choose jewelry with **large charms** or in chunky styles, which are in scale with your plus-size frame. Wear accessories with **feminine details** such as flowery appliques, ruffles, and ribbon bows at the waist to add a soft touch to your look.

SHOES

Wear a **substantial pump** in proportion to your frame. Choose shoes in bold colors or interesting styles, such as **cut-away arches** or **peep-toe heels,** to draw attention to your lovely legs. At the very least, try a **kitten heel** to add a slight, slimming lift.

FIGURE 12.1.1
You, only sexier.

12.1

WHAT NOT TO WEAR

Really. I mean it.

DRESSES

Avoid topping your dresses with **blazers** or **boleros,** which add too much volume on top. Don't wear **straight dresses** or **short dresses** that will make you look top-heavy. Avoid dresses made of Lycra®-based stretch fabrics; as your body moves, stretchy fabric creates unflattering pockets and bulges that make you look larger than you are. Avoid **dainty spaghetti straps** or tiny halter straps, which are too delicate for your frame.

TOPS	SKIRTS
Avoid **puffed sleeves** or **kimono sleeves** that flare out from your shoulders and create unnecessary volume there. Steer clear of **crew necks, turtlenecks,** and **boatnecks,** which will only make you appear even more top-heavy—and if you have very large breasts, it can create the fattening "uniboob" effect.	Steer clear of **dark colored skirts** on the bottom if you're wearing light colors on top. Don't wear fitted **pencil skirts** unless they flare out even slightly. Avoid wearing **miniskirts,** which reveal too much of your legs and cut the line of your silhouette in half, which makes you look wider.

PANTS & JEANS	COATS & JACKET	JEWELRY & ACCESSORIES
Don't hide in your clothes by wearing **loose baggy pants.** On the other extreme, don't wear **leggings;** though it's tempting to show off your thinner bottom half, this will only make your shoulders look even larger and make you look more top-heavy.	Avoid **cap sleeve jackets** that widen your shoulders, and **short-sleeve boleros** that hit at the widest part of your arms, making them appear heavier. Don't wear jackets made of **thin, lightweight materials** such as thin cotton or linen, as it won't help hold in and structure your wide torso.	Don't cover up your chest area with **scarves** or **chokers,** which make your torso look thicker. Steer clear of **tiny clutches** and **dainty earrings,** which will look out of proportion on you. Don't carry a **large purse** that rests under your arm, which adds extra bulk to your larger top half.

SHOES

Don't wear shoes in drastically contrasting colors from your outfit, which breaks your look in half, widening you. Avoid heels that look too delicate, such as **thin, strappy stiletto sandals;** these will look out of proportion on your plus-size frame. Also, skip **plain flats** that don't add a slight lift to your look.

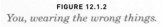

FIGURE 12.1.2
You, wearing the wrong things.

THE NEW YOU

Three ways to put your dress-sexy rules into play.

CASUAL	CAREER	FORMAL
The V-neck of this long top shows some skin at your neck, which is slimming. The vertical stitching down the front of the shirt is slimming. The horizontal stripe at your hips balances your wide shoulders. The dark, boot cut pants creates subtle volume below the knees to balance your shoulders.	The light layering of the scoop neck sweater over the tailored shirt helps smooth out any imperfections in your middle. The V-created by the shirt helps slim you. The pattern and flared style of the semi-circle skirt adds necessary volume on your bottom half.	The V-neck of this dress and the bold beaded necklace both draw the eye up to your chest, at the center of your body. The single color of the dress is slimming overall. The horizontal detailing at the hem of this godet skirt helps widen your silhouette where you need it.

YOUR ONE FASHION MUST-HAVE: *boot cut pants*

The very subtle flare below the knee helps to add volume to your bottom half to match your shoulders. Choose a pair in a dark color to help slim your look overall.

TALL
PLUS
RECTANGLE

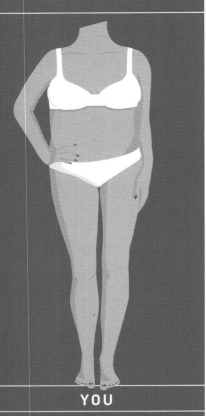

YOU

You are **TALL**.
[5'8" OR MORE]

You are **PLUS**-sized.
[OVER 205 LBS.]

Your body forms a
RECTANGLE
as your shoulders are the
same width as your hips.

You have broad shoulders.
You have equally wide hips.
Your waist is wide and undefined.

YOUR BLESSING

Your first blessing is that you were born with a balanced body! Because your hips and shoulders are the same width, all you need to do is create the illusion of a waist between the two, so you'll appear to have an hourglass silhouette. Also, you're tall. Since your weight is distributed on a longer frame, you have a lot to work with when it comes to balancing your body. And looking taller is your key to looking slimmer. Your other blessing? Because you're plus-sized, you may have one of the most sexy features of all: a sexy chest! With even a little bit to work with, you can turn what you have into eye-catching cleavage. Finally, your legs are slim in relation to the rest of your body, which means you can play them up and show them off—nothing says sexy like a little bit of leg on display.

YOUR CURSE

As a TALL, PLUS, RECTANGLE, you lack a defined waist. That gives your silhouette a slightly male shape. In fact, the extra weight around your middle turns your rectangle shape into more of an oval one. This means you have to find clothes that slim down your figure overall. Also, because you're both tall and plus-sized, it can be hard to find clothes that fit you. Chances are, you often shop at specialty plus-sized stores, or have clothes custom made to fit you. That can make for a frustrating shopping experience, because it's hard to dress in the style you want in the size you need. Finally, pay some serious attention when choosing bras and underwear—make sure they hold in and support your plus-size figure.

YOUR CELEBRITY BODY STAND-IN: *Mia Tyler*

WHAT TO WEAR

*Your fashion challenge is to define a waist where
there isn't one by widening your shoulders and hips so
your waist looks smaller in comparison.*

TOPS

Wear **wrap tops, surplice tops,** and **V-necks** to show a triangle
of skin at your chest, mimicking the angle you want to create
toward your waist. Or widen your shoulders with **boatneck tops**
paired with flared skirts. Wear **monochromatic tops and bottoms**
to make you appear slimmer overall. Wear **three-quarter-length
or flutter sleeves** to cover the heaviest part of your arms.

DRESSES

Choose **empire dresses** that
create the appearance of a high,
defined waist. Wear dresses with
wide open necks, like **boatnecks**
and **scoop necks,** as well as full
bottoms that bell or taper out from
the waist to create the illusion of
an hourglass. Wear jackets over
your dresses that hit at the waist.

SKIRTS

Pick **semi-circle skirts, gored
skirts,** or other **flared skirts** that
invent necessary fullness around
your hips and bottom and make your
waist look smaller in comparison.
Wear skirts in **medium-to-large-
sized patterns** that are in scale with
your size; choose patterns with a
dark background to slim you down.

PANTS & JEANS

Wear **straight-leg** or **subtle boot cut pants** that elongate your
body overall and will make you look slimmer. Wear pants in
the same tone or color as your top half to elongate your
look. Try **trouser pants** that add a bit of fullness around the
hip area, so your waist looks smaller in comparison;
pair them with high heels for a sexy professional look.

COATS & JACKETS

Choose jackets with
princess seams
that cinch in slightly
at your waist.
Exaggerate the width
of your shoulders
just slightly with small
shoulder pads or
puffed-sleeves that
will make your
waist look smaller
in comparison.

JEWELRY & ACCESSORIES

Wear sizeable **pendant
necklaces** that draw
the eye to the center
of your body. Or
wear **long, dangling
earrings** that add
vertical lines to your
silhouettte. Wear a
large shoulder bag
that sits under your
arm or at your hips.

SHOES

Wear **pointy-toed
heels, peep-toe
heels,** or heels
with **cut-away
arches,** all of
which will
instantly make
you appear
slimmer.

FIGURE 12.2.1
You, only sexier.

WHAT NOT TO WEAR

Really. I mean it.

TOPS

Steer clear of **high crew necks and turtlenecks with horizontal patterns,** which can create a "uniboob" and make your torso look thick. Don't wear tops with **big patterns** around your middle that draw attention there. Don't wear **cap sleeves** that make your arms look thicker than they are. Avoid tops that cling to your torso and accentuate the thickness in your middle.

DRESSES

Avoid dresses in **shiny fabrics** such as satin and charmeuse that will accentuate lumps in your middle. Similarly, avoid dresses in **stretchy fabrics** that will buckle around your middle as you move, adding weight there. Avoid **drop-waist dresses** that widen your torso, slip dresses that show too much, and **ankle-length dresses** that make you look heavy.

SKIRTS

Don't wear a **pegged skirt** that tapers in below your hips. Avoid **pencil skirts** that square off your boxy frame. Also, don't wear skirts that are overly **poufy or pleated** on the bottom, which adds too much volume to your hips and makes you look heavier. Don't wear bright colored or **large-patterned skirts** without balancing the fullness out on top.

PANTS & JEANS

Avoid **cropped pants** or **Capris,** as they will cut off the vertical line of your legs and make them seem wider and heavier; instead, wear pants that run the length of your legs. Avoid **leggings** or other Lycra®-based pants which will accentuate your lack of hips and make you appear top-heavy.

SHOES

Don't wear **square-toed shoes** that mimic your boxy frame. Don't wear shoes with very **delicate straps** and details, which aren't in scale with your frame.

COATS & JACKETS

Avoid jackets made from **thin fabrics** such as linen that don't have strong shoulder lines. Avoid **double-breasted blazers** and **pea coats** which will add weight to your torso. Steer clear of **long, straight coats** that don't taper in toward your waist and don't reveal some leg.

JEWELRY & ACCESSORIES

Don't carry handbags that hit at your waist, making your middle seem wider than it is. Avoid **tiny clutches** will look too small in proportion to your frame. Don't force **tight belts** around your middle, which may only create bulges and accentuate your middle.

FIGURE 12.2.2
You, wearing the wrong things.

THE NEW YOU

Three ways to put your dress-sexy rules into play.

| CASUAL | CAREER | FORMAL |

The wide-set V-neck of this wrap top widens your shoulders to make your waist seem smaller in comparison. The half-sleeve of the top covers the widest part your arms. The trouser cut jeans create volume below your knees, to balance your figure overall.

The boatneck top also has horizontal details at the neckline, widening your shoulders. Paired with a flouncy, gored skirt, your waist looks slim in between. The skirt hits just below the knee, at the smallest part of your calf, to make your legs look slimmer and sexier.

The half-sleeve of this dress covers up the largest part of your arms and adds fullness to your top half in comparison to your waist. The wide V-neck creates a flattering peek of skin. The empire style hugs your chest, creating the look of a small, high waist.

YOUR ONE FASHION MUST-HAVE: *an empire top*

Because you have extra weight around your middle, it's hard to cinch your waist in. An empire top hugs you bust, then flares out, creating the illusion of a high, shapely waist.

TALL
PLUS
TRIANGLE

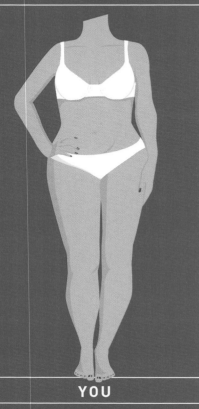

YOU

You are **TALL**.
[5'8" OR MORE]

You are **PLUS**-sized.
[OVER 205 LBS.]

Your body forms a
TRIANGLE
as your hips are broader
than your shoulders.

You have a slim upper body.
Your hips are wide-set.
You have a shapely bottom.

YOUR BLESSING

A sexy silhouette is all about gorgeous, soft curves, and you have lots of them! The place you carry most of those curves is in your bottom, which is a great place to carry it. You definitely have something to be proud of there. Your other blessing? Your torso is slimmer than your hips and thighs, which means you can show off your chest and collarbone. In fact, at first glance, your proportionally smaller top half can make you look as though you carry less on your frame than you actually do. Finally, you're tall. Since your weight is distributed on a longer frame, you have a lot to work with when it comes to balancing your body. And looking taller is your key to looking slimmer. Thank goodness for high heels, because you can slip on a pair of heels and you'll lengthen your look even more!

YOUR CURSE

As a TALL, PLUS, TRIANGLE, you have what's called a low balance. This means that the visual line of your silhouette reaches its broadest point at your hips. You can look very bottom-heavy if you choose the wrong clothes. Your other curse? Though your top half is smaller than your bottom half, your shoulders are narrow. If your arms are also heavy, that makes for a difficult combination. Finally, due to your tall frame and your plus-sized weight, it can be difficult for you to find clothes that fit. Chances are, you're not finding much of what you want in the department store, so you have to hit specialty stores to get what you need. That can be limiting and frustrating when you can't find the styles you want in the sizes you need.

YOUR CELEBRITY BODY STAND-IN: *Jill Ragee*

WHAT TO WEAR

Your fashion challenge is to downplay your oversized lower half and to bring out your shoulders so it balances with your bottom. You also want to look slimmer overall.

TOPS

Wear **off-the-shoulder tops, boatnecks, wide-set V-necks,** or a **cowl neck sweater** to widen your shoulders. Choose **tailored shirts** to create clean, elongating vertical lines; tuck in your shirt so that it doesn't draw the eye to the hem, right at your hips, making you appear wider there. Wear tops with **kimono cuts** or **fluted sleeves** to add volume to your upper half.

DRESSES

Choose **corset dresses** that cinch in your waist. Wear dreses with **princess seams** or **shirt-dresses** with buttons or other vertical details to slenderize your look. Wear dresses with **sweetheart necklines** that add shapely curves to your torso to match your curvy hips. Choose dresses with **fluted hems** to bring attention away from the hip area.

SKIRTS

Wear **dark-colored skirts** or **monochromatic looks** to slenderize your look. Choose **A-line skirts** that taper over your trouble zone, **wrap skirts,** or **gored skirts** that hug your hips, then flare out gently from there. Or try skirts with **handkerchief hems** to show off a bit of leg. Also, try **straight skirts** that fall straight down over your hips.

PANTS & JEANS

Try **boot cut** or **straight-leg pants** that add volume to the bottom half of your legs to balance your hips from below. Wear **flat front, wide-legged trousers,** such as **palazzo pants** in a lightweight fabric, that drapes gently over your hips without bunching or clinging. Aim for pants with **large back pockets** that are proportional to your frame.

COATS & JACKETS

Wear **boleros** over dresses to add some extra volume to your torso. Wear collarless jackets like **Chanel-style jackets,** worn open to create a long vertical line down your front, slimming you. Choose **military jackets** or coats with small **shoulder pads** to balance your hips.

JEWELRY & ACCESSORIES

Carry a handbag that is in proportion to your plus-size frame, such as a **saddle bag** or a **hobo bag** that fits at your chest or your waist to balance your larger bottom half. Choose **large, beaded necklaces** or large pendants in proportion to your frame.

SHOES

Wear **pointy-toed heels, slingbacks** or **open-toed heels** to lengthen the look of your legs. If high heels are uncomfortable for you, even a **kitten heel** will give you a lift that slims you down.

FIGURE 12.3.1
You, only sexier.

WHAT NOT TO WEAR

Really. I mean it.

TOPS

Don't wear **turtlenecks**, which can make your neck disappear and double your chin—especially **sleeveless turtlenecks** that reveal the heaviest part of your arms. Avoid **raglan tops** and **crew neck sweaters** that narrow your shoulders. Avoid **ponchos** that mask your entire torso and leave you looking shapeless. Don't let the hem of your shirt hit at your hips, widening you.

DRESSES	SKIRTS
Steer clear of **sheath dresses** that bring your silhouette line out to its widest point with no defined waist. Don't choose **drop-waist dresses** or those with horizontal details at the hip line that widen your widest part. Steer clear of **spaghetti straps** that will look too delicate for your frame. Avoid **shiny slip dresses,** which will reveal all your bumps and bulges.	Skip **light colored skirts** that draw attention to your bottom-heavy proportions. Avoid **shiny, volumizing fabrics** as well as rigid stiff fabrics such as crinoline, which widen your hips. Don't wear **prairie skirts** that add bulk to your bottom half. Avoid **tulip skirts** that taper in below the hips before flaring out, making your hips seem larger.

PANTS & JEANS

Avoid **khaki or light-colored pants,** which will add unwanted volume to your lower half. Don't choose pants with **side or angled pockets** or with other details at the hips. Avoid **flared jeans,** which will add too many curves to your frame and shorten your stature. Don't wear trousers with **front pockets, whiskering, or bleaching** on the thighs that draw attention there.

SHOES	COATS & JACKETS	JEWELRY & ACCESSORIES
Don't wear shoes in contrasting colors from your outfit, braking up the slimming, vertical line you want to create. Steer clear of **chunky heels,** which make you seem heavier.	Don't wear jackets made of **lightweight materials** such as linen and light cotton, as these will accentuate your narrow shoulders. Avoid jackets that hit at the mid-hip, the broadest point on your body. Keep in mind that **fur or faux fur** coats have a volumizing effect on your figure.	Don't wear **choker necklaces** that cut off your neck. Don't carry **too-small purses** that seem tiny in relation to your figure. Avoid **messenger bags, shoppers,** and **totes** that hit at your hip, as well as hip belts, which will bring too much attention to the widest part of your body.

FIGURE 12.3.2
You, wearing the wrong things.

THE NEW YOU

Three ways to put your dress-sexy rules into play.

CASUAL

The three-quarter-length sleeve on this cropped jacket covers up the thickest part of your arm. The layering and full shoulders add volume to your shoulders and torso to match your hips. The straight-leg jean adds a bit of volume below the knee to balance out your hips.

CAREER

The monochromatic skirt suit creates a slimming effect. The peplum jacket flares out over the hips, smoothing out the transition to your wider area. The godet skirt flares out at your knees, to balance your hips from below. The hem just below your knee elongates your figure, while still showing some leg.

FORMAL

The wide set V-neck of this dress widens your shoulders to match your hips. The corset cinches in your middle. The circle skirt flows gently over your hips and bottom without clinging to your curves.

YOUR ONE FASHION MUST-HAVE: *a tailored jacket*

Choose one with strong shoulders and shaped princess seams so your torso balances your hips. Make sure the jacket hits above your hips so you don't add extra weight in that area.

TALL PLUS HOURGLASS

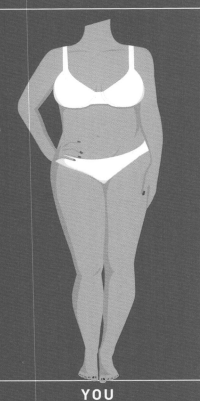

YOU

You are **TALL**.
[5'8" OR MORE]

You are **PLUS**-sized.
[OVER 205 LBS.]

Your body forms an
HOURGLASS
as your shoulders are the
same width as your hips,
with a tiny waist in between.

You have very broad shoulders
and a shapely bust.
Your hips and butt are curvy.
Your waist is defined compared
to your shoulders and hips.

YOUR BLESSING

Your biggest blessing is a great one: You have an hourglass silhouette! Basically, your top half and bottom half are perfectly balanced, and that is the essence of the sexy silhouette. You have a gorgeous, full bottom. You have broad shoulders. You have a sexy chest that you can make either larger or smaller depending on what you choose to reveal. Basically, you have a voluptuous figure like the one artists have been painting for centuries. Your other blessing? You're tall. Since your weight is distributed on a longer frame, you have a lot to work with when it comes to balancing your body. And looking taller is your key to looking slimmer. (Bring on the high heels!) Finally, you have a defined waist. Consider it your perfect optical illusion. Even though your body is plus-sized, you can show off your waist, which helps you appear a size or two smaller than you actually are.

YOUR CURSE

As a TALL, PLUS, HOURGLASS, you have large shoulders. You also have sizeable hips and a big bottom. Yes, you're proportional, but the combination of your plus-size shape combined with your height can make it difficult for you to find clothes that fit you properly. Since it's hard for you to find clothes that fit you in department stores, you have to hit specialty shops or select custom garments, and that can make for a frustrating shopping experience, as it's difficult to find the styles you like in the size you need. Your other curse? You need to pay extra attention in choosing undergarments that hold in your plus-size curves.

YOUR CELEBRITY BODY STAND-IN: *Kirstie Alley*

WHAT TO WEAR

Your fashion challenge is to keep your broad shoulders and wide hips balanced, while defining your waist. You also want to look slimmer overall.

TOPS

Wear **open-neck wrap tops** and **surplice tops,** which bring the eye up to your cleavage and show off your waist. Wear fitted **V-neck sweaters** over bright-colored camisoles to bring attention to the center of your body—especially your gorgeous cleavage! Choose tops with **three-quarter-length sleeves** that conceal the widest part of your arm.

DRESSES

Choose **wrap** or **surplice dresses** that follow your hourglass curves from shoulder to hem. Wear **A-line dresses** with a strong, wide waistline. Or wear a **corseted dress** in a sturdy fabric such as taffeta to smooth out your curves. Wear **dark, single-colored dresses** that create a long vertical line from head to toe, making you look long and lean.

PANTS & JEANS

Wear **straight-leg pants and trousers** or subtle **boot cut jeans** that elongate you. Or wear **pressed-crease pants** to create a strong vertical line on your lower half. Choose **mid-rise jeans,** which create a smooth line to your hips without adding bulk. Choose jeans with **large, round back pockets** that are in scale with your body.

SKIRTS

Wear **dark colored skirts** that diminish your bottom half. Choose **straight skirts** that lengthen your look. Or wear **godet skirts** or **tulip skirts** that hug your curves before flaring out at the bottom. Hem your skirts at or just below your knee; showing off a bit of your legs will make you look taller.

COATS & JACKETS

Wear **peplum jackets** or **corseted blazers,** which cinch in at your waist then flare out toward your hips. Choose jackets with **princess seams** that mimic your shape. Try **trench coats** that hit at your knee or above; showing a bit of leg will make you seem taller and slimmer.

JEWELRY & ACCESSORIES

Wear necklaces that feature a single focal point—like a medium **pendant necklace** that falls in a V-shape. Wear **wide belts or sashes;** skinny belts will be dwarfed by your size. Carry a **large handbag** in scale with your frame.

SHOES

Wear a **pointy-toed, heel** in the same color as your outfit to elongate your look. Or wear a **substantial pump** or **wedge heel.**

FIGURE 12.4.1
You, only sexier.

WHAT NOT TO WEAR

Really. I mean it.

TOPS

Avoid **square necks, crew necks,** and other **high-necked styles** that cover up the skin on your chest and can morph into the dreaded "uniboob" that will make you appear top-heavy. Steer clear of baggy tops, such as **peasant tops** and **empire tops** that flow too freely over your torso, both of which cover up the skinniest part of your waist and will make you look boxy.

DRESSES

Don't wear dresses that hit at the **mid calf** or **ankle** and make your legs look heavy. Steer clear of **drop-waist dresses** that hide your natural curves, or dresses with belts or sashes at your hips instead of at your waist. Avoid dresses with **large patterns,** such as florals, this will draw too much attention to your figure in general.

PANTS & JEANS

Avoid **cropped pants** or **gauchos** which cut a horizontal line through the widest point of your lower legs, making you look heavier. Avoid pants with **angled or diagonal side pockets** that land at the hip and make you look bottom-heavy. Don't wear **low-rise jeans** because your figure is bound to spill over.

SKIRTS

Steer clear of skirts with details at the hips, adding width where you don't want it. Avoid **bell-shaped circle skirts** in thick fabrics that are too poufy and add unwanted volume to your hip area. Don't wear pleats that aren't stitched in up to the hip, as this will also create too much fullness at the area. Avoid **shiny fabrics** and **busy patterns** on your bottom half.

SHOES

Don't wear **strappy stiletto sandals** that are so delicate they seem tiny next to your plus-size frame. Avoid **ankle straps** that will make your ankles look wider.

COATS & JACKETS

Skip **long jackets** that land at the hip, as this adds weight to your broadest point and covers up your defined waist. Avoid **boxy jackets** such as double-breasted coats and pea coats with front or side pockets that widen your hip area.

JEWELRY & ACCESSORIES

Don't cover the skin area around your neck and cleavage with **scarves** or **wide choker necklaces**. Avoid long necklaces that add weight to the middle of your torso. Don't carry too-tiny clutches which will seem out of proportion with your plus-size frame.

FIGURE 12.4.2
You, wearing the wrong things.

THE NEW YOU

Three ways to put your dress-sexy rules into play.

CASUAL

The V-neck top draws
the eye toward your center.
The princess seams
in the top show off your
natural waist. The straight-
leg jean adds volume
to the bottom of your legs,
balancing your hips
and making you seem taller.

CAREER

The monochromatic
skirt suit elongates your
figure, slimming you.
The peplum jacket creates
a flattering V-neck
and mimics your hourglass
curves. The gored skirt is
hemmed at the knee, showing
some of your lovely legs
and elongating your look.

FORMAL

The V-neck draws
the eye to the center of your
body, toward your
cleavage. The dress lightly
grazes your hips, fitting
the hourglass curves of your
body perfectly. The half-
sleeves cover the largest part
of your arm. The flare
at the hem balances your
hips from below.

YOUR ONE FASHION MUST-HAVE: *a wrap dress*

**A wrap dress creates a flattering V-neck, cinches your natural
waist, defining the best feature of your silhouette. Choose one in a mid-weight
fabric and it will smooth out any bulges you have.**

THE GLOSSARY

Have any questions about the items I recommend in the book? Check out the definitions and illustrations for many of them here.

TOPS AND SWEATERS

BOATNECK

This top has a high, straight neckline that opens across the collarbone and meets at the tip of the shoulders. It is cut equally high along the front and in back.

CAMISOLE

Shaped like a bra with fabric draping from the bottom of the bust to the waist, this sleeveless, fitted top is often made of thin fabrics such as silk, satin, or light cotton.

CARDIGAN

This collarless sweater opens down the full-length of the front and often closes with buttons or snaps. You can take it on and off without pulling it over your head.

COWL NECK

The neckline of this top or sweater has loose-fitting, extra fabric that drapes naturally in the front. It can be either high-necked or open to reveal more skin around the neck.

CREW NECK

This round-necked top or sweater has a band of ribbing around the base of the neck that is curved in the shape of a circle.

HALTER

This sleeveless top attaches behind the neck, rather than over the shoulders, revealing an open upper back.

KIMONO

The sleeve of this top is part of the main bodice, rather than separately sewn on. It has a wide cut at the armpits and tapers out toward the wrists, like Japanese kimono robes.

RAGLAN

The sleeve seams of this top extend up to the base of the neck, instead of meeting over the shoulders (like baseball jersey tops with colored sleeves on a white shell).

SQUARE NECK

This top has an open neck shaped like half a square (as opposed to the U-neck, which is shaped like half of a circle).

SURPLICE

Like a permanent version of a wrap top, this style is created by cross-wrapping fabric across the front and securing it (most often in the seam) to create a V-shape neckline.

SWEETHEART NECK

The open neck of this top is shaped like the crown of a heart as it meets in a small point in the center of the bust line.

TAILORED DRESS SHIRT

This structured dress shirt has a separate sewn-in collar at the neck and buttons running down the length of the front.

TURTLENECK

The neckline of this top (usually a sweater) reaches from the shoulders up to the base of the chin with enough fabric to fold over to the neckline.

U-NECK

This top has a deep open neck that dips into a half-circle. (A wider version of this is called a "scoop neck.")

V-NECK

This top has an open neck shaped into a "V" at the bust line, like an upside-down triangle.

WRAP TOP

This top is created by cross-wrapping fabric and securing it (usually with a tie or button) on the front, side, or back of the top, which creates a V-shape neckline.

A-LINE

This dress steadily tapers out from the waist to the hem in strong, straight lines, revealing a silhouette like the edges of a capital letter *A*.

PRINCESS SEAMS

These are form-fitting, curved seams that mimic the hourglass shape, running down the right and left front of the dress.

CORSET

The focus of this dress is in the tight, torso-hugging band from the navel to the bottom of the bust; it is often reinforced with boning inserted into the stiff fabric to pull in the stomach and push up the bust.

SHEATH

This dress features a figure-hugging silhouette with a defined waist and is most often designed as a sleeveless shell that hits at or just below the knee.

EMPIRE

The bodice of this dress hugs the bust, then gathers just below the bustline and tapers out to the hem, as if from a very high waist.

SLIP DRESS

Originally worn as a sleep garment or undergarment, this dress—usually made of very lightweight fabrics such as silk, satin, or thin cotton—has spaghetti straps and a low-cut neckline and can be "slipped" on and off over the head.

HALTER

The straps of this sleeveless dress start toward the front center of the garment, then attach behind the neck, rather than over the shoulders, revealing an open upper back.

STRAPLESS

Quite simply, this dress has no straps running over the shoulders or arms, thus creating a horizontal or a sweetheart neckline.

OFF-THE-SHOULDER

The straps of this dress are designed to wrap around the arms, below the shoulders, revealing bare shoulders and an open neck area.

SURPLICE

Like a permanent version of a wrap dress, this style is created by cross-wrapping fabric across the front and securing it (most often in the seam) to create a V-shape neckline.

POLO DRESS

The T-shirt shaped, collared top of this casual dress has two or three buttons on the front that open to a V-shaped neck, then fall to the knee.

WRAP

This dress is created by cross-wrapping fabric and securing it (usually with a tie or bow) on the front, side, or back of the top, which creates a V-shape neckline.

PANTS

BOOT CUT

The cut of these pants runs straight from the hip to the knee, then flares slightly from the knee to the ankle.

CARGO PANTS

Originally created to hold gear for the military, these casual pants are known for the numerous pockets sewn onto the outside of the pants, often at the hip, thigh, and/or knees.

CROPPED PANTS

These straight-leg pants can be hemmed anywhere from just above the ankle to just below the knee. (Similarly, short pants that are more fitted and tapered to the knee are called "Capri pants.")

CUFFED TROUSER

The hem of these pants is doubled-back and stitched, revealing a folded cuff that can be anywhere from short to a few inches tall.

FLARED

The cut of these pants runs straight from the hip to the knee, then flares dramatically from the knee, steadily outward to the ankle. (They're also called "bell-bottoms.")

LOW RISE

Because the "rise" between the crotch and waistband is low, the fastening button or snap of these pants hits a few inches below the navel, and the top of the pant hits just above the hips.

MEN'S TROUSER PANTS

Styled just like traditional men's trousers, these dress pants are cut to fall straight from the hip with slanted side pockets and cuffs.

PALAZZO PANTS

This versatile pant with extra wide flare is often mistaken for a skirt and is available in a variety of styles that go from casual to evening. (The cropped version of these are called "gauchos.")

PRESSED-CREASE

These dress slacks feature a strong ironed crease running down the front of both legs, from hip height to ankle.

SKINNY JEAN

This style of jeans is tight-fitting through the waist, hips, and thighs, then tapers down, hugging the calves and ankles. (It's also called a "cigarette pant.")

STOVEPIPE

Basically, a slightly tighter version of straight leg pants, this style is fitted to the knee, then falls straight to the ankle.

STRAIGHT LEG

The cut of these pants runs straight from the hip to the knee, then straight from the knee to the ankle, with no taper or flare.

A-LINE

This skirt steadily tapers out from the waist to the hem in strong, straight lines, revealing a silhouette like the edges of a capital letter *A*.

ASYMETRICAL HEM

Rather than running straight across the skirt bottom in an even line, this hem is slanted on the diagonal, revealing more leg on one side than the other.

CIRCLE

Named for the fact that the hem of this skirt, stretched out, forms a large, complete circle, this style is very full. (A less full version of this is called a "semi-circle skirt.")

DENIM

Made from cotton denim, this casual skirt shares the hip-styling of a pair of jeans: belt loops, angled pockets, and a button or zipper closure.

GATHERED

The waistband of this skirt consists of small fabric folds gathered and sewn together into an elastic waistband or a separate fabric waistband.

GODET

Similar to the gored skirt, this style hugs the hips, then features triangular swaths of fabric, called godets, sewn between the panels, to create more fullness at the hem.

GORED

This skirt is constructed from any number of vertical panels of fabric, called gores. Fitted through the hip, the panels have flare on the bottom to create a flirty flounce at the hem.

HANDKERCHIEF HEM

Rather than running straight across the skirt bottom in an even line, this hem falls in various length points around the base, the way a handkerchief would when held in the center.

HIGH-WAISTED

The fastening button or snap of this skirt hits above the navel, making one's waist appear higher than it is.

PENCIL

Most often worn with suit jackets or as professional attire, the cut of this skirt runs straight from hip to hem and is hemmed just above, at, or just below the knee. (It's also called a "straight skirt.")

PLEATED

Though there are varied types of pleated skirts, the general style features permanent vertical folds in the fabric (This illustration shows a box pleat from the waist to the hip, where the pleat then releases.)

PRAIRIE

A western-inspired skirt made from tiers of ruffles. It comes in various lengths and can be either a knit or a woven fabric for a variety of effects.

TRUMPET

This style is slim-fitting from the waist through the hips, then flares or ruffles outward, like a trumpet, at the knee. (One that tapers in just slightly before flaring out is called a "tulip skirt.")

WRAP

This skirt is created by cross-wrapping fabric and securing it (usually with a tie or belt) on the side, back, or front of the skirt, thus creating a soft flare or an A-line silhouette.

JACKETS

BOLERO

This is a light, extremely cropped jacket meant to be worn open; the styles are varied enough so some can be paired with a dressy evening gown—others with a casual top.

CHANEL STYLE JACKET

A boxy-cut, button-up jacket, most recognizable in tweed.

CORSETED BLAZER

The bodice of this blazer contains a torso-hugging band often reinforced with boning inserted into the stiff fabric; when closed the blazer helps define the waist.

DENIM STYLE JACKET

Usually made from cotton denim, this style, hemmed to hit at the waist, features two front buttoned pockets on the chest and two slanted pockets above the hip area.

CROPPED JACKET

This jacket's hem hits just above your natural waist.

HIGH STANCE BLAZER

A blazer in which the top closure fastens around the bust or higher.

LOW STANCE BLAZER

A blazer in which the top closure fastens below the bust or lower.

MANDARIN COLLAR

Like the Asian collar from which the style is adapted, this is short band collar that runs an inch or two straight up the neck, with a notch in the center that may or may not close with a button.

MILITARY JACKET

This casual jacket can take on a variety of military-inspired embellishments, such as epaulets, oversized buttons, pockets, etc.

PEA COAT

This is a hip-length jacket with a wide-notch collar featuring a double-breasted closure, in which one flap of fabric completely crosses over another and attaches with a double row of buttons on the front of the coat.

PEPLUM JACKET

This style tapers in snugly to the waist, with a flounce flaring out toward the hips.

PRINCESS SEAM BLAZER

These seams are curved, form-fitting seams running down the right and left sides of the coat, mimicking the hourglass shape.

SHAWL COLLAR

Instead of using a separate piece of fabric for the collar, this style features one continuous piece of fabric that folds over at the neck in one elegant line.

TRENCH COAT

This coat can take on a variety of military-inspired embellishments, such as epaulets, oversized buttons, or pockets; it ties at the waist, with an A-line shape from the waist to the knees.

ANKLE STRAPS

This style of shoe is fastened around the ankle with a strap made of fabric or leather.

PEEP TOE SHOE

The front section of this shoe is cut away into either a small or sizeable hole to reveal the toes.

CHUNKY HEEL

This type of heel is thick and wide and covers more surface area on the ground than a skinny stiletto heel. (A version with a strap across the top of the foot is called a "Mary Jane.")

POINTY-TOED HEEL

This style is named literally, with a triangular-shaped toe. (The heel is also called a "pump" or a "stiletto.")

CUTAWAY ARCH

Because the material between the heel and toe is cut away on each side of this shoe, this style reveals the arch of the foot. (It's also called a "d'Orsay" pump.)

ROUND-TOED HEEL

This style is named literally, with a toe that rounds off in a smooth semi-circle, as opposed to a point or a square. (The heel is also called a "pump" or a "stiletto.")

FLAT

This style of shoe has a flat sole and does not lift the heel of the foot above the ground.

SQUARE-TOED HEEL

This style is named literally, with a toe shaped like half of a sqaure, as opposed to a round or pointy toe. (The heel is also called a "pump" or a "stiletto.")

KITTEN HEEL

Considered as an in-between to high heels and flats, this style of shoe has skinny, short heel that lifts the heel of the foot no higher than 2" above the ground.

SLING BACK

Instead of a full piece of material around the back of this shoe, this style provides a small belt or piece of leather that hugs just at the back of the ankle.

KNEE-HIGH BOOT

This style of boot covers your ankles and calves, topping off just below the knee; most styles have a zipper running down one side.

STRAPPY STILETTO

A skinny, high heel that is also designed like a sandal to reveal a lot of skin around the foot. (It's also called a "heel." A tall stiletto is also called a "spike heel.")

WEDGE

The triangle formed at the base of this shoe is a slowly rising extension of the sole of the shoe that lifts the heel like a high heel.

JEWELRY AND ACCESSORIES

BANGLES

These bracelets are rigid, round pieces without a clasp that slide onto the arm and remain in solid form.

BARREL

This round handbag is named literally, as it is shaped like a barrel, with straps that wrap around the body of the bag.

CHANDELIER EARRINGS

With small drops of beads or crystals dangling in various styles, these long, fluid earrings look like miniature versions of chandeliers.

CLUTCH PURSE

As it is meant to be "clutched" under the arm, this small or medium sized purse comes without a large handle and can't be carried on the shoulder.

CHOKER

This tight-fitting necklace is any style that closely hugs the neck.

HOBO BAG

This crescent-shaped purse has a shoulder strap just long enough so that, when worn, the bag sits just under the arm.

CHUNKY BEADS

This necklace features oversized drops of wood, plastic, crystal, or another stylish material, linked together in a draping necklace.

MESSENGER BAG

This oversized bag closes via a large flap that folds over the top. It is either worn over the shoulder or across the chest, landing at the hip.

CUFF

This wide, solid bracelet wraps tightly around the wrist, resembling the cuff of a shirt.

SATCHEL

This large handbag is known for having two handles or straps so that it must be carried by hand at the hips.

DRAPEY NECKLACE

This necklace, which can be made of a gold or silver chain or a string of small beads, drapes long and low down the front of the chest.

SHOPPER

Created to carry large loads, this oversized bag has an open top and a large open interior, without many extra compartments.

PENDANT NECKLACE

This tight-fitting necklace is any style that closely hugs the neck.

TOTE

This large handbag is considered a complete carry-all, as it contains many individual compartments both outside and inside the bag.

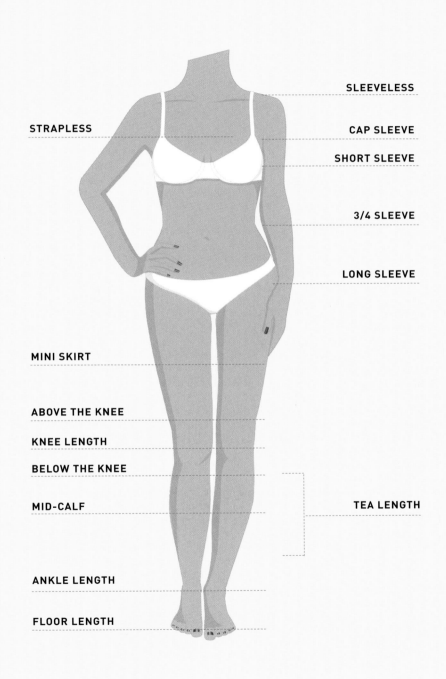

SLEEVELESS

STRAPLESS

CAP SLEEVE

SHORT SLEEVE

3/4 SLEEVE

LONG SLEEVE

MINI SKIRT

ABOVE THE KNEE

KNEE LENGTH

BELOW THE KNEE

MID-CALF

TEA LENGTH

ANKLE LENGTH

FLOOR LENGTH

YOUR DREAM CLOSET CHECKLIST

Have you ever opened your stuffed closet and thought, "I don't have a thing to wear!" Of course you have, and I can help you change that. Now that you know about your unique silhouette, here's a list of the must-have basics—wear them every day, and you'll be dressing sexy. Grab a pen and go through the list to see what you already have, what you can edit out, and what you might need to buy.

If you have these items, in the shapes that most flatter you, you'll never again open your closet and think, "I don't have a thing to wear!"

TOPS AND SWEATERS

☐ 1 BASIC **WHITE** COTTON TAILORED SHIRT

☐ 1 **COLORED** TAILORED SHIRT *(that flatters either your eye color or your skin color)*

☐ 7 COTTON **T-SHIRTS** *(one for every day of the week; choose some in long-sleeve styles that best suit your shape, and some in short-sleeve or tank styles that best suit your shape)*

☐ 1 **SEXY** PARTY TOP *(that can be dressed up with the right accessories)*

☐ 1 SHINY, SILK **CAMISOLE** *(one that can be layered under your structured jackets or, for some of you, worn casually alone)*

☐ 1 PRETTY TOP WITH **SPECIAL DETAILS** *(refer to your Fitting Room to see what types of details work best on you)*

☐ 1 BLACK **SWEATER** *(ideally, a cashmere one that works for your shape; it's expensive, but it's worth it)*

☐ 1 SOLID-**COLORED SWEATER** *(again, buy a cashmere one in a color that flatters your eye color or your skin color)*

DRESSES

☐ 1 TIMELESS **BLACK DRESS** *(choose the shape that flatters your silhouette so you can dress up, from cocktail parties to weddings)*

☐ 1 **DAYTIME DRESS** *(it should have a simple neckline and be in a color or pattern that best flatters you)*

☐ 1 UNIQUE **SEXY PARTY DRESS** *(either in a bold color, with interesting details that work with your silhouette, or in a print that flatters you)*

SKIRTS

☐ 1 **BLACK SKIRT** THAT FITS YOUR FIGURE *(check your Fitting Room to find out which style best suits you)*

☐ 1 FLIRTY, **DRESSY SKIRT**

☐ 1 KNEE-LENGTH **BUSINESS SKIRT** *(again, check your Fitting Room to see what's best—pencil skirts don't work for everyone!)*

PANTS AND JEANS

☐ 1 **CASUAL** PANT *(it should flatter your figure and be tailored to a perfect fit)*

☐ 1 PAIR OF **BLACK** PANTS *(these should also flatter your figure and be tailored to your length when you're wearing heels)*

☐ 3 PAIRS OF **JEANS** *(they should flatter your figure and one should be hemmed to wear with a pair of heels, for casually dressing up)*

COATS AND JACKETS

☐ 1 **BASIC BLACK SUIT** WITH MATCHING SKIRT OR PANTS

☐ 1 **BLAZER** THAT LOOKS GREAT WITH PANTS

☐ 1 THREE-QUARTER-LENGTH **LIGHT COAT** *(this length looks great on most figures)*

☐ 1 **OVERCOAT** *(this is a serious investment for many winters to come, so don't skimp on fabric here!)*

☐ 1 CASUAL, LIGHT **JACKET** *(check your fitting room to find out which style best suits you)*

SHOES

☐ 1 PAIR OF **HEELS** *(in the right style for your height and weight as recommended in your Fitting Room)*

☐ 1 PAIR OF **FLATS** *(for a comfortable day of shopping!)*

Thank you Moms and Pops for everything, and I mean everything.

Thank you Mundi Male, Chanelle Embrey, Holly Leygraff & Fanny Penny—I couldn't have done it without you. Thank you Natalie Andrody for always coming through. Susan Moses for being a friend and inspiration. Jennifer Walsh and Andy McNicol for supporting my vision. Bill Shinker, Lauren Marino, and Hilary Terrell at Gotham Books for making it happen. Emily Oberman, Bonnie Siegler, Allison Henry, and Lizzy Ferraro at Number Seventeen for all your hard work. Amy Spencer and Liz Ruckdeschel for getting me.

Thank you to my incredible daughters Alexis and Natalie; thank you Dudley and Theodore, and the biggest thanks to Mark for always being there.

Lastly, a special thank, you to all the women I've ever dressed.